Prelude

I started writing about my marriage, relationship and divorce to a narcissist in an effort to release the poison from my soul and to free myself of all the ugly memories that I remembered and the ones that I had suppressed. Since finishing my story I realized how essential my memoirs would be to other people who are in narcissistic marriages or relationships that feel completely helpless, hopeless and desolate. I am hopeful that my story, which emphasizes the pain, suffering and psychological warfare endured in living with a narcissist, can help women and men stuck in narcissistic marriages to muster the courage to leave their toxic relationships for the sake of their sanity. I also hope that sharing my insight and experiences with a narcissist might help any single woman or man who sees the same traits and behavior in their partner to think twice about marrying or having children with them, thus saving them years of misery and abuse, as well as sparing the unborn children the same suffering that goes along with it.

Victims of narcissism have little to no support system. They have no place to turn to because narcissism is so complex and those who have not lived or been married to a narcissist do not understand their wrath. My narcissist husband displayed a fake image to everyone around him; it was hard and still is for most people to believe I was the victim since my husband could be so charming and impressive with everyone else.

Along with releasing my pain I wanted to document my suffering so that one day, when my children become adults and I feel that the time is right, I want them to know exactly why I left their father, which at the time left them confused and very hateful towards me. Their immense anger and hate originated from the lies that their father went on to tell them and the fear of me that he implanted in them during our divorce. Classic child abuse or, in legal terms, child alienation.

Also, I want victim readers to know this: you are not alone in your misery, there are many out there suffering like I did and like you are now. I want you to know that you can leave – and you must. Your narcissist partner will fight you viciously on your way out of the relationship and, I assure you, you will have to swim through some turbulent and torturous waves and protect your children with therapy to boot. Upon reaching the shore, you will have a chance to live a normal life again, you will have grown from your pain but, most importantly, you will have survived the curse of a narcissist.

While you are reading this book, you might very well wonder why I stayed in my seventeen-year abusive marriage for as long as I did. You may even wonder what was wrong with me. Did I lack self-respect? Did I lack self-esteem? Did I enjoy abusive behavior? No to all. However, during those seventeen years I lost some self-respect, I lost my self-esteem and I learned coping tools to endure the abuse. What I lacked was the knowledge of the psychological brutality and destruction to my soul by choosing a narcissist as my mate. Prior to meeting Peter, I was a fun and carefree and loved meeting and engaging with people. I did not fear anything. I had crossed the ocean alone at a young age to explore new land. I was not the kind of girl who was going to allow myself to be the victim of abuse; I was in control.

Despite all that, I put up with way too much abusive behavior and I stayed. I stayed because I desperately wanted my marriage to work, especially since we had children together. We were a family. I believed that you made a marriage work "through thick or thin" as the saying goes. I was married to a hard-working, handsome man, we had three wonderful boys, a successful business, a great life ahead of us (financially speaking), and I was in love with the whole concept of being married and being a family. I didn't want to be divorced. I didn't want a broken home for our children. I didn't want to share our boys for weekends and holidays with an ex-husband. I didn't want to have the children grow up and have to make that horrible decision of who they would visit for Christmas, Mum or Dad. I didn't want them to have to tell people, "My Mum and Dad are divorced". Instead, I lived, admittedly for way too long, in a cold, loveless, and abusive marriage that lacked any emotion, intimacy, sex, or friendship.

I realized very early on that I was nothing more to my husband than a marital contract. I did not feel loved, did not feel special and was always walking uncomfortably in his presence as he gazed flirtingly at other women throughout our marriage. Consequently, I created an image for our marriage to compensate this loss. One that made us look perfect, normal, happy and functional. I had built such an impressive image, that at times, I actually believed that Peter and I were happy. Sadly, all I was doing was living in a lie. One to my children, my family, my community, but most importantly to myself. I was terribly unhappy. I was tired of walking on eggshells, tired of pretending to be a happy couple, tired of protecting my boys from his anger and rage, tired of trying to be noticed by him, tired of sharing him with other women (a chronic problem that lasted most of our marriage); it became one long, tiring, draining and empty existence.

I mastered several coping mechanisms that kept things calm and argument-free for the sake of my own sanity and for the sake of our boys. One was to leave him alone or practically ignore him, which was so unhealthy and yet it worked well for years. I did this to protect the boys from unexpected outbursts of rage which had happened often since the birth of our first son and often for reasons that were unfounded. I protected the fake image that I had created for years, one that I paid very dearly for in terms of my happiness, my health and later, my children.

Peter is not aware I am writing this book. I have changed our names for legal protection since the first thing he would do is to sue me and take everything from me with great satisfaction. The second thing he would do is deny everything and say that I was making it all up and blame bitterness or instability. There are a couple of people who know I am writing this book who fear it might push him over the edge and attempt to kill me. I am not afraid. I prefer to warn women and men of this ugly sickness and plan to advocate for women and men who are currently suffering at the side of these evil personalities. I want to support the woman or man whose partner has alienated their children from them and coach them through how to survive during a time that they feel death is less painful. So, I couldn't care less about how Peter feels or what he might do. I have a mission to help people and if I lose my life over it...then so be it.

I married an incredibly handsome man and seventeen years later, I divorced a monster.

Chapter 1

... I was blown away by how incredibly handsome he was. He was tall, had chiseled features, a great body, was not loud and obnoxious (like many men his age at that time) and seemed friendly. There was something about him... I felt right there and then that he had to be mine. He was everything desirable to me. He had a physical look that I was very attracted to, and he ran his own small business which I very much respected, especially at his young age. He played a little hard to get and I enjoyed the challenge. I did not consider his lack of honesty during those early days, I was too smitten with his exterior image. I was introduced to Peter at the gym by my friend, Jose. Jose and I had been steadfast and loyal friends for four years. He was my best friend. I was throwing a party that night and Jose pulled me aside and asked me if I thought we should invite him. I thought he was gorgeous, so I did, and he accepted.

When he arrived I remember thinking again that he was the most handsome man that I had ever met in my life. Here he was, in my home. What could be better than that? During that evening, trying my best not to ignore the rest of my friends, I found myself drawn to his side. Each time I left to tend to food or drinks I made my way back, not wanting to miss one moment with him. I wanted him to know that I was interested in him and I could not have made it more obvious. It felt like he had shown up at my home specifically to see me and his arrival had left me feeling euphoric. He brought three of his friends along, which was great, until they said that they were going on to another party. I was hoping they would stay all evening. The thought of this gorgeous man leaving prematurely led me to intensify my sultry flirtation. I was in a dwindling, meaningless and dull marriage at the time so when Peter came along it left me feeling invigorated. It all started with his incredibly striking look. He gave the impression that he was interested in me though he was acting very cool about it. I found that to be profoundly intriguing and sexy. It felt exhilarating to be around him.

He didn't stay as long as I hoped. I was disappointed when he left although I knew I could find him again through Jose. I had given Peter my phone number at the gym the first time I met him but I didn't hear from him after my party, not even a call to say thank you. Had I not impressed him? I was a very flirtatious woman at the time and had no problem seducing a man, especially one like him. I had put on such a wonderful party with great friends, delicious food (I'm a good cook), paid him lots of attention...and no follow up? I was not prepared to lower my own principles and call him because I very much believed that a man should pursue a woman if he were really interested.

A couple of weeks later while I was painting in my home, I received a call. I answered and a man said," Who is this?" I remember thinking that was a little weird to call someone and ask them who they were but I knew it was him; I recognized his voice. I played with him a little and replied, "You called me, who is this?" He said, 'It's Peter, I found your name and number on a piece of paper and I couldn't remember how I knew you." Ouch! That hurt. I was just a name and number on a piece of paper. At least that is what he wanted me to believe: he turned out to be a pathological liar so it was probably untrue and his intent was to make me feel good by calling, but not too good because he didn't remember who I was. This would be the first of hundreds of hurtful comments that would be coming my way. Still, I was so smitten by him and so happy to hear from him that I ignored his disrespectful approach. This phone call had been a red flag about his treatment of a woman and I had ignored it. The problem was that I was young and was too inexperienced to recognize the warning signs. We spoke for a while and ended the call not making any plans to see each other. On one hand I was disappointed and yet, on the other, was thrilled that he now knew me as the owner of the name and number on that piece of paper.

I was married at the time. My marriage was on life support and had been for some time. I had not been married very long before realizing that my husband did not have the qualities that I had hoped for as far as being financially responsible and someone I could count on as a hard worker and a provider, not just for us but for our future. We were both young and were just starting out in life. Immediately after our wedding we put a deposit on a home together, a wedding gift compliments of both of our parents. We contributed equally to all the bills except for one major problem that soon after arose. My husband would wait until final notices on all of our home bills before making his part of the payment. This practice left me feeling uneasy. I started working part time when I was twelve years old. I had never had a problem finding work and I worked very hard throughout my school years working two jobs most of the time. I worked most nights at a local restaurant throughout college and continued working nights during my first full-time accounting job. I had paid off the electronic equipment for my bedroom and loans for two cars before the age of twenty-one years old simply from working hard and being financially responsible. My husband, on the other hand, turned out to be financially irresponsible at the age of twenty-seven, which I had not counted on especially after purchasing our home. He worked as a medical sales rep when I met him and his job entitled him to a company car and medical insurance. It was a great job and suited him well since he was gifted in people skills, something that I liked very much about him when I first met him.

He also played in a band at night. Prior to our marriage, I used to go with my friends to the bars that he played at. It was a lot of fun and I remember those days fondly. However, those nights turned into a lot of drinking for everyone especially the band. The meager salary they were payed only just covered the bar bill. Those late nights led to tired mornings and that interfered with his daytime sales job. He used to sleep all morning and lie to his boss that he had been making sales calls. I would hear him lie often which made me lose some respect for him since he was compromising a good job over late nights, a band and beer. His boss fired him soon after and, thanks to

3

a loyal friend, he was hired at another medical company with the same benefits. I assumed his band playing would dwindle after we married and that building a solid home and future would set precedence over a band. However, after buying our home, the same pattern of financial irresponsibility became evident. He continued to play in the band, continued to sleep all morning, and not long after lost that job too.

As I watched the bills sit month after month waiting for final notices, I realized only too quickly that this was not the life or the future I had envisioned and one I no longer wanted. I could not afford to pay for both of us and was angry that he drove himself into financial debt by being irresponsible. Not only was I driven and responsible in my work, I was equally driven and dedicated to my health. I exercised regularly, ate healthy food and took pride in my appearance. My husband had recently put on a lot of weight and told a friend--in front of me--that he did not have to worry about his weight or how he looked any longer because he was married.

One night, Jose brought Peter as his guest to a dinner party at my home. There were eight of us around the table that night but it might as well have been just Peter and me. I learned new things about Peter that night which caused me to become more drawn to him. Unlike the puerility of the man at the end of the table—yes, my husband, who was drinking tons of beer, and probably not planning to go to work the next day-- Peter was very responsible. He had his own place, his own car, worked out, had a small business which he owned with a partner, and seemed to have his head screwed on the right way. This realization prompted me to look at my husband at the end of the table, and I knew right then, at that very moment, it had to end fast; like that night.

Peter had all the qualities I was looking for in a mate. As I've said, he was physically attractive, he was not loud, he was nice to talk to, he had a job and he appeared to be financially responsible; he'd also been helpful by taking out the garbage that night.

I had long forgotten his initial call to me wondering who I was and figured that I had been wrong about him. I grew up in a family, in a town and in a culture where it was expected that people were responsible, both socially and monetarily. Peter had come across as having both of these qualities, which made my attraction to him stronger. Recognizing that evening that this man had drawn me to him in every single way, my relationship with Mr. Puerile ended days later.

Being single meant spending more time with my best friend Jose. Jose loved throwing dinner parties and would always invite Peter. He would tell Peter I was going and would tell me that Peter was coming. Even though Peter knew I was interested in him and he with me, according to Jose, on some of those occasions he would show up with a date. Really? We both had an attraction to each other, so why the girl? If he was interested in me, really interested, he would have come alone. He was not pursuing me at all and yet in a way he was. He would show so much interest in me at those dinner parties and then leave with his date. That behavior had made no sense. In hindsight, it was extremely disrespectful to both me and the woman. It was another red flag which I chose to ignore as I continued my pursuit to get this man. He was playing hard to get and I was stupidly playing the game with him. Years later I would visit with a very wise man who would tell me that if you have to chase something it's because it is running from you. It's running for a reason – because you are not supposed to be with it. That spiritual wisdom would not have resonated with me at the time.

I would ask Jose why Peter was bringing other women to the party if he was interested in me. He was equally confused because Peter was asking a lot about me. My bafflement would dissipate fast when I heard this, and was quickly replaced with a surge of euphoria at the thought of him being interested in me after all. Ha, I would think, he's not really that happy with the woman he is with else why was he asking about me. I figured he was playing hard to get which drove me to want him more. Unfortunately, I did not consider this behavior as unacceptable at the time. I was too focused on wanting him for myself which made me just as bad and my desire to be with him equally unacceptable.

After my divorce I would meet up with my friends a few times a week where we'd watch some great local bands, eat crappy bar food, drink beer, laugh and stay out as long as we could bear. I still have that same circle of friends, except it's gone from cool bars, loud music, single men, fashion clothing, tight tops, tight pants and hangovers, to dinner parties, card games, movies, shows, and Friday night cheese and wine.

One of those nights in my twenties out with the girls I bumped into Peter, the first time I'd seen him out at a bar. Never missing an opportunity to let him know I was interested, I walked over to him. Wasn't he supposed to come over to me if he was interested? Drat, I was so dumb back then. He was there with a friend who later became a friend of mine too – or so I thought. Peter asked if I wanted to go back to his place for a drink along with his friend and another woman. Yes, of course I did. What I hadn't realized at that time was that the woman was with him! I drove back to his apartment and all four of us continued to drink and chat. I felt very comfortable in Peter's house and had known him for almost a year at this point. After realizing that I had had way too much to drink and drive, I asked if I could crash on his couch. He had no problem whatsoever with my request. In fact, his friend ended up sleeping on the other couch. Just before I fell asleep, I watched the woman go into the bedroom with Peter.

When I woke up in the morning, the friend was gone and the woman was gone. When I asked Peter if they were dating, he told me that she was a "pain in the ass and he couldn't get rid of her." He said there was no place for her crash so she had slept in his bed. He insinuated that she had passed out and that nothing had happened between them, and I believed him because I wanted to believe him. I was clearly naïve and gullible.

He had been so incredibly convincing as he was lying to me, and since we were still only friends, there had been no reason to lie! He had had no reason to lie except for the fact he was a liar. This would be the first of many times that he would look straight into my eyes and lie to me.

Chapter 2

A week or so later, Peter called me and asked if I wanted to go out to lunch. Oh my gosh! Was this a date? I couldn't say yes fast enough. The following day, Peter picked me up, opened and closed my door for me, (nice!) and took me to a local restaurant. He was kind of goofy in a cool way and lunch with him turned out to be really comfortable with neither of us having to try too hard at all. He had always come across as a cool dude and our circle of friends all seemed to feel that way too. As I sat with him that day I realized that he was not a dude at all. In fact he was very much in control of his life, had some pretty significant goals set for himself and his future, had had some early success in starting a business with a college friend, had his home in order, his finances in order, and seemed very intelligent and smart. There was a lot more to Peter than met the eye. He was mysterious and secretive which unhealthily enhanced my attraction; it was exciting and seemed to keep me on my toes searching for more about him. Who was he?

I, on the other hand, am an open book with no secrets whatsoever, so this locked book of secrets and mystery was becoming more and more intriguing. There was a dysfunctional excitement being around Peter. As a child I grew up always in search of excitement, fun, risk and even danger. I was not afraid to approach anything or anyone, and it was from this pattern of braveries that I marched forward and pursued a man who was clearly secretive and mysterious for a reason.

I had known him for over a year at this point; what was hiding behind the subdued image? He was so much greater than that but I could not figure out what it was. I would learn about hiding behind an image soon enough; I was about to live behind one for the next seventeen years. All the same, I was with a super-hot guy who was extremely responsible in his life who had just taken me out on a date, and I felt like I was walking on water. He drove me home, opened my door, and gave me a kiss on the cheek. He was very charming that day.

It was only a few nights later until I saw him again. He called and told me he was going to meet some friends at a restaurant which had a fun bar and did I want to go along. OK, I thought, I don't know why he bothers to ask, the answer is always going to be "Yes, yes, yes." So, I said yes. He picked me up and I felt like I was on a second date. He was already including me with his friends, showing me off (or so I had thought). There were a few guys at the bar that I recognized from the beach. Peter hung out at the beach on the weekends with a bunch of real "dudes" and one in particular made me feel very welcome that evening. His name was Alan. He was also handsome, not nearly as handsome as my guy, but sweet, warm, friendly and kind.

Peter seemed to behave differently towards me at the bar that night. Had I misunderstood? I thought it was a date. It seemed like I was just part of the group and nothing more. I had thought that I was going as "his girl". I noticed that Peter was spending a lot of time with a girl a few bar stools away from us. A short time into being there, the girl started crying hysterically. I remember thinking that she was embarrassing herself and that I would never conduct myself in that way publicly. Why was she crying and why to Peter? It was starting to bother me, not because I was jealous but because I was feeling abandoned and ignored by the very man who brought me there. He finally came over to me after what seemed way too long and I asked him what was wrong with the girl and asked who she was. Why was he listening to her blubber when he was supposed to be with me? I felt that he was treating me poorly that night and showing me no respect. Something felt really wrong.

He told me that Alan had just broken up with her and that she was really upset and wouldn't leave the bar. He was just trying to calm her down hoping she would leave. Phew, I felt relieved. She had

9

belonged to someone else and that made me feel a little more secure. He stayed with me for only moments and went back over to her. I was left not knowing what to do with myself and continued to make small talk with his friends. I could tell that Alan sensed my being uncomfortable (or felt sorry for me) because he came over and talked with me for a while. I liked him, he felt safe to be with. I asked him why he had broken up with the girl that Peter was talking to.

"She's not *my* girlfriend!" he said. "She's Peter's; he's trying to break up with her."

WHAT! Thoughts started racing through my head. Why am I here, why am I here, why am I here? I felt like an idiot, deceived, gullible, foolish, and hurt. I don't recall if I told Alan that night that Peter had lied to me but I think it had been obvious by my reaction. I walked over to Peter and told him that I wanted to leave and I needed him to drive me home. Where was my self-respect back then? Why had I wanted *him* to give me a ride home? I should have called a taxi and never ever looked back. It must have been a matter of pride, I suppose you brought me, you take me home. He had shown me zero consideration that night. It was another red flag. One of sheer disrespect towards me. There would be many more of these episodes lying ahead for me with one leading to a massive panic attack which would end up with my being hospitalized. Ten minutes before we actually left, the girl stormed out the bar. I should have felt sorry for her. I should have felt some compassion for this hurt and rejected woman yet all I could do was feel that she deserved it for ruining my night. She hadn't ruined it, she had showed up there thinking she was with him and he had brought another woman. I knew how that felt from the dinner parties and here he was doing it to her using me!

I did not talk to Peter for most of the ride home nor did he to me. It felt too vulnerable to admit that I had felt abandoned, humiliated, or misled about the evening so instead I asked him why he had lied to

10

me about the girl belonging to Alan.

"That's what *he* told you?" he yelled. "I saw him hitting on you all night; he only told you that because he wants to be with you!"

He went on a complete rampage the rest of the drive back diverting the focus from himself and his actions to Alan. He was very convincing. I had found Alan to be kind, nice, and safe but after Peter finished his rampage on Alan and his antics, I started to believe that Alan was the one being deceitful and his surreptitious conversation with me was a skeevy way of stealing me. Peter brought me home but I was still really angry. Before he left he continued to tell me how wrong I was about the whole evening and that he had really wanted to help his friend by getting rid of the girl. He was extremely upset that I was mad at him for something he hadn't done. I conceded that I had been wrong and that my perception of the situation was what caused the problem that night. In truth, he was angry because he had been caught.

The more I confronted and quizzed him on what *really* happened, the more I felt that I sounded jealous and insecure. I was neither. I had felt disrespected and hurt by his behavior and I should never have spoken to him again after that night. However, I was young and inexperienced and wanted to be with him so much that I was willing to look past that night. I felt that I could change him or tweak certain behaviors since everything else seemed so perfect. We seemed good for each other. I cooked for him, I helped him with general household chores and organization, I cared for him, I admired him and I represented him with pride and integrity in front of his business partner, clients, and later his family and friends. He, on the other hand, fulfilled areas in my life that were important to me like his being a hard worker, financially responsible, organized, a problem solver, and with his 6-foot 2-inch height I felt safe with him. For weeks after this episode he was very considerate and treated me to nice meals and evenings out together. It helped propel my emotions back from angry and guarded to loving and safe in his presence.

11

Shortly after the bar encounter I returned to the U.K. to visit with my family. Peter had driven me down to the airport. He could not find a place to park. He was becoming irritable and claimed it was because he wanted to spend time with me in the airport before I left. He slowed down at a parking space that had a temporary sign saying no parking. He got out of the car and ripped the sign out of the hole, threw it on the ground behind other cars and parked his car. Even though it was wrong, it was his way of showing me that he was doing it for me, for us. It was naughtily romantic and I was most impressed by it. A week later I returned from my trip. Peter met me at the airport with a bunch of red roses. I was so flattered and elated. It was like I was drowning in pride. This tall, handsome, romantic man was here for me, with roses to boot. I felt like the luckiest girl in the world.

There was a back and forth manipulation and control of my emotions forming and was going to be the crux of a very long, miserable, unhealthy relationship. I had just entered a life of on again/off again abuse that was about to bring with it years of misery and strife. I had an unhappy and unloving relationship with my own mother which is what made travelling to another continent an easy transition for me. Psychologically speaking I had unconsciously recreated and continued this wretched pattern of existence on the other side of the pond with Peter.

There was no question whatsoever that it was Peter breaking up with the girl that night. I know this as a fact because the girl Alan was dating at the time turned out to be my dearest friend to this day. I was not accustomed to being deceived by people close to me. I was masterfully being psychologically manipulated to believe I had not seen what I had seen and known what I had known.

Chapter 3

I had started to see Peter a little more frequently. We never formally announced we were dating to our friends, or each other for that matter, we just kind of were.

Peter used to hang out at the beach during the weekends and play volleyball with his beach friends, including Alan. He was dating a girl called Lara who became a dear long-time friend who lived with her brother Art and my friend, Jose. Jose and Art are gorgeous and gay. Peter often went out with Jose but not so much after we started getting together. Peter used to tell me that he went out with Jose because he was a chick magnet and it helped him pick up girls. Hang on! He was way more handsome than Jose. That made no sense, but at the time everything Peter told me made sense because I wanted it to.

One night early on in our relationship, Peter and I went out together and had a great night. I was really starting to enjoy our time together. We had started to stay over with each other frequently at this point nearly always ending up at Peter's place. We stopped at a red light and there was a flashy red car next to us. I am not a car person but this was the kind of car that made you do a double take. A muscular guy sat in the driver's seat of his red prestigious convertible wearing his personality right there under his butt looking around in sad desperation on a Friday night to see who he had attracted. He caught me looking at the car and then, seeing Peter, turned away. I was just about to tell Peter how typical that it was to see a guy in hot car without a date when all of a sudden, my window started going down. "Why don't you get his fucking number?" Peter said in the most vicious voice I had ever heard. It frightened me because I had not heard this type of tone from him before. I was so flustered from the random angry outburst that all I could think of was to raise the window so the guy couldn't hear him. He held his finger down on the window button to prevent me closing it and yelled it again, "Why don't you get his fucking number?" I was horrified. I couldn't even speak from humiliation. What was wrong with him? I was disturbed by his behavior and couldn't understand what had triggered it. I explained that I was looking at the car and had no interest in the guy at all. He couldn't hear me. He was livid. There seemed nothing I could say that would snap him out of the rage. This was the first time he had gone completely nuts over nothing. It scared me. I decided to take comfort in silence until we arrived home. How dare he humiliate me in public that way and I told him so. We went back and forth about the situation where nothing had happened for too long. I eventually went back to silence, a place where he couldn't reach me. I emotionally shut down. This would not be the first time that I had to emotionally shut down for the sake of sanity and, along the way, social humiliation would continue causing such stress that I would start experiencing anxiety and feelings of despair.

The following day after seeing how very upset I was he told me that he had been angry because he thought I was flirting with the other man. It was an excuse and a pathetic one at that. He knew how much I loved being with him and he knew that I had not been flirting so it left me wondering what the real trigger that caused this violent outburst. The romantic in me wanted to believe that he reacted in a protective way and had felt threatened, but it was dangerously unhealthy. It was like he was making his mark on me almost like a form of ownership. He had also shown me one very concerning thing that night: insecurity. It is one thing to be insecure, it is another thing to act on it in a mean and vicious way. The outburst also highlighted another surfacing trait which was that a bad incident happened *"because of something I did"*. Or didn't do in most cases.

Any time there was strife, it was followed with good times. The weather was so beautiful at night that Peter pulled the mattress out of the bedroom of where I was staying and we slept outside for a few nights. It was so romantic, spontaneous and fun. This was a side of him that I liked. That was the good stuff that followed the bad.

Some weeks went by filled with friends, bars, and dinner parties. Boy, was I proud to be with Peter, this whopping tall gorgeous man by my side. We had good times when we were out with our friends-- in the beginning that is--and the distraction of being with them prevented me from analyzing those things that were starting to trouble me. I made the best of every time we were out with our friends because I am such a people person and loved socializing. We were going through some really happy times. I would always sit on Peter's knee if I could, not to keep people away or to ward women off, but because I loved the intimacy and I wanted to be as close to him as possible. Even though we had had some set-backs, I wanted this relationship to work out more than anything in the world. I thoroughly enjoyed being with Peter, especially now that everything was good again.

One night, Jose asked me if I wanted to go out with him to The Copa, a local gay bar. I was starting to see less of him now that Peter and I were together. I had just moved in with him. It was way too soon to have moved in together, hindsight being just beautiful, but I had been looking for a new place and Peter asked me if I wanted to move my stuff into his home. I was over the moon and moved in almost immediately. We were officially a couple. We were living together and I was on top of the world. The Copa was having a show that night. Shows at gay bars are the best. Drag queens prancing around on stage as Madonna, Cher, Diana Ross, Lisa Minnelli, fabulously loud music, and safe when you're straight! I wore my jeans and my new white sweater. It was my favorite top. I remember it looked great on me and was why I loved it. I asked Peter if he would like to come with us. He said he did not feel comfortable in gay bars (how would he know?) and did not want to come.

I was kind of hoping he would say no because Jose and I had so much fun together and I was starting to miss him a little.

Peter and I had a good relationship at the time but I had noticed it seemed to lack laughter. There are some people in your life who you always have a good time with and laugh when you are around them; that was Jose. Peter was not happy about me going out that night even though we pressed him to join us. I have always held my friends in high regard and though I didn't want to put a friend ahead of my boyfriend and feel like I was disrespecting him, I felt that Peter was being a little selfish knowing the history of our friendship. After all, Jose introduced us. He was not about to break us up.

Even though I knew Peter wasn't pleased with me going, I went anyway. I didn't think it was a healthy way to start a relationship where your partner decides where you can go and who you can go with. Way too controlling. Jose and I had the best night just as I had expected. I laughed a lot that night. I always felt good after spending the evening with him. I would laugh for days, sometimes weeks and occasionally years afterwards recalling some of the things he did. That's how healthy going out with a good friend is and that is exactly why I went out that night. I returned to Peter's place around 1am. Gay clubs finish late and yet I think we were one of the earliest to leave that night. Peter was sleeping so I tiptoed into bed and went straight to sleep.

The following morning when I woke Peter had already left for work. I wished he would have woken me even if it were just to say goodbye. Maybe he was being respectful and allowing me to sleep. I walked out of the bedroom and the white sweater that I had worn was torn into small pieces and were scattered all over the living room floor. When I say small pieces, it had not been cut into small pieces but torn into small pieces. That must have taken some strength...no, rage. Have you ever tried to rip fabric into pieces? He had been so upset that I had gone out. This was his way of punishing me, by ripping up my new white sweater. How weird is that? This was the first thing that had been of some value to me that I recall him destroying, and there'd be more. This was just the first.

I was so angry about my sweater but more troubled about why he would do it. Why not talk to me? "I don't like you going out that late." Or, "I don't like you going out without me." Or, "I don't like you going out with another man." I don't know, anything. Why would he keep quiet and then punish me? I did not make very much money back then and it had been an expensive purchase. It was an issue that I felt needed a discussion but, as I was discovering, conversations involving emotion or explanation were impossible. When I asked him why he had ripped up my new sweater, he simply refused to answer. Either it was learned behavior from his childhood where things were broken during episodes of family fighting, spiteful revenge towards me for having the audacity to go out and leave him at home, or perhaps it was *him who really wanted to go*. I will never know because he refused to discuss it. I was becoming anxious about his behavior and rage because not only was it completely foreign to me but it was frightening.

Seeing how deeply upset I was by his behavior he agreed to purchase some new towels for the bathroom that I had been suggesting we needed for several weeks and which he had refused to buy. This purchase was his way of apologizing. He wouldn't sit down and discuss anything that was "bad behavior" with me – ever. He ran from it and bought it out of the way. Over the years to come, there would be some very expensive apologies.

A few months later he broke another gift that was special and sentimental to me from my longest and dearest friend. She is an essential therapeutic oil specialist and is proficient in the natural healing and organic world. I had told her a little about what was going on at home.

She herself had married and divorced a narcissist several years earlier; she knew exactly what I was going through and what I was facing. The next time I saw her she gave me the most beautiful clay pot filled with essential oils. She designed the mixture to bring me spiritual peace, safety, and strength. I remember it had smelt wonderful. I kept it in my car. Peter knew Wendy had given me the gift.

One day we were bickering over something stupid in the car when he lowered the car window, grabbed the pot and with great force, threw it out of the window where it shattered into tiny pieces on the street. He wanted to hurt me as badly as he possibly could and knew that breaking my gift would devastate me, just as it had with the sweater.

I hated him for what he did. His face was full of rage and pleasure at the same time. This must have been how it worked in his family growing up, but not in mine. Around that time, Peter had been sharing a little about his abusive childhood and how his mother had played psychological games, how she never fed him properly and how she had moved him from school to school to prevent him making friends and being around other children. He was being held hostage and mentally tortured at the same time. It sounded like such a lonely childhood filled with psychological cruelty. When I looked at Peter I had started to envision that little boy within him yearning to be loved and instead being treated with an abundance of distain. I should have been concerned about my own well-being with him, but I found myself starting to forgive his behavior, feeling sorry for him and for what he had been through. I've always wanted to help those suffering or less fortunate around me. I wanted to help him, to fix him, to make up for what had happened to him. I was greatly mistaken, since he was the only one that could do that.

Chapter 4

Peter told me that he was adopted and that the family who had adopted him were weird and fought constantly throughout his life. They were full of secrets and nobody could talk about certain things like age, memories, or past events. When they did, they fought about them like they had just occurred and they always exploded into vicious fights. I met them for the first time when Peter and I decided to take a trip to New York. It was early December of 1995. We did not have much money at the time. We had a nice time in New York; we went sightseeing, had snowball fights and idly walked about the city with no cares in the world. Except one. He was extremely anxious about the upcoming lunch visit with his family. We had arranged to take a train from the city and his family was going to pick us up from the station. His family was his mother, his father and his adopted sister. The entire train ride he talked about how strange they were. I had wondered why we were visiting with them if he felt so anxious. We exited the train and walked towards the parking lot. Something didn't seem right.

They were all there. His father, an older man who seemed genuinely happy to see both of us, his sister who scowled unhappily as we approached, and his mother. She said hello and seemed as uncomfortable as Peter. I was unable to read his mother or even connect with her because she wore a pair of extra-large black glasses with very dark lenses that covered most of her face. She kept them on the entire time she was with us, including over lunch. I literally couldn't see her, but I knew she was watching me.

We all squashed into his Dad's car and proceeded out of the train station. There had been no warm greeting from the women, no hug, no handshake, no smile. I had the uncomfortable feeling that I was being judged. The father gave me a hug but most likely got into trouble for it after we left, according to Peter.

"Kiss ass piece of shit...kissing her ass" would be the kind of dialogue that most likely took place. Peter told me that his mother often accusing them of kissing peoples' ass when one of them was trying to be nice to someone, especially a non-family person. Yes, he would pay dearly for this act of kindness by these viscous and hateful women. Peter heard this kind of hateful and disparaging attack on his father for most of his young life, and not only to his father but to anyone that was not the mother's family. During that short ride to the restaurant, they argued and nitpicked the father's driving the entire time. They attacked him for the way he drove, which way he had gone, the place he was planning to park, and just about anything they could do to belittle him. He did not speak up or defend himself once. It had been from years of witnessing this despicable treatment of his father, along with other things that I would learn later in our relationship, that built immense anger in Peter towards his mother, his sister and subsequently, towards women.

His mother only spoke once to me during lunch, asking me where I was from. The sister came across worse than her mother. This was my first time meeting her and she was unfriendly, rude, ignored me most of the meal, was difficult to engage when I did try to talk to her and seemed very angry. I believe she was not angry or upset with me at all, but because I was Peter's girlfriend she would treat me the same way that she treated him, and the reason she treated him so badly was because she had not got past how he had treated her growing up. She was obviously very hurt and expressed her hurt in the form of anger, just like him.

The discomfort I felt being around them morphed into entertainment. This family was totally dysfunctional and very angry. I was mesmerized as I watched them, and completely confused as to how they operated as a family. One of them would say something to needle the other which set off a trigger, and next minute they were fighting and it was usually about something from years past. That little insight confirmed why Peter was unable to resolve any of our issues with me. As a family they had been unable to resolve conflicts and this held up their maturity and spiritual growth; they were unable to move on. This was his family. This is how he grew up.

Peter needled them equally over lunch. There was no sign of any warmth, kindness, love or respect for one another. It was clear to me that their family dynamic was in shambles and that these women were mean and angry as a result. I felt that they were holding back a little in front of me and that the fighting might have become more war-like had I not been there. I was pretty relieved when we left. The unhealthy energy was making me feel unsettled and I felt like I needed to wash them off me.

Peter and I made fun of them on the train. It wasn't that hard to do, to be honest, because they gave us so much material, but really, I should have taken a step back and felt sorry for them. Not just for them but for Peter also. They all had to be living with a lot of unresolved pain if this was how they were behaving. I missed the signs from this encounter of Peter's own lack of maturity and lack of empathy and kindness which was in the beginning stages. This would be projected at me full force.

I was intrigued by this dysfunctional family dynamic and asked Peter many questions. He was always vague and often told me that he couldn't remember what they were referring to when they'd talked about an incident. He only shared a handful of stories about his past and they were usually filled with miserable, angry or hurtful accounts. I don't ever recall hearing a nice story about his childhood. I felt so sorry for him not having a normal childhood and that feeling of sorrow for him allowed him to get away with some unacceptable behavior in our early years together because I would find myself excusing it due to his past. I kept seeing a sad and lonely little boy in him that was resulted in my allowing him to get away with too much, and that was my fault. His childhood experiences had started to impact his adult life and his unresolved anger towards his mother and sister was about to become mine.

21

Peter owned a small profitable business with his partner Doug. Doug and his wife, Duchess were a lot of fun. They were very warm and kind towards me. They were older than we were but they both had an incredible vibrant and energetic personality. I always enjoyed being around them because Peter and I would get along well in their company. That was because he was on his best behavior. He was developing what I call "the image" and he did it well. They seemed to mentor Peter in a parental kind of way. Peter and Doug worked well together but Peter definitely was the harder worker of the two during the latter years of their business relationship. I loved Doug's carefree appearance and behavior in and out of the office, but Peter wanted to intensify the working relationship and the growth of the company and that desire led to a disconnect between the two. Making more money was extremely important to Peter. That desire to become financially successful would soon overtake everything in his life, including me. Peter was not happy with Doug's efforts and lack of presence at the company and started making plans to remove him.

Jose called me and asked if he could come over that night. Yes, of course. Peter and I were home and the phone rang from the guardhouse announcing his arrival. "Jose's here!" I called to Peter. What happened next was startling. He went berserk. He literally went from normal to livid in one second. He was pacing up and down in a rage I just could not comprehend. I was totally dumb-founded. Jose was our good friend, he introduced us, and he was gay! I might have understood some of his reaction if it were a straight man making plans with me and even then not have condoned this behavior, but he wasn't. We had no plans that night, no children, no other guests, what could possibly have upset him so much? If I were guilty of anything, it was that I had not considered Peter before inviting Jose over that evening.

I tried to stay away from him during this outburst and went into the bedroom. He followed me, completely enraged. He came over to me and with his towering height and strength, put his hands around my throat and pinned my body up against the bedroom wall. His face was raging red and he was so out of control that he was spitting through his clenched teeth as he asked me what the fuck Jose was doing at *his* house. His grip was so tight around my neck that I could not move. I was very conscious that any minute Jose would be coming through the front door and I did not want him to see what was happening. That's when I heard him yell hello. Peter immediately released his grip around my neck and opened the bedroom door. What he did next was as equally disturbing to me as what had just happened. He greeted Jose with a big hug, a slap on the back and told him how happy he was to see him. He offered him a beer and welcomed him with such phoniness that it literally made me feel sick. I came out of the bedroom trying my best to be authentic and hugged Jose. I was still shaking. I wanted to vomit. That had been Peter's intention. He wanted to sabotage my night because it had not been what *he* wanted and this was payback for not asking him. For the few hours Jose was there, Peter behaved like he was really pleased. He had completely sucked my energy dry and had fed off it like a vampire. I don't recall how I got through that night without falling apart but I do know that I had just started a new and unhealthy way of dealing with abuse. I hid it.

He would not talk about this episode except to say only that it had happened because of me. He had been angry because he had not wanted anyone there that night and because I had not discussed it with him. So, the attack was justified and was my fault. He left for work the next morning like nothing had happened. That day I went over everything in my head a hundred times. Why had he done that to me? Not only was it abusive, it was dangerous. I took ownership of the fact I had not been considerate of him in his own home, and that my flamboyant personality and carefree ways that he once seemed to like so much were now the crux of his tantrums. But why did I have to change who I was at my core to ward off future outbursts? How could I change who I was in my heart? How do I stop welcoming my friends into my home and nurturing my friendships? I loved the spontaneity of friends popping by for no reason than to say hi, or stay for a drink or two, especially if we were free. That's how I grew up. It was a warm, friendly and normal thing to do when you have friends. I was struggling with the memory of his hands around my neck and could not believe for one minute that inviting our friend over and thoughtlessly not checking in with Peter first would lead to such a massive reaction of rage.

This led to me being a little fearful at times especially when there was an occasion involving my friends and socializing. Many times, everything went well and there were no problems, but I never knew what and who would cause the fuse to ignite. It was stressful for me.

I had kept every episode of what happened in a personal vault, one kept private from everyone that knew me or us. I was keeping this unspeakable behavior a secret because I was ashamed of it, and because of that secret, I had nowhere to turn. Before I met Peter, I would never have put up with this kind of treatment and would have frowned on anyone I knew who did put up with it. I would have told him in the most unpleasant words ever what I thought of him and left.

However, that compassionate carer in me, the one who felt sorry for him, was holding on to what I thought was great about him and praying that I could change the rest. If we stayed together long enough I knew I could help him. If he grew to realize that I was not like his family and that his family were his enemy, and not me, we would be just fine. I wanted us to work even if it meant slow progress and I was willing to stay by his side to achieve it. Having just left a two-year marriage I did not want to fail at this relationship too. I was more determined to make it work and prove that I was not the common denominator in failed relationships. In fact, I *was* the common denominator, not in failed relationships, but in choosing the wrong people.

When you meet a narcissist – man or woman - they are very

charming. They are nice to you and make you feel good. That is why women date and marry narcissist men and why men date and marry a narcissist woman. At first you don't see who they really are or, in my case, don't want to. I had been so happy with my tall, handsome man who worked hard that I had forgotten to find out who *he* was. He had not exposed his true self to me and I had fallen in love with his mask. I also didn't know there was such a thing as a personality disorder and maybe from naiveté thought it manifested itself in a first encounter.

A few weeks went by following this incident. They were usually great weeks after an anger related outburst. However, this one had been serious. He was trying to control me and the fact that he couldn't was causing him to intensify his behaviors in an effort to make me fear him and this, I believe, is was what led to his first physical attack, because he wasn't making any ground.

Part of why I was able to put up with him and stand up to him was from my own past and tough stance to life. I grew up in a family with parents that lacked affection of any kind. We were given very little healthy attention, guidance or protection. My brothers and I were pretty much on our own during our childhood lacking the fundamental parenting required for psychologically healthy children. The way I dealt with the absence of feeling nurtured and protected was to face life aggressively which ultimately led to my becoming somewhat tough and unafraid. As a young girl, I had felt that I had no one in my corner, nobody to stand up for me, which left me with no choice but to stand up for myself. It was my fearless and valiant adult self that kept me from cowering to Peter during the early times of adversity. I was too strong for him, but also for my own good.

Christmas had arrived and things had been going really well. We had our first Christmas party at Peter's home. I love to entertain and cook for my friends so I could not have been happier. We had all our favorite friends at our party that night; it was a blast. Jose was the life and soul of the party. We danced, we drank, and Peter and I really looked wonderful together. I was back to loving life with Peter. It's amazing how quickly you can forget about bad times when you want to. I wanted to. Christmas Day arrived. I prepared a gourmet breakfast for Peter and I and we opened a bottle of Dom Perignon to celebrate. Life was great. We were going to be just fine. I wanted us to be fine.

Two months after Christmas I looked down at the pregnancy test and it very clearly read "positive". I was pregnant.

Chapter 5

When I found out I was pregnant I was totally over the moon. Peter seemed happy about it also. We were not married and yet it didn't seem to bother either one of us. I had been ready for motherhood for so long that expecting a baby had felt more jubilant to me than anything in the world, including feeling like we had to get married because we were pregnant. Finding out that we were having a baby together had given me a feeling of security with Peter and the fact we would be raising a child together cemented our relationship.

Ironically, I had just finished working at a restaurant full time and was asked to leave for not taking it seriously. They had been right to let me go. I had no intention of being a career server. I had just become a citizen of the US and had taken the job as a stepping stone during a time when I was debating returning to the UK to be closer to my family or staying in the USA and re-evaluating my future. That was when I met Peter.

Upon becoming pregnant there was some relief for me in knowing that Peter made enough money to take care of us. I was a very hard worker and knew that I would find work eventually but was devastated to observe how angry Peter had become that I was not making an income. He became excessively focused on me finding work instead of celebrating our pregnancy and making me feel pampered, which is all I had wanted.

We didn't really care about any of the logistics of the pregnancy at the time, we were just happy about it. Especially me. I was going to be the best mom ever. Peter had asked me when we found out that I was pregnant if we should get married. I had not wanted to at the time because I did not want our marriage to be about "getting married because she was pregnant". I preferred to get married for romantic reasons and not because a child was coming. I am not sure it that was selfish but it was how I felt at the time.

Peter started taking some strategic steps to outline a future for us now that it included a child. It was such an exciting time for us and we should have felt joyfully ecstatic...but shortly after our news I felt that Peter was becoming a little distant. When I woke up most mornings Peter had already left for work. This would have been completely OK with me being that I supported his hard work ethic, but he rarely called during the day which I found to be somewhat uncaring considering our new pregnancy. If I called him he would usually tell me that he was busy and had to go. How busy could he be to not take a few minutes to say, "Hi, how is your day, how are you feeling?" His office was only a few miles away and the few times I had gone there he made me feel unwelcome and gave me only a few minutes of his time. I stopped doing it after a month or so because of the disappointment and rejected feelings that I would leave with. I was a very independent young woman and this relationship was starting to make me feel insecure. It was as though he was deliberately wanting to hurt me and I could never figure out why. Worse, I would wonder what I was doing to deserve it. I think it was from the failed marriage before meeting Peter that I felt that I had to try harder and that maybe I was the problem in relationships. When there were early issues between us I inevitably looked at myself instead of looking at the despicable and disrespectful way I was being treated. I had no idea at that time what I was dealing with.

I was baffled by the emerging insecurity because insecurities with men during my teens had long been a part of my past and I did not like how it made me feel. I had one special man in my life in high school who treated me so wonderfully and came from a loving and functional family. Even though he had chosen me to be his, I was so afraid of losing him that I said or did insecure things that actually caused me to lose him. I adored him and had felt secure with him. It was a sense of security I had lacked as a young girl and was so desperately in search of. It was from losing this wonderful relationship early in my adulthood that made me avoid the behaviors of insecurity for years until I met Peter. I felt weakened around him, but not because of my insecurities, it was from his well-planned attempt to control me and to remain in control of everything we did because of *his* insecurities.

Peter would often take a lunch break from the office and preferred to drive past our home for lunch alone than offer to eat lunch with me, meet me for lunch or even to come home and see if I was OK. My vision of a loving and caring man in my life had just had a little chip taken from it. When I talked to him about it he would make me feel bad and point out that he had 3 people to take care of now and that I was selfish not to see that. I was made to feel so guilty that I was not working at the time that I overly compensated by decorating the home with monies that I had, making the most amazing three-course meals for our dinner almost every night and hand making bedding and quilts for our baby.

Jose helped me achieve this home decorating goal by painting some beautiful canvases for our home and he painted the most beautiful mural for our baby's bedroom filled with angels and clouds. Though my efforts were obvious, they seemed to go unappreciated by Peter. I always chalked his inability to be available to me to the fact that he was working so hard and such long hours to get us financially stable for our future. While this was wise and admirable, it would turn out that he was about to become a workaholic and was going to work harder to get more, and more, and more at any cost. Money was going to become his primary focus and would be more important to him than anything.

When I was growing up my parents started off their days together, usually over a quick coffee and breakfast and then on to work. However chaotic it might have been with two parents trying to get out of the door, with three children to boot, we seemed to make that short morning time in the kitchen work. I missed that family time in the morning, so I asked Peter if he would stay home for five minutes in the morning or wake me up a little earlier so we could drink coffee together or have a quick breakfast. I had felt that it might be healthy for us to spend some time together, being that we hardly saw each other except for late at night, and by then we were both tired. I remember we got into a fight over this request. I pointed out that it meant something to me, and he pointed out that "one of us has to work". I was searching for a little more intimacy in our relationship and I couldn't even get him to drink a cup of coffee with me. I had started to get round and full and was feeling less attractive but might have felt wonderful if he had treated me differently. Any time I broached the subject of "us" all I got back was how hard he was working for the roof over my head, and how hard he needed to work to support our child, and how much harder he needed to work to support me to stay home with our baby. Then I would feel guilty for putting pressure on him to spend some time together and that was the end of another conversation seeking intimacy. He diminished my needs by acting as a victim of hard work because of me.

This was the first time since I was twelve years old that I was not earning an income. I came to the U.S. initially for travel experience and should have been back long before but was taking advantage of being free and single in a warm and sunny climate where I was having a blast. I had fallen in love with America. It felt powerful. I felt safe, I felt free, I felt empowered. I enjoyed the sun, the beaches were beautiful, it was warm, stores were open late; it was like living the dream. I started looking for work immediately to fund my travel plans. After two weeks, I had steady work. I started as a nanny (the easiest job to find at that time) and used that to save money and travel. I was shortly thereafter introduced to a tele-marketing position through a friend. I really enjoyed selling over the phone and did very well. I was often complimented by my prospects for having an attractive accent. I started selling my product very quickly and was paid handsomely for it. I had been astonished when I was offered the top marketing position and surprised by how quickly it had come. I learned a lot about people during that time and I also became adept at the art of selling.

My arduous decision about living in America or going home changed when I met Peter. Although Peter was able to support me, I had been presented with a challenge because I was pregnant and without a job. I had saved some money and had a large amount of cash. I did not owe anybody anything and never bought something unless I had the money for it, subsequently leaving me debt free. I hid my cash (a few thousand, I believe) under the mattress in the guestroom. It was not because I was hiding it from Peter; it was more to have easy access to money being that I was not working at the time. If I wanted to hide it from Peter, I would have taken it to my bank. I was also a little concerned that since I became pregnant, there had been no conversation between us about finances, our bills, a budget for the home, or anything. When I asked him how we would address finances (because I hated asking him for it), he told me that he didn't have any to budget for me and decided he would ask me how much I needed for groceries that day and give me only that much. I felt like a child asking for pocket money; it felt demeaning. This aspect of our relationship quickly became contentious, with a building resentment of having to constantly ask for money for food and home needs. I could not understand why we couldn't come up with a financial budget for the home where I could manage it independently of him. He was trying to convince me that he didn't have money, and yet I knew he did. He was lying. After some heated discussions, I accused him of enjoying that I had to ask him for money. He told me that he did and that it made him feel good when I had to ask him for it! I was disgusted that he even acknowledged it to be true. If he had respected me on any level, he would never have put me in a humiliating position, especially during my pregnancy. It was a sick and selfish game of needing to feel superior. If I had had family living close by I would have left Peter. If not that particular time, certainly during one of the many distressing times that followed. I felt vulnerable; I was not employed, I was pregnant and with nowhere to turn, I stayed.

Not long after that day, I came home and Peter confronted me about finding my cash in between the mattress. He was angry about it. All I could think of was how the heck had he found it. What could he have been looking for between the mattresses? He was so angry that I had hidden the money that he kept it and refused to give it back to me. With the exception of a small savings account, it was all I had. I had been using it little by little to sustain my personal needs. I had bought a couple of pieces of maternity clothes now that I was growing and had to discreetly incorporate them into my closet so he did not see the purchase. He felt that I should wear his large tee shirts as my maternity clothing and a pair of stretchy pants. He told me that if he had to use his money for the home, then my money (that he stole from me) would be used towards the same. I was not familiar with this type of treatment at all and naively continued to believe that he was treating me unkindly because he was angry that I was not contributing. Now it was my turn to be angry. He had just stolen my money without any conversation or agreement; he just took it and that was that.

I have a feisty nature and I usually don't back down from anyone, including him. I was about to learn that my strength would become my enemy and would enhance the intensity of his cruelty. I hadn't realized it at the time but the more you stand up to a narcissist, a psychopath, or a misogynist the more it will infuriate them and their behavior will worsen. If I behaved submissive to Peter, the verbal, mental, emotional and psychological attacks would not nearly have been so ferocious, but I was feisty. The fighting escalated; I tried to grab at my money and he pushed me so hard that I fell against the bed post of the guest bed and my arm slammed into the corner. I saw stars and almost fainted from the pain. I thought my arm was broken. I looked at my arm in the bathroom mirror through my tears. There was a blood-red welt the size of a plum on my arm. I thought it was my bone protruding and in shear horror and fear I ran to the phone and dialed 911. Peter ran after me and hung up the phone as they answered. He changed his demeanor instantly and calmly suggested that we go for a walk. I was upset, I was angry, I was afraid, I was crying, I couldn't move my arm due to the huge welt growing by the minute and he wanted to go for a walk? "Come on," he said, "let's get out of here." He was being really nice to me, but how was that possible? How was he able to change that quickly? He had just been irate and physically assaulted me.

We left the house and took the back paths behind the pool area and around the back of the community and found a bench. We sat and talked about what had happened. It was the first time we had actually sat and discussed a problem. That was progress for us. Ugly but progress...except for one thing. It had not been authentic. The reason Peter whisked me out of that house so quickly coupled with the demeanor change was because the police were on their way. Any time you call 911 and they answer and you hang up, they consider you in immense danger and radio out to all units in the area for immediate assistance. They came quickly and silently to our home to help me, except I wasn't there. Peter knew this and it was why he became psychopathically nice and suggested this beautiful make up walk and talk. It was bullshit. The police would have taken one look at my arm and he would have been arrested, and he knew it. It was after this physical attack that I started to fear him.

Chapter 6

The following day, after Peter left for work, I packed up all my belongings. I was so shocked at what had happened the night before that I had to get out, and fast. I wanted to be gone before he came home. I was done in a little over an hour and I cried the entire time. I felt like a total failure. Pregnant to a man who had the audacity to physically assault me...again. I felt pathetic and felt that I would be viewed as such by those who knew me. In fact, contrary to what I had been feeling at that time, I would have been viewed as having courage, being brave and strong to have walked away from an abusive partner. I called Jose and told him that I needed to come and stay with him.

I was getting myself ready to leave when, to my surprise, I heard Peter. He had come home from work midmorning unexpectedly. I was around five months pregnant at the time. I was as surprised to see him as he was to see me with my packed boxes. His arrival had totally ruined my plans to be gone. I wondered if he was feeling remorse about what had happened because he never came home early. I picked up a box to take down to my car and Peter stood in front of me, not allowing me past. After pleading with him to move, I put the box down and left with my bag and keys. I got into my car with Peter right behind me. He told me that I was being ridiculous and that we should talk. Why was it that he was always ready to talk when things had become a crisis and practically reached the end? I started the car and reversed out the driveway. Peter suddenly jumped onto the hood of the car. I continued to reverse thinking he would jump off. He didn't. I started to drive down the street and he remained on the hood of the car. I was closing in on a major road and he was still holding onto the hood. He was not planning on getting off. I became afraid that I would be stopped by the police and quite frankly, the fact that I had a man on the hood of my car as I was driving was quite embarrassing. So I stopped the car. He got in and begged me to turn back, and finally I did. We went back upstairs and talked. We resolved the financial budget issue and after many tears, from me, I unpacked my boxes and stayed. It took that ugly ordeal to win me a financial budget.

Things were great again for a while. They always were for long periods after abusive episodes. I didn't tell anyone about what happened that night. I was ashamed of it. It went into the closet with the last physical attack. It was easier to forget the bad times when things were going well. I refused to look back and kept my vision forward but never forgot. The bizarre and abusive behavior was becoming a pattern and I was choosing to ignore it because it required less effort and less conflict. I wanted our relationship to work so deeply because of my life-long desire to start and become a part of a happy and functional family. Everything between us had started to normalize again, with the exception of the fact that I had started to tread delicately around Peter at certain times. This was not who I was, and I did not like how it made me feel. I was not a timid person and feeling compelled to tread carefully around my own partner because I feared upsetting him was stressful, ridiculous and had started to affect my confidence. I was accepting the very unpredictable and unfolding cruelty that I would seriously caution any other person about. My first strike back against the abuse had been to leave, however, the power of his manipulation had brought me back. After returning I mentally struggled for some time with where I would go alone, pregnant and without an income. I was afraid of this scenario and of forcing it upon our unborn child. Not having any family in the country to move in with during that difficult time was a huge factor to my staying. There is no question whatsoever that if I was not pregnant with Peter's child that I would have left him because of the bizarre behavior. However, there was a greater responsibility at hand; I was not going to let our child down by bringing him into the world with a major disadvantage, or at least that is how I felt.

I became so determined to make our relationship work for our child that I conveniently ignored the increasing severity of Peter's behavior and remained hopeful that I could eventually change him. All I wanted was for him to show me that he loved and cherished me--kind of like what I had hoped my own mother would do but never did. I had unconsciously beckoned in and was reliving the very void that encompassed my childhood. I poured love and care into Peter, attempting to earn his respect, and his trust, but I got nothing back.

I believed in the sanctity of family and now that we had carelessly just started one, I was determined to show responsibility and raise our child in a loving two-parent family, even if it was a constant work in progress, fully believing that once our child was born things would work out. I also believed that when Peter witnessed my abundance of unconditional love and care for both him and our child that it could help to heal his childhood wounds, and my own.

I had a wonderful pregnancy with our first child. I was very excited and eagerly awaited the arrival. Peter and I decided to take a last minute month-long car trip when I was around six months pregnant. We thought it would be a good idea to fly to LA and take a car to visit several west coast states and then spend a week in Hawaii before our baby came along. I did not complain about sitting in that car for two weeks even at six months pregnant. I was enjoying our time together, though it continued to lack intimacy and though work could no longer be blamed for it. This was the most time we had spent together in a long while.

One day Peter and I were talking and he told me that he had sent a man to the hospital for trying to date his girlfriend. It was not the kind of story I wanted to hear, nor did it make me feel good. He said that the guy had tried to ask his girlfriend out and Peter took his motorcycle helmet and hit him across the head with it almost fracturing his skull. The guy spent some time in the hospital. I don't think he expected my reaction to his story to be of horror and shock, and quite frankly it sickened me. He quickly tried to soften the story but I had already heard it. The action he took was not normal. It was wrong and it was violent. He was obviously a dangerous person, or at least had been at some point. The story left me feeling wary about him and who he was, especially since the same behavior had expressed itself early in our relationship. I had also just learned that it was not only because of my actions that he lost control and became violent, it had happened before with others.

When we arrived home from our trip, Peter continued his long work hours. I was starting to get really bored and asked Peter if I could help at the office. I really enjoy working and, being that I had finished decorating and preparing our home for our new family, I was ready to do something else. Peter was uncomfortable with it initially but since he had some very unreliable staff he begrudgingly welcomed it. I am a fast learner and a hard worker so I picked up the work very quickly. I was happy that I was working and around other people, and not just at home all day. My belly was pretty big at this point but it did not stop my performance. I continued to work at the office right up until the day that I delivered our first child.

One day around lunchtime, a pretty girl walked into the office. She asked if Peter was there. He came into the front of the office and, I have to say, based on his and her reaction, it was like I had caught him in bed with her. "Oh, this is my girlfriend," he said to her. It was clear from her reaction even as she tried to mask it, that she was shocked to learn of me, especially with my beautiful round eight-month pregnant belly. It was an uncomfortable few minutes where she claimed she was just passing and had stopped by to say hello. I asked him about her after she left and he told me that she was just a friend that he used to know and that was all he would say. I would not be at all surprised if he was having some kind of relationship with her but I chose not to press the issue because we were getting along so well at the time I did not want to upset anything. Of course, I knew something was going on.

Since we had been getting along well and everything seemed better,

I wanted to enhance our romance and intimacy. I bought Peter a beautiful Hallmark card that expressed words of gratitude and love for him. I was coming close to bearing our first child and I was becoming soppy and soft and wanted to share my feelings with him. I was appreciative of his hard work and long days and wanted him to know that. Since he was uncomfortable with emotional conversations, I said them to him in the card. I left the card on the steps up to our home. I thought it was very romantic and sweet. He came in the house and said nothing about the card. I asked him if he found it and he told me he had. I asked him if he'd read it. He told me that he had. I asked him if he liked it. He told me that it was a card. It hurt me but I decided to leave the issue alone. A couple of weeks later I saw another card with uplifting and less romantic wording. Since the words expressed how I felt I bought it. It was a card that had a little more humor to it and I thought he would enjoy it. I left it on the steps again. He told me to stop wasting money on cards. That was the last time I ever bought him a card expressing sentiment. As hurt as I had felt, I forgave him and felt that I was pushing intimacy on a man unable to receive or give it.

That was until around six months later when I found an envelope in the storage room with love letters between Peter and a former girlfriend expressing intense feelings to one another in one letter after another. Was it that he had absolutely no feelings for me or was it that he was faking it with her? I would continue through the majority of our years together to be romantic through lighting candles, setting a beautiful table with fresh flowers, cooking wonderful meals and serving nice wine. I didn't do this so much for him; I was doing it for us and especially for me. I'm not sure what happened to the man who met me at the airport with roses, but then the narcissist has a way of being charming with his victim during the beginning of a relationship and will expose his authentic self-loathing self when he feels he has you in place.

My pregnancy was going fantastic even though I was close to the end. I continued to exercise, I was in good shape, I ate well and there were absolutely no complications. I was totally in love with my unborn baby. I would talk to it, sing to it, play with it while it was in my belly, tickle its feet and would have to constantly push those feet out from under my ribs as the baby became bigger. I dreamt I gave birth to a boy one night close to the end of my pregnancy. I did not receive a lot of TLC from Peter during my pregnancy. He was not tender at. He was too busy into himself, his work, and our future…so he said. All Peter did was work. He either always was or had become a workaholic. It was around this time that I noticed Peter was looking at other women in a lascivious way. I asked him about it and he would tell me that he wasn't. That was that. It wasn't that I was insecure, because I was far from it. I came into this relationship with an abundance of authentic confidence. Though he tried to convince me many times that I was jealous and insecure, it was really him that was both. A classic narcissistic trait is to blame the other entirely for what you are yourself. However, his guileful flirting with other women in my presence had started to make me feel insecure and rejected.

When Martin was born, it was the best day of my life. Nothing had come even close to this moment. I could not stop looking at him, I was wholeheartedly in love. When he was placed into my arms I told the nurse that he had an old soul. I don't know why I said it or where it came from but I believe it was said because it was so. We were inseparable. He was such a good baby and so very calm. I couldn't believe that I was finally a Mom; I was flooded with euphoria.

We arrived home completely elated with our new baby. I swaddled him and placed him into his new crib in his new room that Jose had painted for us. Jose, who is an amazing artist, had painted angels against a blue sky with puffs of white clouds; it seemed so appropriate for a new soul coming into the world. There he lay, fast asleep, so beautiful, so peaceful, so calm, and I was so grateful to be blessed with him. Peter and I sat in the next room and watched TV. I wanted so much for him to fuss so I could have a reason to go in and pick him up but he didn't; he slept contently. I remember feeling that first night home like I was going to cry, wondering why I felt like crying, trying not to cry, but crying anyway. Peter looked at me and asked why I was crying. I told him that I had no idea why I was crying. He said, "Then stop." I felt so hurt and embarrassed at the same time, that I did. What a callous and cruel remark to make to the mother of your child. Not one hug, not one word of comfort, just, "Stop crying."

I was a great new mother, if I say so myself. I was not overly protective and was very generous when it came to allowing people to hold and snuggle with Martin. He was put onto a schedule immediately and slept and ate very well. My parents came to stay with us for a few weeks and he was given a lot of attention from all of us. Martin was their first grandchild and they were ecstatic. They gave us lots of relief during that stay, taking him for walks every night, helping me to bathe him, rocking him, playing with him and just being there to help with whatever I needed. My Dad was so patient and would sit with him for hours.

Peter and I were invited to a dinner party while my parents were staying with us. My mother urged us to go and take advantage of her being there. So, we did. The dinner party was being thrown by a woman named Fanny that I had known only a short while. The lunch girls (as they were known) were all older than me, which didn't bother me in the slightest. I liked being in their company; I found them to be most interesting. We arrived at her gorgeous condo that overlooked the ocean. There was a quartet playing classical music that night, delicious food, a full moon, nice guests and the most spectacular view. After giving birth to Martin, I went back to my original shape in around two weeks. I am the woman that most women hate. My stomach was as flat as it had been before my pregnancy. I could see how it would be difficult for those at the party who didn't know me to believe I had an eight-week old baby. One of the lunch girls, Marian, was there with her husband, Victor. She happened to be one of my favorites because she was so kind, so warm and so friendly, as was her husband. They are from Venezuela. This was my first time meeting Victor. He was an older man around sixty. Marian told him that I had just had a baby and he could not believe it. They were quite a funny couple. He told me that Marian took two years to lose the fifty pounds she put on with each of her children and they laughed lovingly together at the memory. He told Peter that he was a very lucky man to have a beautiful woman that looked that amazing after childbirth. This should have been such a compliment to Peter, but, unbeknownst to me and them, he was getting angry. I was not sure what made him so angry at the time but if I had to guess today I'd say that he did not like me getting complimented, it made him jealous. He likes the attention on himself although I did not know that at the time.

The night went on. Peter was never really comfortable in social gatherings so I was keeping my eye on him and aware that he might not be having the best time. I would leave early on his behalf. I was on the balcony with the Venezuelans for some time, even though it had gotten chilly. We were talking about their children, their grandchildren, where they lived, and the funny things the grandchildren were doing. It was light and easy conversation. I remember thinking how cool they were and how wonderful it would be to have grandparents like them; I told them that their children were very lucky to have them.

I had worn a dress and did not come prepared for the cold and I shivered from the drop in the temperature. Victor saw this and very kindly took off his jacket and put it around my shoulders. I started to walk inside the condo to warm up, and what happened next made time stand still. I saw Victor fly past me and land on the floor. You know when you see something and it happens in slow motion because your brain can't comprehend the vision? That happened to me right then. I turned and saw Peter and he had a violent look of his face. I was in a state of shock and was completely mortified. I took off Victor's jacket, put it on the back of a chair, and walked straight ahead to the elevator. I did not look back once.

41

I had never seen anything like that happen before. A thirty-year-old man attacking a sixty-year-old grandfather just for being kind to me? I was so angry with Peter. How dare he hurt this man? How dare he disrespect the host? How dare he humiliate me? He humiliated himself, to be honest, but I felt that he took me down with him. This was the first time he had exposed his violent side in public, at least since being with me. I waited until we were in the car and as far away as possible before unleashing my anger. Instead of any remorse of any kind he told me that Victor was hitting on me. "How many times did he have to tell me about your body?" he yelled. "Putting his jacket around your shoulders...fuck him." If only he had been friendly enough to join us and heard our conversations about family, he would know that he was not flirting with me at all. I never saw the lunch girls again; I was ashamed and could not face them.

My mother brought a beautiful crotched blanket with her from England that my seventy-year-old Aunt Betty had made for Martin. My aunt lives in the same village that I grew up in and is a wonderful and kind person. She goes to the same church as my mother and father and is an active member of the church community. She had made the most beautiful blanket I had ever seen in the shape of a large circle almost like spider's web. It was unique and was made with a fine yarn and a fancy crotchet stitch. I crotchet myself and I know the love, time and effort that went into this gorgeous blanket. One evening I draped it lightly over Martin in his crib. The following morning Peter told me that he had removed it because Martins finger had been caught in one the holes of the blanket and that it was too dangerous for me to put over him in his crib any longer. The chances of a four-week-old baby taking a thread in his finger and pulling it hard enough to endanger himself seemed a little far-fetched to me. However, acknowledging safety and picking my battles, I agreed that I would only use it as a cover when he was in his stroller and I was with him. It was too beautiful a blanket to put away.

The following week I took Martin to the mall in his stroller. The beautiful blanket was draped lightly over his body. A few days later I went to look for the blanket but I could not find it. Frantic, I looked in the car, in the stroller, in the baby bag, in his crib, in his closet, in my closet, in every room in the house. I called the stores in the mall that I had visited just in case it had slipped off. I knew that was not possible because I would have noticed when I took him out of the stroller and into the car. But where else could it be? Peter came home from work and I asked him if he had seen it. He told me he had not and started looking with me. Our townhome was quite small and I kept it immaculately organized, so there really weren't too many places for Peter to check that I hadn't already checked. He checked the cars, the garage, and the pool area that was close to our unit, under beds, behind the washing machine, the dryer, opened up the stroller, checked in the towel closet and even checked the garbage bags. He walked around the surrounding neighborhood looking for the blanket. For over two hours Peter facetiously helped me look for a blanket that he had already thrown in the trash the week before. He finally admitted this to me a few days later when he saw that I was not prepared to give up. He had thrown it away because he had warned me not to use it again and I had. I was heartbroken. Peter, who had no connection to sentiment, was able to throw it in the trash like it had no value whatsoever just to punish me. Knowing how much I had liked it, and knowing how sentimental it was to me was more reason for him to get rid of it.

That is what a heartless narcissist does.

I never told anyone about the blanket, not even my mother, family or friends. I was too ashamed and knew if I told them that they would not only worry about me, but start to dislike Peter.

Chapter 7

Martin became my entire world. I could not wait to get out of bed every morning to be with him and would miss him once he slept at night. In a way, he was filling the void that I was feeling in my relationship with Peter. We were at the park one day and a friendly girl came over to me and asked me if I would like to join her and her friends once a week at different parks. I was not really into the idea of hanging out with "Mommy and me" groups but she had been so warm and inviting that I agreed. Most of my friends at that time were not in the same boat as me. I was the first one in my group that had a baby. I had found myself feeling a little alone as a new mother for a while, so I was really grateful for these new mothers. We are still friends to this day.

Peter and I got into a routine each week that seemed to work for the both of us. Peter would come home from work and I would tell him about my day with Martin. I told him about all the cute and funny things Martin did, what words he was trying to sound, what he ate, who we saw, where we went, what ideas I had for the weekend, who's invited us over for dinner etc. Peter rarely shared much back with me. I would ask him where he went for lunch and like always, he had spent it alone – or at least that's what he told me. I wondered many times why he chose to be alone all the time. When I had met him, he portrayed himself as a guy who enjoyed going out, enjoyed socializing, liked to have fun and had several friends. He was not this guy any more. The friends I thought he had were just people he met at the beach to play volleyball with; he never kept in contact with them after we got together. They had not been friends after all. Nothing about Peter made sense to me...only his rising desire to be powerful and successful.

If I didn't expect any conversation about his day, if I was content with no emotional or intimate engagement whatsoever, and things were good at home as he wanted them, we were in a comfortable place. However, I wanted so much more than this. I wanted him to show an interest in me, in my day, how I was doing, etc. If he didn't want it in return that was his loss, but I needed it, if nothing else just to feel human to him. I found it incredibly odd that he required nothing of substance from me but would perk up in conversations about business and money. He was empty of anything tender or intimate and only ever interested in himself.

If I played along with our new reality which was not a reality that I was used to or was happy with, we got along just fine. He did not feel like a true friend or partner to me. I felt like we were under contract, like we had to act as a family and create an impressive image to those around us. Our dynamic appeared pretty nice I admit, but the dynamics behind the closed door were of loneliness and disconnect.

When Peter came home on a typical work day he would change his clothes, tend to Martin for a while, eat dinner with me and then go to bed. We were approaching two years together at this point, with a baby, and when Peter and I were together all I felt was an intense feeling of loneliness. I was with him physically, yet alone, something I had never experienced before. I had hoped that our beautiful son would bind us together and improve the disconnect between us but to my shear disappointment, it hadn't. He behaved like he was very unhappy being with me and I was behaving like I was the luckiest girl ever. I would wonder if he was feeling resentment at the fact we had a child together and that he felt that he *had* to be with me. It took me years to realize that I wasn't really doing anything wrong, and took me a lot longer to comprehend that I was with a malignant narcissist, a sadistic psychopath, a pathological liar, one that would become wealthier and in turn, crueler.

Jose was the only person at the time that I really trusted. I started sharing some of my struggles with him and he was equally shocked at Peter's behavior as I had been. I told him that Peter rarely smiled or laughed, which I had not found normal for a young and relatively successful man. I excused it constantly by convincing myself that he was under pressure, working too hard, working to secure our future – all the things he was telling me. But the truth is that there are many men who wake up every morning to do the same for their families and don't treat their partners with the same avoidance and disrespect as he did to me. The only way I could handle this reality was to channel my loneliness into forcing myself into feeling gratitude for all his hard efforts for us. I was not lonely on any other level than within my relationship. I had nice friends who were a lot of fun, a group of moms that I saw weekly, family and friends from the UK who I spoke with frequently, and a disciplined gym schedule which I would look forward to and, most important, I had Martin.

I nearly always had a wonderful meal waiting for Peter after he arrived home from work. The table would be set beautifully, the food would be ready, and I would pour him a beer or a glass of wine as we sat. You would think that he would be elated with this kind of nightly greeting, but he reacted like he had to tolerate me. I would have to remind myself that I had chosen to bear a child with him and that we would have to make it work at any cost for Martin's sake.

Peter took me to hang out with a few of his beach friends shortly after we moved in together. We had driven up to a home on the ocean which I had found to be quite impressive. The house belonged to the parents of his friend, Richard, the guy who had slept on the couch at Peter's house the same night I had stayed over on that first night. His new wife, Sarah was with him. She could not have been more unpleasant. She was harsh, abrasive and a mean gossip. She had a habit of saying things to me that left me feeling stung and uncomfortable. She would bring up Peter's old girlfriends often, and regularly allude to something Peter had told me as not being quite the truth. She was trouble and it was obvious. She was an angry, mean, and bitter woman. Since they were Peter's friends, I would end up keeping her close for years...the devil you know, right?

Sarah became pregnant a month after I did and at her baby shower I met a fabulous girl, Lorraine. She had this magnetic energy that made everyone around her feel good. She reminded me of Jose. She and I would end up becoming very good friends. She was generous, interesting, an avid listener, and she was kind. Kindness to me is a precious gift and one that I admire. I really liked her. Tall, pretty, intelligent, an attentive mother, had a healthy baby, a great marriage, a gorgeous home on the beach, and financial success. I have to admit that I very much envied her life; we would spend some great years together which unknowing to her, helped me through some difficult times... right up to the day she told me she was dying.

A new struggle that I was facing with Peter in addition to the violent outbursts and avoidance was his addiction to looking at other women. I call it an addiction because I caught him doing it all the time. If we were committed and in a loving and respectful relationship, why was he looking to attract the opposite sex while he was out with me? Clearly because we were not.

When I first brought up this behavior, I was told that I was insecure and jealous. Insecure I was not, and neither was I jealous. I was hurt. I was hurt by his insensitivity. Not only did he chastise me for broaching this subject more than once, he denied it every time and told me it was all in my head. Thank God, I know who I am. I could have been in severe danger if I had believed what he wanted me to believe which was that I was not seeing what I *was* seeing. I could easily have been brainwashed by his dangerous manipulation if I were of a weaker nature. The danger I was facing with this emerging psychopathic personality was that I was too strong spiritually and mentally to be defeated by his psychological tactics. In turn, my strength only elevated his inner rage which is where the danger lay.

When Martin was around 6 months old, we took him to the U.K. to see my family. We decided to get him christened at my parent's church during this trip. My mother had been working on me to take a few days and go on vacation with Peter. I knew she meant well and was trying to give us some time together alone as a couple but I had no desire to go. I was happy right there with all my family and friends. I did not have family in the U.S. and had not left Martin with anyone except my parents since he was born so, reluctantly, since my family were on hand, I decided to travel to Paris for 4 days with Peter. I looked at the trip as a four-day break, but sadly not as a romantic getaway. The worst part of getting ready for that trip, aside from what was to come while we were there, was leaving Martin.

We arrived in Paris and, after walking aimlessly for too long along the crowded Paris streets with suitcases in hand, a kind man stopped and asked us if we were lost. We were. We could not find our hotel. Not only did he offer to help us, he walked us right to the front door of our hotel. He had completely gone out of his way to help us. It was such a nice gesture and I had noted how kind he had been. I had never seen Peter go out of his way to help anyone unless there was something in it for him. I dreamed of being with a kind man, especially since our relationship had been suffering and Peter was treating me so poorly. It was around this time that I looked at the man I was with and realized that he really wasn't as handsome as he had initially appeared. I struggled each day I was in Paris because I was missing Martin. He was the only person at the time who I was truly connected with and shared unconditional love with. I felt like I had abandoned him and what made that feeling worse was that Peter and I were not particularly getting along.

The women in Paris were incredibly beautiful. They seem to live to be beautiful. They dressed with such finesse, their hair was stylish and they had a way about them that was very sexy. It wasn't long before I noticed Peter being more interested in them than Paris. We ate dinner that night at a restaurant that reminded me of a cavern. It had long banquet tables that you shared with other guests. You just slid in wherever there was a spot and that was your place at the table. I felt insecure that night since Peter and I did not have new people skills when we were together. When I was alone or with my friends it would not be unusual for me to leave with names and phone numbers in an effort to form relationships, especially with nice people. Peter found this behavior strange so I just didn't reach out to people when I was with him. It made me so uncomfortable to have to be so distant from the people at our table, coupled with the lack of intimacy or communication that night between us, that I asked to leave as soon as we were finished. Not only was our relationship lacking in intimacy but it lacked sex too. I was only thirty years old. I knew this was not a good sign and did not know what to do about it. I would reach out and hold Peter's hand but he would soon drop it. I was never sure if it was that he just didn't like holding my hand or if it interfered too much with the chemistry between him and all the different women we passed.

The following morning, we decided to go for a walk. Two men passed us that morning on our way to a local bakery to get coffee and a croissant. They did the pssst, pssst thing as they passed me, which is what French men seem to do. It was a compliment that I acknowledged, but I did not engage. Peter was furious. He gave them a terrifying glare. He didn't like the attention that they had given me. Somehow, I knew that I might pay for what they did. It had made him very angry, and yet he was guilty of the very same and worse.

As we walked to the Champs-Elysees I noticed that Peter had gone from looking at other women to smiling at other women. He was doing it on purpose to hurt me. He was still angry about the guys making whistle calls at me. I did not have Martin as a distraction and I felt I had nothing to lose so I warned him that I would not spend the rest of the day with him if he continued to flirt with other women. He became mean and started putting me down and telling me what I had heard so many times, that he wasn't looking at other women. He continued to be verbally mean so I kept my word and crossed the street to head back to the hotel. The sidewalks were crowded and I quickly slipped into the waves of people and picked up my pace to get away from him. I was pining for my baby and here I was in Paris

49

as miserable as could be; all I wanted was to go home. I was not prepared to tolerate his poor treatment of me any longer and I sent what I thought was a strong message by leaving him alone in the middle of Paris with absolutely no intention of seeing him for the rest of the day. I was startled when a hand grabbed me from behind and shoved me to the side of the sidewalk. It was Peter. I was mortified. A man came over to me and asked me if I needed help. Yes, yes, of course I did, but I said no. I was so embarrassed and ashamed of this awful scene he was causing and wanted to get as far away as possible. I shook Peter off and ran as far as possible before taking a narrow side street and. After I realized that he hadn't followed, I slowed down and spent a few hours walking alone in this beautiful city that was supposed to be the city of love. I went back to the hotel and called my mother to see how Martin was doing. I wouldn't dare mention what had just happened. I was ashamed of all the bad incidents that happened between us and hid them from everyone.

The rest of our stay was uneasy. Peter always seemed to know when he'd crossed the line because he was unusually nice for long periods afterwards. He would also buy me something pricey as his way of apologizing. He bought me a beautiful leather bag the following day which made me feel a little better, but only temporarily. After the mortifying sidewalk drama, I spent the rest of our time in Paris counting down the hours to get home to be with Martin. I vowed I would go back one day with a man I loved, a kind man. I can't even tell you how the rest of the trip went because I really don't remember. I have chosen to suppress any other memory of that trip. All I recall from that trip was landing in the UK and being greeted by the only person that mattered to me at the time, and that was Martin. I had missed him and since he had been a distraction from my distress up to that point, I found great solace and peace when I was with him.

After we returned to the US, Peter's parents came to visit us for the weekend with his sister. His father was always nice to me. He was pretty feeble most likely from years of being trodden down not just from the mother but from the sister too. They ganged up on him all the time. His sister was sullen and moody and unfriendly. She would always make unpleasant comments to Peter which he dutifully returned. Obviously, this had been their communication style since childhood. His mother reminded me of a woman who had emotionally stopped growing at twelve years old. She was childlike and immature in her conversation but never missed an opportunity to start trouble. One night at the dinner table Peter said to her jokingly, "Alison doesn't want much, she just wants everything." She went back home after that trip and told a member of the family that I was spending all Peter's money. She was delusional. Another night at an Italian restaurant, Peter and his sister, Joy, started going at each other. They were both in their late thirties at the time. They were starting to draw attention from the tables around us. Our table had become quite entertaining, but not to me. Their behavior was humiliating and not good for Martin, who was sitting in a high chair at the end of the table. I told Peter and his family that if they continued to argue in front of Martin that I was going to leave. Not only did they continue to fight, but Joy punched Peter really hard in the arm. The anger just exploded from nowhere. I got up from the table and left. Peter followed me and we drove home. His parents and his sister arrived at our home ten minutes later and continued to fight. When they told me that Peter had been in therapy when he was five years old, he told them to shut up. He called them liars and, after they continued to pressure him, he literally threw them out of our home. Though I tried my very best to prevent Martin from seeing this despicable scene, he was very much aware of it. He was agitated and crying. I loved my son more than anyone in that room and hated them all at that moment for causing him upset. After everything died down, I asked Peter why he had gone to therapy as a child. He told me that he hadn't and that they were liars. Maybe but he was too. I never did find out if he went or why.

Though this family was clearly dysfunctional on an unprecedented level, it wouldn't stop me from doing the right thing for them as grandparents. I sent them photos of Martin every month or so during his first year and even sent them letters that were written by me but spoken like they were from Martin. They never acknowledged my letters or photos. After a year of sending them, I stopped.

Chapter 8

I had fallen for Peter from the first minute I had seen him. I had been physically attracted to him, had loved his work ethic, and had loved that he was very responsible, I'd thought, in all aspects of his life. When I met him, he had showed that he liked to be social, something that would change pretty quickly. All these qualities had been very important to me. However, as time went on I realized that he was missing the very fundamental qualities that were more important in life, especially to me, the very ones that I had omitted to seek in him. I had fallen in love with the image of this man. We had peaks and valleys in our friendship but there had not been any display of compassion, of empathy, or of sincere and authentic kindness. After Martin was born I had felt that we would work things out eventually and that we would grow to be closer over time. Now that we had a child together I figured he would want us to work as much as I did for Martin's sake.

Martin was around 9 months old and we had decided to invite my parents over from England for his first birthday. Since we had been getting along better, we had resumed marriage discussions. We decided to get married while my family was in town, and before I knew it my brothers and their wives were booking flights to attend our wedding. A month before our wedding day Peter and I had a very bad argument. It had been over the man I had dated before Peter. We had not dated for very long but during the months we were together we shared an intense relationship filled with spirituality and amazing sex. His name was Patrick. He did not want children therefore I had to accept early that we were not going to be a long-term relationship. I was drawn to him more than I had ever been drawn to any man before. Unlike Peter, he was short, petite and ordinary looking. Peter ridiculed him early on in our relationship and I had felt compelled to defend him by retorting that it was not his looks that I was enamored with but his personality, his kindness and his lovemaking qualities. It was the worst thing I could have said to Peter since he was erotically clueless. After an argument between Peter and I early in our relationship I had gone to see Patrick. We had parted respectfully as great friends and there was nothing weird about my going to see him. Peter went berserk. He was the reason I had gone to see Patrick since I was looking to feel comforted. He could not forget my visit to Patrick, he very much kept it at the forefront of every issue we had for months. He would taunt me at any opportunity about my going to see Patrick for sex which was only a figment of his own delusion. When he started another fight over Patrick and how I had slept with him on that day I went to see him, as though if he said it enough I would confess, it almost led to my calling off our marriage.

Peter's business partner, Doug was marrying us, being that he was a notary and his longtime business friend and mentor. I had been so shaken by this last argument that I called Doug's wife and told her that I was not going to move forward with the wedding. She spoke with me at length and I had shared with her that we were not getting along and it just didn't feel right to me. When Peter found out that I had called her he was furious. He was more upset that I had shared our shaky relationship with her than the shaky relationship itself. Seeing that I was serious about my decision, the other side of Peter that surfaced in a crisis appeared. The softer and kinder side. The side I would only ever get to see when there was a big problem, a fight, or he was looking to manipulate things his way. The deceiving Peter convinced me that we were going to be just fine and that we needed to think of Martin now and not ourselves.

Peter and I were married the day before Martin's first birthday. Ironically, I was 4 weeks pregnant. I wanted so much for my wedding day to be genuine that I beamed with pride at Peter, but I felt that I was trying too hard to make it what I wanted it to be verses what it was. We invited most of our friends, my family and Peter's cousin to our wedding; we excluded Peter's family as per his request. It had been a great evening amongst our friends and family and I recall feeling as happy as I could with the secrets I was hiding. That night we stayed in an oceanfront hotel as husband and wife.

One of the secrets I was hiding had to do with Peter's friend, Richard. During the summer of 1997, before we were married, we spent the weekend with Richard and Sarah at his mother's house on the beach. His mother and father were out of town and we had the home to ourselves. Sarah and Richard had a son, Ryan, who was the same age as Martin. I liked Richard. He felt like a brother to me. Martin was almost walking at the time. It was so relaxing and refreshing to be staying in a beautiful home on the beach with friends. We stayed a second night because we were enjoying our time there plus it was a great home but honestly, going home was a lonelier option. The following morning Peter told me he had to leave for work. I told him that I was going to stay for a little while longer so that the boys play together and then I would return home. Peter had not liked this idea at all. Why did he care that I was there for a while? This was *his* friend after all, not a stranger, and the purpose was for the enjoyment for our child. I remained firm and did not leave. He left and he was really angry. Only I knew how mad he was. He had pretended to Richard that everything was OK, shook his hand and left with a big smile. I knew what kind of smile that was; it warned me that I was going to pay for staying there, and I did.

Richard and I hung out with the boys and watched them play on the beach. They were having so much fun sitting on the shoreline letting the waves wash into them and giggling. I had not heard from Peter that day which was not unusual, but when he came home he was livid. "How dare you stay there!" Then he accused me of sleeping with Richard. That was a ludicrous statement and completely delusional. I had never shown any interest in Richard. But he would not sit and discuss this issue with maturity. How would we ever get past this incident that didn't happen if we didn't discuss it? I would later introduce coping tools that would alleviate or even prevent this kind of episode regarding other men, but they were not in place in time for this incident. Peter continued to accuse me of having sex with Richard that morning and was furious with me for weeks for staying that Monday morning.

That first week, afterwards, was horrible. Peter barely spoke to me and living in such a tense environment, extremely aware of his angry energy was very unsettling. Peter would insist for years that I had been unfaithful to him that morning with Richard and subsequently I had to start avoiding any kind of genuine friendship with Richard, which was difficult because we got together with him and his family so frequently, plus I liked him. Not once did he confront Richard with this ridiculous allegation. What he had really done was push me away from Richard so that he could have him as a friend independently of me. He had used this issue as a way to control my relationship with his friend.

The intensity of his rage to my staying with Richard that morning was a grave warning. The fact that I had to change my social behavior and who I was to appease Peter's insecurities was absurd, and yet that is exactly what I started to do. I would avoid Richard as best I could, which was hard to do when we were out as friends and because he was so genuinely nice to me. Peter seemed content with having Richard back to himself which is what I let him believe. I had found a way to cope with his insanity, and that would be to pretend. The pretend coping tool worked but was a sign of weakness to me. Having to find a way to cope with an overpowering psychotic force was a huge indication that he was in fact weakening me.

When I had found out that I was pregnant with our second child, even though my relationship with Peter was still rocky here and there, I was completely delighted. Sadly, I would hear from Peter over and over again that the child belonged to Richard.

Shortly before our marriage, Peter bought his business partner out of the business. He moved the company an hour away from our home closer to where he said it needed to be. The timing of the buy-out had been devious and was preemptively and meticulously orchestrated to protect his future – not from an outside entity or enemy – but from *me*. I would find this out many years later.

Just after Peter and I were married we started looking for our first home together. We looked every weekend for around four months. I remember this search being quite enjoyable. We were getting along beautifully at that time and the fact that we both had the same home goals helped us to remain happy in that moment. After an exhausting hunt, we finally found a home in a gated community which needed to be completely renovated. We both agreed that it would be worth it because it had wonderful potential. There were a lot of children in the neighborhood and our quieter cul-de-sac street would be a perfect street for young children. Once we had bought our home, I rarely saw Peter-- with the exception of weekends-- right up until the birth of our second child.

When I would wake up in the morning Peter had already left for work. He would arrive home long after I had gone to bed at night. Often, he would come home in the early hours of the morning, would sleep for a few hours and be gone again before I woke up. It felt like he had completely abandoned me. I was around 5 months pregnant at the time. I wondered if he was deliberately avoiding me or that there was someone else that he was spending time with. He never invited me down to see his office or to meet his new staff. It was clear he did not want me there. Now and again he would sting me with a cruel comment like, "Look up and tell me what is over your head and tell me who is paying for that" or, 'if you didn't bother me all the time I could get more work done." Work seemed to be more important to him than us. I was pregnant and alone.

When I met Peter I was completely self-confident, strong-willed and independent. Since we had become husband and wife, I strongly believed that we needed to do so much more to build a loving and respectful relationship between us. I still wanted and needed a functional, caring and communicative relationship with my husband and the father of my children. I constantly yearned for our marriage to self-correct. I was starting to feel lonely and, worse, ugly and unappealing to him. It had started to chip away at my self-confidence. I felt like I was not good enough. When friends or family asked how things were going I would pretend and tell them that things were great. I would paint a picture of a happy family, not because it was, but because it was what I wanted so desperately. Unlike anything I had done prior to that moment, I had started to lie to everyone around us, but most of all, to myself.

I grew up in a home and a culture where our parents came home at night and ate dinner together as a family. It seemed so simple and beautiful, and here I couldn't even get my husband to come home! In a way it was killing me. This was not the kind of family dynamic that was going to make me happy. Where was the balance between work and family? For the year or so that he spent at his new office, he was completely evasive when I asked him about his day. If I pressed him he would get upset and asked me what I wanted to know. His behavior was leading me into suspicion and his on-going, hurtful comments had started chipping away into the friendship that I thought we had. When I looked at him I no longer saw a friend. This was not the kind of marriage that I had wanted. I could not figure out how to reach Peter on any level and was tired of feeling alone and hurt. After weeks of research and finding someone that sounded suitable, I made a call to a divorce attorney. I felt that I had tried everything I could to connect with my husband. I was completely exhausted and tired of feeling so alone, humiliated and rejected. He, on the other hand, seemed quite happy with the image that I had painfully created to our friends and family. He preferred to work all hours for financial success, of which there was never enough, avoiding me when possible, and looking at other women to hurt and disrespect me. I couldn't take any more.

I walked into her office seven months pregnant, feeling incredibly vulnerable and embarrassed. "I need to divorce my husband," I told her. I was so ashamed of the way things were at home with Peter and how coldly he treated me that I couldn't even tell this woman half of what went on. I told her that I was unhappy and that my husband was often unkind to me. I told her that he had rage outbursts that troubled and scared me and that we had tried to get along but we just couldn't. She listened to my story and then smiled at me. She told me that we had one young child and a baby on the way and that I was probably feeling very hormonal. She suggested that I go home and try to work on my marriage and that we seek therapy together. Perhaps my calmness and tone had led her to feel that my request for a divorce lacked validity. There was a weakness to my spiritual strength and that was how I came across.

I was a lot stronger than Peter in many ways and that made him want to hurt me more. The truth is that he did hurt me, tremendously, but most of the time I would practice self-control and not let him know it. I hadn't wanted to give him the satisfaction of seeing the pain he was causing me. I was worried that if he did, he would note the trigger and use it over and over again, just like he had done when he knew how much it bothered me when he looked and flirted with other women. Instead of standing up to his abusive goading and taunting I had started to enable it by ignoring it. I was very resentful and angry but refused to let him know. Living this way was inevitably going to be dangerous to my health. That divorce attorney had no idea of the repercussions of the advice she had given me.

Towards the end of my pregnancy I decided to make some meals and freeze them. I remember after giving birth to Martin how I had wished I had prepared a little more when it came to eating. It's hard to stand and cook for long periods of time days after giving birth, so this time I would prepare. We could not afford to eat out much at the time so making meals at home was what we did and what I loved. I knew if I made four or five day' worth of meals that we would be good for a while. I could defrost one each morning and have dinner that night. I will never forget the meals I made. There was chicken parmesan, eggplant parmesan, meatballs and a cottage pie. As easy as they are to make, they are extremely time consuming. I love to cook so that didn't bother me at all. It took me most of the day to make them. I decided that I was going to freeze all of them, but first they needed to cool down before I could. I left all the dishes on the kitchen counter to cool. Peter complained that he had no room on the kitchen counter top to put some papers. We lived in just under 4,000 square feet of house and he had to start a fight with me over the fact there was no counter space for some documents.

It was a very hot day that day and I needed to leave for a few hours to run some errands. When I returned, I was utterly astounded with what I saw when I entered my home. He had placed all the dishes around the pool in the blazing sun to spoil. I was so incredibly hurt by this that I actually suppressed any reaction. "I need room in this kitchen for my stuff," was all he said. I felt emotionally sick. Only a sociopath could behave this way and want to inflict this kind of pain on another.

At times when I reflect on this kind of behavior I wonder why I stayed. There was no one answer. If I had to guess, it was partly from the shame of having a second chance to meet and marry someone more compatible, and failing again. There was some pride being married to Peter due to his appearance, hard work and success. The fact that we did not seem to be happy together made me determined to find a way. I did not want to be a single mother since I truly believed in marriage and did not want my child to be a child of divorce. Most of all, I would never leave my son for one day and end up in a time-sharing situation where I lost time with him. The mere thought was terrifying and was never going to happen, even though I suffered as a result. I had to let my self-confidence and self-reliance lay low around Peter for many years so that I could fulfil my role as an unconditionally loving, protective and nurturing mother. When my strength and self-respect emerged there was always an issue. It was always challenged.

As I approached my last few weeks of pregnancy, Peter told me that he was going out of town for business. I remember thinking that it was a really odd time for him to leave for a few days and told him so. Only a few days earlier at a doctor's visit, we had found a little amniotic fluid which had concerned my doctor and elevated me to a slightly higher risk pregnancy. I only had a few weeks left, plus as easy as Martin was, this was the time I needed more help. I felt that he was being inconsiderate of my needs. He was evasive about the nature of the trip just calling it work. He said that I was insecure for asking his whereabouts. I was getting close to giving birth and he was leaving with no travel details or consideration about my situation. I had suspected for some time that Peter had another woman (or man) that he was hiding from me. His long days at work for months on end and his secretiveness led me to suspect that there was someone else in his life. He went on that trip despite my feelings. I remember thinking that this was just the price of being with a businessman. He left on Monday and came home on Thursday morning. When he arrived home, he absolutely stunk of alcohol. I could smell it as he stood at the end of our bed I told him that he smelled of alcohol. He told me that he had had a beer on the plane on the way home. I knew he was lying. He was totally hungover. Why was he lying to me? I didn't care that he went out with people and got drunk the night before, I cared that he was lying to me. He was a pathological liar. I believe this was one of many times that Peter was cheating on me.

I had a doctor's appointment the morning Peter came home hungover. My doctor told me that I was still leaking amniotic fluid and that they needed to induce our baby that afternoon. Michael, beautiful, beautiful Michael was born prematurely and was taken away to ICU. That was one of the worst days of my life. Bearing a baby and then it being taken from you with no opportunity to bond. I understood why but it didn't make me feel better. It was a brutal time for me. All I did was cry. Here I was with a premature baby in ICU, a lying hungover husband, and seemingly, an empty and loveless marriage. I asked for an early discharge from the hospital and left the next day. I needed to be with Martin. He compensated for the void I was feeling. I would spend a couple of hours with Martin and head back to the hospital to see Michael and feed him. The back and forth would go on for days. I would stand and stare at him through tears and hold his hand for hours. I hated the noise of the beeping machines and the coldness of his surroundings. I took a tape recorder and would play soft and spiritual music to help drown out the machine noises around him. It was sheer torture to see him there. It was just as unbearable for me to leave Martin with a friend of mine as often as I had to. I couldn't leave him with Peter. He showed absolutely no emotion to any of what was going on and nor was he there to help me. I had just given birth to our second child and he had not been there for me physically, mentally or emotionally. He told me that he would take some time off when Michael was discharged but I needed him then.

Peter would visit with Michael on his way home from work late at night. I had been terrified of Michael's lack of progress during his first few days. I was facing baby blues, was back and forth to the hospital every few hours, I felt alone, I felt scared, and felt like I had no one to turn to. I sat there sobbing with Martin on one knee, my heart in the hospital, in such need of emotional support that I asked my parents to fly over to help me. They had planned to give Peter and I some time together with our new baby in a week or two but he hadn't been there so they came earlier. I made excuses for his absence telling them that he had some very important work that had to get done because I was ashamed to admit that this had been the pattern for some time. I received a 5am call from the hospital the following morning to say that they were moving Michael to another hospital and that he was not improving. I went back to the bedroom to tell Peter the news but the bed was empty, he was already gone. I was so relieved when my parents arrived. I was able to visit Michael all the time and know Martin was in safe hands. During one of the most emotionally challenging times that I have faced as a parent, Peter had been physically and emotionally absent.

After Michael was born, I considered myself no different than a single parent, even though I still lived in the same home as the other parent. We continued to pretend that we had a functional and somewhat happy marriage to those on the outside which had become easy for me. I had emotionally shut down around Peter and would move forward since this was the easiest way to cope with the disappointments and purposeful pain that I was enduring. I found myself looking for ways to cope when things cropped up and I was succeeding but it was not a blissful way to live.

Chapter 9

Once Michael was born I found myself very busy. I did not have any help nor did I want any. I submerged myself into being the best mother I could possibly be. Having the distraction of two infant boys and all the work that went with it, helped drown out some of the loneliness and neglect that I was feeling in my relationship. The two boys became my world. I did everything with them. I was not a controlling mother, far from it. However, I always insisted on good manners and good behavior - that was non-negotiable. It paid off for these young boys as they grew up because their manners were impeccable.

I was still seeing my "Mommy and me" group every week. It was great to have a place to go to once a week and meet up with the same friends that were in the same child-rearing stages. It was also important to me that the boys developed friendships and understood the concept of loyalty, especially since we didn't have family members living anywhere close to us. I took the boys to music classes, gymnastic classes, water parks, the zoo, the park, the science park, the aquarium, to Disneyworld, to Butterfly World, and even taught them to cook at a very young age. These activities were fun but exhausting for a stay-at-home mother hoping for well-rounded and well-behaved children prepared, stable and ready for their educational futures.

We had just moved into our new home. It needed a complete renovation and much work lay ahead which we knew prior to the purchase. We were able to get the house at a great price due to its distressed condition and it had been good for us at the time with two young children. It was a large house with a pool on a quiet cul-de-sac. It was a perfect home for raising children.

Martin and Michael were growing beautifully and were so much fun. Peter was gone most of the week and rarely spoke with me during the day. He would come home and was very good with the boys when they were little. His order of importance at the time was himself, work, the boys, then me. It seems that over time I slowly started adapting to this reality of not feeling important to or loved by Peter, and sadly started living my life on a more singular plane. Inevitably an image had to form to cover this disconnected marriage and that was where I was excellent. I would behave around Peter like we were relatively functional, knowing full well we were disconnected. It was important for me to have our boys think we had a decent relationship, even if it were mostly an act and a lie. It was easy to do when they were young. The same image spilled over to our social life at the weekend where I felt like I did a very good job covering up the fact that we were unhappy. If my unauthentic behavior, my new coping tool, saved our boys from seeing parental conflict and helped us stay afloat in our social circles then it was what I had to do.

I was seeing a lot of Lorraine and her son during this time. She was a fun, vibrant and intelligent friend; I trusted her and felt safe around her. She was a fabulous and devoted mother who was remarkably attentive to her son, Bobby, at all times. It was an easy friendship lacking any effort which made it very special. We would also see each other on weekends with our husbands and other couples. One weekend we were invited to Lorraine's house for the day. She had invited two friends of mine, Barbara and Tommy, who were married and who came from the same city as me in the U.K. They had been at the same party where Peter had pushed the older man to the floor. Tommy was quite loud and abrasive, but a heck of a lot of fun to be around. Peter didn't like them. I'm not sure why he disliked them so much but suspected it was because they were my friends before we met, or because they were too unlike him.

We had not known that they would be at Lorraine's home that day until we arrived. Peter was instantly angry and not at the situation, but with me! I was the only one who knew he was angry about it because he conveniently hid it from everyone else. He was going to make me pay for it by ignoring me when I spoke to him, or staying far away from me, or even asking me when we were alone why they were there. Since there was absolutely nothing I could do about it, and knowing how angry he was, I had no choice but to switch him off if I was going to enjoy the day. I hadn't gone there to be miserable so I fell in with my friends and stayed away from Peter. He did not like that I was continuing to enjoy myself without showing any kind of remorse.

I stood in the kitchen talking with Barbara for some time. We had been friends for eight years and I found her very funny. I also really needed the pick-me-up. Out of nowhere, Peter came and stood next to me and pinched me really hard when no one was looking. It hurt. I asked him, quietly, why he pinched me. He didn't answer. He smiled and engaged with the group like nothing had happened. Why had he felt the need to hurt me? He was obviously angry and yet standing there pretending he was happy to the others was making me feel sick. I was having a great time with our friends until he pinched me. He pinched me, hard, a second time and this time I was mad. I asked him in front of everyone in the kitchen why he was pinching me and that he was hurting me. I did not like having to call him out in front of everyone, nor was it my style but I had had enough. He was being physically abusive. How brave and manly he had been to do it in secret. He said that he didn't know what I was talking about. Barbara believed me especially when I showed her the two small bruises on my thigh later that night. She had also witnessed him pushing an elderly man to the ground so she knew what he was capable of.

I always made sure we went out on a Friday or Saturday night, or both. I felt it was healthy to maintain a social life I had found the most amazing and loving babysitter, so it was very easy for us. One Saturday night we were invited to a party at my cousin Nest's house. Her guests were always interesting and usually from different countries. Her husband is Brazilian so you could always count on a fun group of Brazilian friends dancing and having fun. Soon after arriving, she pointed out a guy and told me that I really had to go and talk to him. She said that he was very funny and she knew I loved funny people. She pointed to a short tubby Indian in her living room talking to some of her guests. I could tell from his audience that he was a man of charisma. He had such a friendly smile. I went over to introduce myself and he could not have been nicer. He was telling a hilarious story that had us all laughing. He was a marvelous storyteller. His personality was magnetic, with great positive energy and he was completely full of life. I encouraged Peter to come and talk with the Indian but he walked away. I didn't care one little bit because my new Indian friend was so invigorating and it made me feel good to be around him.

To avoid any issue on the way home in the car, I came up with a plan and told Peter that the Indian was an idiot. I added that he was pompous and arrogant. What was I doing? I thought he was absolutely fantastic. Why did I have to say that? It was clear why I had to say it. If Peter found anyone to be a threat (a man particularly and not necessarily sexually), he would be mean to that person or to me. Therefore, I pre-emptively diffused any potential incident of rage by ridiculing, mocking or putting down the person that might be the cause of that trigger. What a tiring and dishonest way to live. But it worked. Peter did not get upset that night. Whilst I was disheartened that I had to be dishonest about my feelings, I'd found a coping mechanism that would work for me over and over again. The fact that I was starting to lie to him was not indicative of who I was. It kept us free of unnecessary conflict when we were around our friends which is all I felt I had at the time but did not make me feel good. I was becoming devious around Peter when we socialized but certainly not because I wanted to be. I could talk to other men now that I had my new tool. It worked every time.

I confided in Lorraine about the problems I was having with Peter. She was such a great listener and I trusted her. She seemed to give me very fair advice but it was based on what I was telling her and not the whole truth. I was ashamed of the whole truth. She would tell me to come and stay in her home for a few days to get a break but I knew that wasn't the answer. That would make him mad. Since she didn't really know the scope of our problems, she had no idea that staying with her would only escalate our situation. I was so ashamed of some of the behavior that I was embarrassed to tell her. I worried that she would wonder what was wrong with me for staying if she knew everything.

I often fantasized about leaving Peter and living life post-Peter, but I couldn't fathom ever leaving my boys for one day and losing valuable childhood time with them. I knew what my options were if we divorced. One weekend the children are with Mum and the next weekend they are with Dad. However, Peter had warned me years earlier that if I ever left him he would fight me and take the boys from me since I couldn't prove I could support them; that threat had terrified me. I felt that the boys needed me the most at the time since they were so young and needed more of a mommy role in their lives. Peter was not a nurturing or loving father and that reality, along with his short temper and anger, prevented me from leaving at their vulnerable and impressionable age. I knew that sharing our boys would be a nightmare. I could not protect them from his anger and coldness if I was not with them. He would have controlled them like a sergeant and not allowed them to express themselves and their individualities. He would have told them what he expected of them and they would have had to conform. They would have been hardened and hurt in my absence since, if he couldn't hurt me any longer, he would start to hurt and abuse them. Since childhood I had longed for these children so I could teach them all the wonderful things in life. I was going to fulfil that dream at any cost. Therefore, the idea of leaving Peter was completely out of the question. Even though it meant tolerating a loveless, unhappy and unhealthy relationship, I would never leave if it meant I would lose time with my children. I just had to make it work. There were long periods of time where things were good but really, I'm not so sure they were necessarily good, they were just free of conflict. A typical good day for us was that we both tackled our respective tasks for the day, tended to the boys at night, ate dinner, talked about his business, and didn't argue about anything. I had known Peter for almost five years at this point and felt that I didn't know him at all.

Peter seemed to like ruining things for me ahead of social functions or even during a social function. It was deliberate and done intentionally to upset me so that he could capitalize on my miserable inner state. He was like a vampire sucking at my energy so that he had an abundance of it for himself. He could thrive by leaving me feeling depleted and miserable.

One example of many that comes to mind was our annual Christmas party. I spent weeks planning our Christmas parties, sparing no detail. The invites went out, the house was decorated inside and out, the tree was beautifully decorated, the staff were booked, the chef was booked, the bartender was booked, the food was prepared by me a full week prior to the party, the music playlist was selected by me and ready to go, the games were ready, my Santa was selected, and my guest list was in check. This was my favorite holiday and party every year.

A few weeks prior to this particular party, I had taken Martin and Michael to Lorraine's house where they swam most of the afternoon in her pool. Sarah was there. She seemed to have it out for me over the years and I was very aware of her troublemaking ability and was very cautious around her. We were sitting along the edge of the pool talking when Sarah pointed to Michael who had waded out a little too far into the pool and had lost his step. He wasn't a proficient swimmer yet and needed to be pulled back. He must have gone under the water for four or five seconds at the very most. Sarah made some snarky comment like, "That was close." I had ignored her.

Our Christmas party day arrived. One of the primary reasons I hosted Christmas parties was not just to have all our friends over; I also wanted the memory of our boys that every year having a wonderful Christmas party with their friends where Santa showed up with a huge bag full of gifts. They were such fun parties. It was such a magical experience to see them look into Santa's eyes with total belief in him. It was worth every bit of my time just to watch that moment. That night, everything was going really well. Our friends all seemed to be having a great time. I rarely saw Peter during our parties since we both did our own thing and I was usually busy making sure everything was going OK. Then I saw Peter walking towards me with *that* face. He told me to get in the bedroom. As soon as the door was closed he grabbed my arm tightly and turned purple with rage. "You almost killed my son," he yelled. "You nearly drowned my son." I knew Sarah had said something to him. I tried to tell him that he only went under the water for seconds and that I had been right there and pulled him back. He did not want to hear what I said at all. I could not believe he was addressing this issue during our party and how irate he had become. There were around eighty of our friends outside that door having a great time, and I was behind the door being verbally and physically attacked. Wanting to maintain the false image, all I wanted to do was go back outside and join my friends. He wouldn't stop. I didn't know what to do. The rest of the evening was a blur to me. Outwardly I put on my best, but inwardly I was devastated and distraught especially knowing that he would continue to attack me later. Peter on the other hand, took full advantage of the despair that he had just inflicted on me by moving on through the party like nothing had happened. He actually appeared like he was enjoying himself, and he most likely was knowing how much he had just upset me. I walked around the rest of the night in a haze.

Lorraine loved birthdays. She made a big deal out of them and always made me feel special on mine. Every year she sent me the most beautiful vase of flowers. She knew I loved flowers. Peter also knew that I loved flowers but very rarely gave me any. He bought them for me on my birthday and Valentine's Day but never handed them to me. He just left them on the kitchen counter along with groceries that he picked up while he was there. He really had an issue with intimacy. He once told me that he remembered his father giving flowers to his mother and his mother saying, "What the hell did you buy me flowers for, it's a waste of money." He told me how angry that had made him. It was probably why he had an issue giving me flowers during our marriage, it was a direct result of his childhood memory.

Lorraine hadn't called me on my birthday that year. I started to wonder if I had upset her. It wasn't like her to forget birthdays, especially mine. She was usually the first to call me every year to wish me Happy Birthday. I called her at home that afternoon and my call went through to voice mail. I called her cell phone which she did not answer. I always worry when I think I have upset a friend so instead of enjoying my birthday I found myself worrying about her. I didn't hear anything from her that night either. The following day I didn't hear anything so I called her home again. A strange woman answered which totally confused me. She took a message and said that Lorraine would call me back. She didn't. I was totally perplexed by her disappearance. A couple of days later she called. I was so relieved but winced when she told me she had something to tell me. She had just found out that she had cancer. Whack! I wasn't sure what to say so I asked all the stupidest questions you ask when you are in shock and you don't know how to act. She told me she had a lot of people to call and promised we'd get together in the next few days with the boys. She hung up and I started to cry.

I met with Lorraine a few days after she told me her news. I gave her the biggest hug and told her that I would stand by her side every step of the way and I did. I wanted her to know she was not alone. We sat in the park for several hours. Life changes pretty quickly when you get news like that. The nonsense stops. She asked me what I had been doing all week. I told her about my week and that we had gone out for dinner on my birthday. Her mouth dropped. She was horrified that she had forgotten my birthday. I didn't care that she had forgotten, it didn't matter anymore. Here she had received the worst news of her life and she was worried about forgetting my birthday. What a friend. She told me that she would be going away for a little while to receive experimental treatment. I was so upset. She told me that her type of cancer was rare. That didn't sound good. I left with such a very heavy heart that day. The following day the hugest vase of the most beautiful flowers arrived. I broke down and sobbed for hours.

After hearing about Lorraine's news, it made me more determined to search for stability in our marriage. I felt it was important for all of us. Lorraine's son was about to lose his mother to something outside of her control. My boys didn't need to lose their family dynamic especially since *we* were in control. When things were settled between Peter and I our home life ran smoothly. We were living under the same roof of a beautiful and warm home and yet very much apart. In an effort to strengthen our relationship I sought out another family counselor. We went to see her and, as with the first therapist, we really didn't get anywhere. She suggested that we see her separately for a few visits. During our first session with her Peter sat with his arms folded tightly. He made it very clear he did not want to be there. Then he slouched on the couch with an air of childishness and insolence like he had in the last therapy office. The topic of him ogling at other women came up which he denied and said that it was all in my head. Any topic that had some relevance to our situation was simply dismissed. He would manipulate the session by cleverly and deceitfully turning the attention back to me with the pretense that I was an annoying, insecure wife who was delusional. I have to admit he sounded pretty good. However, he was lying. He knew he was flirting with women everywhere we went, as he would later confess to marriage counselors number three and five. The worst thing for me about going to therapy with Peter was exposing my vulnerabilities. I would discuss things in therapy that bothered me and I would tell him how much it hurt me: His endless flirtation with other women, the disrespectful way he spoke to me, disagreeing with me in front of people or friends about facts he was completely wrong about, being emotionally neglectful

72

and unavailable. WRONG THING TO DO WITH A NARCISSIST! While therapy is typically a safe space to discuss issues through honesty and vulnerability, to a narcissist it's a jackpot. He now knew how to hurt me more and he did. He used these sessions not to improve what we had, but to enhance his emotional cruelty now that he knew my trigger buttons. He would regularly tell me on our way home from these sessions how much work time he had just lost by being there and what a waste of money and time therapy was. Our marriage was just not that important to him.

Martin and Michael were both in school and doing really well. Martin was wise for his years and was a quiet, sweet, loving and serious child. Michael was sociable, exciting, energetic, empathetic and funny. I had absolutely loved staying home with my boys and raising them during their early years. Shortly after Martin was born, I had gone through a stage where I was worried about not earning an income. I had earned an income since I was 14 years old. It had been difficult for me to go from working, earning an income and feeling productive to becoming a dependent. One night I told Peter that I was thinking about looking for an evening job. It had a lot to do with the fact I didn't liked asking him for money and, even after we resolved a budget, I still wanted to feel that I was contributing. He said that I should raise Martin and tend to the home which would allow him to earn the income. He told me that our roles were very equal, just different. This made sense and made me feel less conscious about my lack of financial productivity. I believe that if you are able to be a stay-at-home mother, it is the most precious, rewarding and sacramental job that a mother will ever have in her lifetime. He told me that I should take on my new role and enjoy it and leave the earning power to him. So, I did just that. My life became a busy routine of breakfast, school drop-off, errands, school pick-up, lunch, naps, activities, bath-time, dinner, book reading, bed and, always, checking in on Lorraine. She was starting to sound a little weak which I could hear when we were on the phone.

Lorraine came home after spending a few months out of town

getting treatment. I had missed her a great deal. We would talk about her treatment and what was coming up. I never pitied her. She told me that it made her feel bad and all she wanted was to feel the same as before. I continued to be the same silly friend always looking for a good laugh with her. Lorraine told me that she had to go back to Boston and I asked her if she'd like me to go with her. I needed to show her how much I supported her and to give her husband and son a break from the back and forth travel. I wasn't sure if Peter would agree but when we discussed my going he was surprisingly OK with it. I was so grateful that I had the opportunity to show my unwavering friendship by supporting her on this daunting trip. I was taken aback by how many people in that treatment ward were around my age. I hadn't really been able to comprehend the reality of cancer until seeing all those people around me that day coming in and out for treatment. While I was waiting for her I sat next to a middle-aged man. He had a kind face with a warm smile. He told me that he felt better because the doctor had just given him another week to live. Wow! I had not expected that. Here was this kind man at my side with no apparent chip on his shoulder sounding truly grateful for another week of life. I couldn't believe it. I told him that I was sorry to hear that and had to turn my head because of the tears welling up in my eyes. He told me not to worry about him. I was overwhelmed by his strength along with his honesty. That short conversation made me think about my own situation at home. If I had one week of life left would I want to spend it with Peter? The answer was no, I wouldn't. The insight and clarity from that incident led me to one conclusion, I had to do something to change my life and my future. Eventually, I would...only it was too many years later. Years filled with humiliation, pain and loneliness.

As I've said, there were layers to why I stayed so long. When we had good periods, it gave me a glimmer of hope into what could be, what could get better and what I could live with. It was such an emotional rollercoaster, feeling that I had to think of a way to get out without impacting the boys one minute, and then seeing some hope and intently looking for a way to build on it. I knew that I had not chosen wisely with Peter. To be fair to myself I was not familiar with the charm and appeal of the devious narcissist. Now that I had made that choice and since we had children together, I firmly believed in fighting for and not giving up on our marriage. I felt like I would be letting the boys down. I wanted to fix the marriage and yet fighting for Peter and to help Peter, who is so psychologically damaged was practically impossible unless he was willing to help himself. Peter did not think there was anything wrong with his behavior or his abuse, which left me nothing to work with. He often told me that I was the problem in our marriage. I had started to distance myself emotionally from Peter, which I found helped me from anguish. It was incredibly unhealthy and very unnatural for me, but as sad as it was, it helped me. During long sustained calmer times, I would let my guard down and resume my dreams of a future that included Peter and a beautiful future with our adult boys, weddings, grandchildren and travel. This push and pull of my future constantly left me in a state of turmoil. I believe my culture and upbringing played a big part in my putting up with way more than I should have. During my childhood in the U.K. there seemed to be a shameful stigma that accompanied divorce. We only knew two divorced families growing up. I grew up during a time where we were told to be quiet, not to ask questions, know your place, not to cry, don't tell people your business, look good in front of the neighbors and the community, and when there's a problem, "just get on with it". I would have to say that the "keep your problems private" and "the soldier on" mentality played a significant role in why I stayed as long as I did in a very unhappy relationship.

I had been getting frequent headaches and they were getting worse; they were becoming a concern. One day my headache became so bad that I literally could not turn my head. I tried to move my head to the left and right and as I did the pain was so excruciating it made me want to throw up. I was so afraid that I drove myself to the emergency room while Peter stayed with Martin and Michael. I don't cry wolf so he knew something was seriously wrong. When I drove away I had no idea I would be gone for almost a week. By the time I arrived at the emergency room I could barely see. After I was admitted, Peter visited for a while but spent more time outside executing demands to the doctors than he did trying to comfort me. I was truly scared. It felt like my body was shutting down. I was injected with a drug and fell asleep. I had a lot of tests while I was there and nothing was found. I couldn't move my head for days and my entire head ached wickedly.

One day when I woke I heard the door close and felt a presence close to me. I opened my eyes and it was my friend, Wendy. She looked like an angel as she stood smiling over me. She was so warm, so friendly, so sincere, so authentic. She had advanced into the spiritual world and had invited God into her life and I could feel it. She looked down at me and asked me what was going on. She didn't mean there in that bed or in that hospital, she meant at home with Peter. She knew exactly why I was there suffering. She knew that what I was experiencing at home was breaking down my physical state. She told me that the only disease that I had was my abusive relationship with Peter. After what seemed to be a short physical or psychological breakdown I went home. There was no question in my mind that our on-again-off-again conflict had brought on my medical incident. I continued to retreat from Peter emotionally by building my spiritual strength, one that he could not compete with, and a wall around an area that I would not allow him to harm. That's not to say that he was unable to hurt me, I just made it harder for him by moving the triggers and trying with all my strength not to give him energy.

That week had proved to be rough for Peter especially trying to take care of the boys and look for a new business at the same time. Before I'd gotten sick, Peter told me that we had to sell the company and quickly. He had heard that a large competitor had moved into our state and were offering the same service we provided in a three-bundle package. We could not compete with this kind of bundling package because we did not provide the other 2 services. The longer we held the company, the more it would depreciate in value, so it went on the market overnight. Within a couple of months, we sold all the assets of the company to a fortune 500 company who had not exercised due diligence. By the skin of our teeth we escaped with enough capital to pay off all Peter's former debt leaving enough surplus to start the renovation of our home.

It occurred to me that we were completely alone as far as needing immediate help in a crisis. This was the second time since Michael's birth where we found ourselves without family or help. I would have reached out to my friends but Peter had decided to keep my hospitalization private and only told Wendy since she had called looking for me. What would happen if I were to get sick again? God times things beautifully. My neighbor told me about a Mexican girl who was looking for work. Peter was not thrilled with the idea but agreed to a short term stay until I was fully recovered. Her name was Rosa and she ended up being wonderful. She took such great care of me and was fantastic and playful with the boys. She ended up staying with us for a little over a year. She had no idea how much comfort she brought to my life. She was kind and loving and friendly. All the things I had been searching for in Peter. She was truly heaven-sent to me during that year.

After selling our company we were ready to start our renovation. We rented a small townhome a few miles away. Peter and I spent a lot of time on our renovation which took close to a year. Rosa was a dream and was always on hand to watch the boys until our home was finished. It felt like Peter and I rarely talked while we lived in that townhome. He was completely stressed not only because of the renovation but also because he was looking for a new business. I was so grateful for Rosa's caring and loving energy and for all her help which brought me great comfort. I had stopped inviting friends over because of how strenuous it had become to pretend that everything was OK between us. Peter was gone all day, every day which had actually become a relief under the circumstances. He said he was looking for work. That was all he would tell me. He was very tense during that time and I would do whatever I had to do to keep him happy, which usually meant staying out of his way. Living in the townhome had been a wonderful experience for me with the boys. It was such a manageable home to live in, requiring no maintenance at all. I spent a lot of valuable time with the boys that year when I was not working on our new home. I would take them to all kinds of activities and introduce them to anything new in the community. As much as I enjoyed my time with them, whenever there was a quiet moment, my mind would wander to a fantasy of a man who loved me unconditionally and whom I could love equally. I would watch my boys play and many times wish that they could see their parents in a loving and respectful relationship. It haunted me that they would go without this fundamentally important role in their childhood. I am only too aware that our childhood shapes our adulthood. What kind of adults would my boys be seeing our marriage is a state of strife over and over again?

One morning at the townhome, Martin accidentally dropped Peter's cell phone in the communal pool. Peter went absolutely berserk. It was like watching molten rage that had been bubbling under the surface just explode. I felt physically sick watching him storm around out of control and felt sorry that Martin and Michael had to witness their father behave this way. Martin became very upset and started crying. Martin was a good child and since this incident was a total accident, I can only imagine how it made him feel to see his father in this state because of something he had done. As Martin sobbed his apologies and told him that it just slipped out of his hand, Peter continued on. I had never seen my father fly off the handle about anything and felt sorrow for the boys for having to see it. He finally left in the worst mood. Martin talked about this incident years later. It had made a huge impact on him. After watching Peter that day, I knew that I would have to tread very carefully and absorb a lot of the boys behavior in an effort to keep him calm and not set him off and that meant watching my own behavior too.

Peter had rented a local office from a friend. I would ask him to call me before he left so I would know when to have dinner ready but he rarely did. He didn't think he should have to so he just didn't. The misogynist that he is at his core was not going to answer to me even if it was a normal thing to do. He also knew it would bother me and he liked that best. There was an obvious and massive amount of abuse that occurred in his past that was so deep and unresolved that it was becoming more and more mine every day that I spent with him. The irony of his reluctance to let me know his arrival home was bizarre since he nearly always came home to a beautifully set table with candles, flowers, wine and a gourmet meal. I was always looking to set a dinner-time example to our boys and yet he seemed to hate it. Often the boys would tell me that they were hungry and yet I would have them wait just a little longer hoping that their dad would call to say he was on his way. His reluctance to call was like a defiant child not answering his mother...and there it was. A child lashing out and punishing me in his adult form against a woman and the women that had hurt him many years before.

Chapter 10

There were many evenings I ate alone with the boys and Rosa when Peter was working late. I always made a plate of food for Peter but, since he didn't have the graciousness to call me with a time of his arrival, it would sit and be heated up for him when he arrived. Rosa would eat with me most of the time and sometimes with us when Peter was there. I am not so sure Peter really liked her at the table. One evening, Rosa, the boys and I were eating dinner. Peter arrived home unexpectedly and appeared angry when he walked in the door. I am not sure what had upset him that particular night, but he seemed angrier than normal. If I had to guess what caused some of that anger, it might have had something to do with seeing us eating happily at the table without him and that Rosa was at the table instead of him. This was his own doing, of course, because of his contemptuous refusal to call on his way home. I enjoyed sitting with Rosa for dinner. I would inquire into her life at home and her community and ask questions about her childhood and life in Mexico with her family.

I knew more about Rosa in one year than I knew about Peter during our entire marriage. He was guarded, private and secretive. The one thing I knew conclusively about him was his apparent hatred towards all the women including me that had been close in his life. He was mean to them, he would deliberately make himself unavailable to them, he would purposely not call his mother or his sister on their birthdays, Mother's Day, or any holiday, and would not help them when they needed financial guidance or financial help. These women included his birth mother, his adopted mother, his adopted sister, his half-sister on his birth father's side, his half-sister on his birth mothers side, and his ex-wife. He was a misogynist. I chose to ignore his cruelty which, at the time, was primarily towards his mother and sister; it was one of the worst mistakes of my life since it was only a matter of time until he would treat me the same. Most of the stories that I heard about his childhood, and there weren't many, were of how a woman had been mean to him. He had a negative story about his birth mother, his adoptive mother, his sister, his half-sister, the nun at school, his grandmother and his aunt. He shared a couple of stories about how his family were twistedly involved with the Catholic Church and how his other aunt had forced her son to become a priest. A lot of his angst, or at least what I picked up on over the years, was related to the Catholic Church. My hypothesis is that there was severe trauma inflicted upon Peter through the church and those demons still haunt him today.

I went to visit Lorraine in hospital that evening. Since Peter had come home so upset I made sure everything was calm and in place before leaving. I had both boys fed, bathed and ready for bed. I felt that I was overly considerate of his busy work days and always tried to make sure I left him with as little to do as possible on evenings that I went out with friends. Lorraine had been admitted to a hospital one mile from our rented townhome. I really couldn't wait to spend the evening with her after the tension that evening at home. She was so vulnerable, open, caring, interested, and happy to see me when I walked in. What a change from what I had just left. Here she lay with only months of life ahead of her and with that reality looming, had the amazing ability of making me feel appreciated, loved and special. After some time, the subject of Peter and I came up. I lied to her. I told her only a little of what was really going on in my unhappy marriage and with that lie came her optimistic suggestions of how we could solve our issues. Those optimistic suggestions would have been grave concerns had I been honest. She actually liked to talk about my marital challenges with me. She told me that it took her mind off her own stuff. How ironic that my misery helped hers! After staying way too long I left the person I very much wanted to stay with and headed home to the one that I didn't.

When I arrived home, everyone was asleep. Rosa's room was quiet so I assumed she was sleeping too. The master bedroom was dark and frustrating to maneuver around without turning on a light. Peter didn't like to be woken up so I had to be very quiet. Throughout our marriage, he claimed that he had insomnia. Instead of finding ways to improve or treat his this, we had to tip-toe around it; hard to do with young children. I turned the light on in the bedroom for about three seconds so that I could get to the bathroom and turn that light on. Peter woke up and roared through gritted teeth that I had woken him up. I was surprised that I woke him since I had been so quiet. I just couldn't understand how he could wake up with instant rage, especially since he knew I had spent the evening with our friend in hospital. Clearly it was just there - always. I told him that I hadn't meant to wake him and closed the bathroom door to prevent any more light from bothering him. I was hopeful that he would go back to sleep. Not a chance. I heard the bedroom door bang. Here we go. I quickly got ready so that I could get into bed and turn all the lights out. I could hear him downstairs. I wondered if Rosa had woken up from the door banging and was hoping that the boys would stay asleep. I could hear him banging kitchen cabinets so loudly that it unnerved me. I was afraid the boys would wake up and see him like that. What the hell was Rosa thinking? It felt so humiliating and embarrassing.

I lay nervously in our bed wondering how long it was going to go on. He continued to bang doors, drawers and cabinets like an angry little boy having a tantrum. I had no choice but to get up and go downstairs. It was making me feel physically sick and I was really concerned about Rosa. This had to be scaring her too. I peeked in on the boys. I prayed they would be asleep and they were. Thank you. I walked downstairs and asked him to calm down and stop banging everything. I told him that he was going to wake the boys. I was really shocked that he was behaving this aggressively with Rosa home and exposing his true self. Unbeknownst to me, she wasn't there and he knew that. I opened her door slightly so I could reassure her that everything was OK and could not have been happier to see that she was not home.

"You woke me!" he yelled over and over. I had not seen him this angry since he had held me by my throat against the wall, and since he had pushed me against the bedpost. I did not like seeing him this angry, it really frightened me. After realizing Rosa was not home I went back upstairs with him following and yelling behind me like a lunatic. I got back into bed and turned out the lights hoping he would calm down. Out of nowhere he flew into the bedroom and yelled that I was not going to sleep that night either. He grabbed the king-sized mattress, with me on it, and yanked it so high that I fell to the floor. He left the room and went downstairs. I was shaking by this point and determined not to engage him. I pulled the mattress back onto the bed. It took every bit of my energy to drag it back on but I was determined to try to make everything as normal as I could as quickly as I could. I put the sheets back on the mattress and made everything look right again. I was boiling mad by this point. He was right, I would not be sleeping that night either. I put the light back on and started to read a magazine. Not that I was really reading it, I just needed something to do until he settled down. I had never been this afraid of a person in my life.

I heard him coming up the stairs two at a time, or at least that's how it sounded. He jumped on the bed and on top of me. I tried to push him off but he was way too strong for me. His face was red with fury. His eyes were bulging out of his sockets and his teeth were gritted tight. Then he put his hands around my neck and started choking me. Through clenched teeth and spitting with anger, he said, "You woke me up. You woke me up." His hands were tight around my throat as I lashed out with everything I had to try to push him away just enough to run. I got away from him and rushed down the stairs. This was the second time he had tried to choke me and this time was more intense than the last. He appeared uncontrollable so I called the police. I told them that my husband was out of control and that I could not calm him down. I couldn't bring myself to tell them he was choking me because I was afraid of what might happen. I had locked myself in Rosa's room to make that call and as I did, Peter was trying to open the door. I told them he was trying to get into the room and that I had to go.

The police arrived minutes later. "Please stay asleep boys" was all I could think.

I was sobbing from sheer anguish. I ended up telling the police what had happened. I also told them that this was not the first time he had put his hands around my neck and tried to choke me. They left me and went to talk with Peter.

The cunning liar told them that we got into an argument because he had told me that I had to fire Rosa. He told them that I had become extremely upset about it. I could hear him outside the front door talking calmly and methodically about what had taken place. He was completely lying to them, of course, but the most disturbing part of that lie was that he actually sounded convincing. You would never had known that he was out of control minutes earlier. It would have been hard for me to believe my story if I was that police officer. They had been given two completely different accounts of what happened that evening. They seemed to have no interest as I tried to explain that he was lying. I can only imagine they get stuck in this kind of domestic situation often; knowing who to believe was simply impossible for them. I felt some relief when they told me that they had recommended that Peter leave for the evening for a hotel or a friend's house so that the situation could calm down. They also suggested that he consider anger management classes. They told him that he was not to return that night and told me to call them if he did. Perhaps they suspected some foul play after all. I knew he wouldn't go to a friend's home. He didn't really have any. I also knew that he wouldn't want anyone to know what happened so he went to a hotel.

I only had a couple of hour's unsettled sleep that night and will be forever grateful that neither of the boys woke up. I actually wondered if I had been to blame that night as I tossed and turned unable to sleep. *What if I hadn't turned on the light, I knew he had problems sleeping...I should have used a flashlight...I should have brushed my teeth in the morning and just slipped into bed.* Who was I kidding? I hadn't committed a crime, I hadn't done anything wrong. *He* had! The whole incident could not have happened at a worse time. We had booked a trip to go down to the Keys for a long weekend with some friends and we were scheduled to leave early the next morning.

That following morning I wondered what to do about our trip. The boys were excited about going to the Keys. We were spending a long weekend with a couple who we really liked and who were also excited about the trip. They were trailing their boat down and we had activities planned for the whole time. What was I going to tell them? I didn't even know if Peter was going to come home. I was very good about hiding our problems, but this one was going to be a challenge. If we went we would have to wing it and pretend there was nothing wrong. It required energy to perform and pretend and fool people, which was so exhausting, especially following the evening before. I was torn between cancelling our trip and wanting to go. I had not wanted to let the boys or our friends down. I also knew that if we stayed home it would be worse for me than if we went.

Peter came home that morning without a word and went up to the bedroom. I went upstairs to ask him about the trip. I had no choice since I would have to let our friends know. We were due to leave in thirty minutes. Somehow, we agreed that we would go. I think that he felt the same way as I did about letting our friends down so late.

It was going to be an absolutely horrible three-hour drive because I was the one who had to pretend everything was OK in front of the boys. We ended up travelling in silence. It was a wonderful and yet agonizing silence. What had happened the night before was really bad. I played a lot of fun music that I knew the boys liked, which helped to mask the silence and the tension. Our boys deserved to see a healthier relationship growing up and it deeply saddened me that they weren't. I wished that we had authenticity and affection towards each other but it was pretty hard for me to do especially after being physically attacked.

I really don't know how I got through that weekend. It was strained, though Peter appeared extremely elated the whole time. It was obvious that he was trying to belittle me with a phony display of happiness, knowing full well how much I was hurting within. I had become adept at creating an image to outsiders when it came to covering up our fractured relationship but the one thing that I never did was use that behavior to intentionally hurt him. I had created the image from a sorry sense of pride. That weekend he capitalized on my pain and thrived off the misery he knew I was experiencing from the choking incident. I was not able to hide my sorrow as well as I usually could because I was so incredibly upset and hurt...really hurt. I talked with my friend at the pool the following day while the men and boys were out on the boat. It was the first little peep I had given anyone, except Lorraine, that we were struggling. I had felt that the anguish showed, plus I had not had anyone to talk about it with since the incident. As usual, I didn't share the whole truth. I was ashamed of the truth. Like anyone else, she would wonder why I stayed with him if she knew what was really happening. I was reacting coldly towards Peter around our friends, Peter was flourishing, at my expense, and it was making me livid. She was very understanding and showed great empathy for my situation. She shared with me some challenges that she had faced in her own marriage, but they had been nothing close to mine.

All I wanted was for the boys to have a good time which, happily, they did. It was strange that Peter and I avoided any conversation whatsoever about the incident but was probably good for the sake of everyone, including ourselves.

On our drive home, shortly after the boys fell asleep, I asked Peter if he wanted to talk about what had happened. It was like the flood gates blew open and he started in on me in a verbally aggressive way. My intention had been to get some clarity and perhaps some closure to a very ugly moment in our marriage. He blasted me for calling the police-- how dare I do that to him. How dare I put us in a situation where a report would be filed which would be made public information for any future clients to see if they did due diligence on him. It was just incredibly disgusting to hear him talk that way about us. He had more concern about his professional image than the fact that he had abused his wife. Unbelievable. He told me that if I wanted out of the marriage that he was going to make sure that I got nothing from him. He meant financially. But the worst threat was the one he made about our boys. He promised me that I would never take them from him for one day, and that he would fight me to the bitter end to make sure that I didn't. And there it was. My greatest fear. He yelled at me most of the car trip home and eventually I just stopped talking to him and disappeared into my own silence. His threats were all designed to intimidate me and to make me afraid to leave.

The pull-push emotional abuse was morphing into a predictable pattern. However, the push was becoming more dangerous and the pull consisted of increased manipulation, control, generous gifts and trips. The worse the abuse, the longer and more rewarding was the apologetic period.

I put my head down for months and focused mostly on finishing our renovation. The hard work had its perk and that was distraction. For months, the days were filled with the building project and raising our boys. Peter was helping with the renovation and still looking for a new business to purchase. Our time together was minimal and sadly that was fine for both of us. Martin and Michael were at a very fun age and I was thoroughly enjoying my time with them, but it was always clouded with a deep sense of sadness at not being able to share that time with their father by my side, even on my side, for that matter.

Peter had finally found a company that he wanted to purchase. It was a local company involved in insurance that was losing money each month. They were not innovative at all regarding technology and had boxes of papers throughout the offices. His goal was to introduce technology, become paperless and become profitable. It was a huge relief for him because he really needed to work. He is a hard worker and enjoys what he does and therefore I had figured it would take the pressure off anything going on at home – or so I had hoped.

Peter was still engaging with women and still insisting he wasn't. The obvious "come-ons" had been, and would always be, a painful thorn in our marriage. We couldn't go anywhere without him scoping out an attractive woman. I always knew when he was doing it. I'd see women smiling at him. They weren't necessarily initiating that smile, they were returning the smile. Apparently, this was all in my imagination according to him. His insatiable need to inflate his ego using attractive women wherever we went was done with absolutely no regard at any time for how it made me feel.

I had considered leaving Peter many times, but each time had talked myself into staying with him mostly for the sake of the boys. I felt very strongly about traditional marriage especially one that included children. I had chosen to be with Peter. I had chosen to marry Peter. I had chosen to have children with Peter. Now my responsibility to my family was to be the matriarch and make it work through thick or thin. That had been a healthy outlook except I had a husband who seemed to have no interest it making it work. How does a person abuse their spouse over and over and over again and expect it to work? Also, I knew Peter would fight me for the boys; he had told me so. He would argue that I had no income, no job and, most likely, lie about my mental state and that threat was too much for me to tackle. At that time, I would rather have died than lose my little boys for no reason other than the intentional cruelty and punishment of my husband. My responsibility was to raise the children that we brought into the world and not leave them for any reason, even at the expense of the abuse I was enduring.

Lorraine had become physically frail although her mind was as sharp as a whip. She called me and asked if she could see our almost finished renovation. I was surprised and yet happy that she wanted to come because she wasn't doing too well at the time. My new home was important for her to see before she was no longer able to, what a wonderful friend she was. She arrived with her husband and son with a gift for me. She excitedly watched as I opened the little box to discover a beautiful Tiffany pearl ring. I absolutely loved it. She told me that it was a little something to remember her by. I hated to hear her say that. But in truth, she was going to be leaving us soon. I thanked her for the sentimental ring and told her that I would cherish it forever and always think of her when I wore it. That was until it disappeared a year later along with everything sentimental in my life that involved Peter.

As odd as it might sound, considering the turbulent relationship Peter and I had endured for the past five years, I was starting to yearn another baby. I had always wanted to be the mother of three children. I silently struggled with this desire for some time, acutely aware of my dysfunctional marriage, and weighing it against the extreme sadness that I would face if I never got the chance for that third child. I had put off broaching the subject of a third child with Peter because we had been experiencing major problems, but after the last incident, we had been stable for some time. I believe that this was mostly due to Peter's long absences from home since he had bought his new business. He was gone from early in the morning until late at night. It left very little time for anything. Handling both the boys alone for me was simple. Lonely at times, but simple. I had such a good routine going with breakfast pre-school, kindergarten, pick-ups, play time, dinner, bath time, book time and bed time that I felt that I was ready for another child. It felt like my soul was yearning for this child with a strength I could not ignore. Even though I had always wanted three children, this child was being called upon by not only me, but also by what felt like a higher spirit. I had succumbed to the fact that my marriage, though contentious, was a commitment I had made for the long haul so, if I was going to have a third child, it was going to be with Peter. Bearing another child was for me and less for us. We were like two different entities living under one roof but I would need him to bear that child with me. I felt like I had our boys under control as far as a healthy and structured life was concerned and was prepared and very ready for another child. While there are some that might have thought that I was mad to want another child with him, it was me that wanted this child not him. I did this for me.

I told him one night that I really wanted another child. He was a little surprised by my desire and, after mulling it over for a day or two, agreed. He had told me that it would be a deep regret for me to not have another child if I wanted one so badly and, on that note, one month later I was pregnant. I have heard many women who are divorced tell me that they had more children knowing that the marriage was not loving or healthy, but did it anyway. I'm not so sure there is a concrete reason why we have more children with full knowledge that something is wrong in our marriages but many of us do. In my case, it was a heartfelt and soul yearning desire.

I never liked our boys witnessing the tension or bickering between Peter and me. I was very conscious of keeping it away from them. I had become quite adept at it. I preferred to stay silent rather than talk with him about something that might trigger a negative reaction that would be felt by the boys. Rosa was still with us. It was hard to pretend to her that Peter and I had a good marriage because it was obvious that she knew it wasn't. Her presence in our home definitely helped our relationship because we both behaved better than we might if she weren't there.

Dinner time was always difficult for Peter. He didn't like sitting around the table and would leave as quickly as he could once we had eaten. I, on the other hand, enjoyed the dinner table with my family. It was our only family get together on a weekday and it upset me that he didn't see any value to it. The times we had at the dinner table were often uncomfortable because I knew he didn't want to be there. So, on many of those nights I would come up with a game where I could hide the discomfort, where we could find some happiness, conversation and, also, keep Peter from leaving the table before we were finished. Dinner time was supposed to be enjoyable. Here was a table with a healthy family and great food and it had baffled me as to why he didn't seem to enjoy that time. Once Peter told me that his mother rarely made dinner for him and when she did, it was a piece of meat or some other nondescript food given to him on a saucer, no different than how you might feed a dog. He hated his mother for not feeding him and once he started with a part-time job, would go on to buy his own food, which was normally fast food because it was cheap and the quantity filled him. However, I was not his mother and I was giving him the complete opposite, and yet he didn't seem to appreciate it.

I brewed coffee every morning since I had met Peter. I used to wish that we could drink coffee together before the busy days commenced, and yet he always seemed to have a reason not to. It was another excuse for avoidance. Considering we rarely spoke during the day, that five minutes together in the morning might have started off our days in a healthier way. Since we didn't eat breakfast together either, coffee was the only time that we would get to discuss what was on our agendas for the day. Just a brief moment of time together. Peter's reluctance was bizarre. He used one excuse after another to not grab a quick coffee with me in our home. He hadn't liked the way the coffee tasted, prompting me to try another coffee maker. Four coffee makers later, and continuously raving about coffee elsewhere, he was basically suggesting the coffee I made sucked. Being a cook and loving finer foods, good coffee was, and still is, extremely important to me. He went from telling me he didn't like the type of coffee I made to saying he had no time for coffee in the morning. For a long period of time he claimed that he didn't drink it any longer. Years later, I found that this was yet another ongoing lie, when I was horrified to find hundreds of Starbucks charges on his Visa bill bought minutes after he left our home.

Rosa told me that she wanted to move in with her boyfriend and a few days later she was gone. Peter decided to use her room as an office. The nice thing about Peter working from home was that the boys got to see him more and on occasion I could run out and do errands when the boys were napping. However, our home was no longer the home we had been used to where we had fun, had friends over, played music, had fun in the pool, watched T.V. and so on. Now we had to change that routine drastically and I did not like it at all. We had to be quiet, no friends over, no music, no T.V. It had suddenly become dismal.

One day after he was done with work he took the boys outside to play in the cul-de-sac. They were around five and six years old at the time. I had been suspicious of Peter and other woman for some time. Since he had no problem womanizing in front of me, how far was he taking it when I wasn't around? He was so private about everything that he could have been getting away with anything as far as I was concerned. I was cleaning up a little while Peter was outside with the boys. When I was straightening up around his office, curiosity got the better of me when I moved the mouse and the screen came on. His inbox was displayed. There were a few business e-mails on the screen but then one popped out at me and nearly knocked the breath out of me. It said, "Two girls waving at you from Fort Lauderdale." I knew he would be livid with me for opening it because I was forbidden to touch his computer but I did it anyway. I clicked the e-mail open. There was a photo of two sultry girls dressed sexily waving at the camera. The e-mail read, "Hi Peter, waving at you from Fort Lauderdale. Come down and see us." It was the first bit of proof that he might be fooling around with other women and it made me nauseous. This accidental discovery would explain his intense secretiveness and evasiveness. He had another side to him, a secret side involving other women. It felt like my marriage was not only abusive, but one big fat lie. I wasn't sure how to handle what I had just found so I left the e-mail open on the monitor. I did not want to confront him in front of the boys, the open e-mail would do it for me. It always worried me that the boys might remember mom and dad arguing because of something mom started, so I would just wait and see what he did. If they witnessed an argument stemming from something I did or said, then their perception would be that I was mean to their dad and that would not seem fair to me since I only ever confronted Peter about very unacceptable things. Only when they got older would they realize the seriousness of my accusations and until then, anything we did in front of them would only hurt them. I never liked them seeing us in conflict.

I went into the kitchen and didn't know what to do with myself. I busied myself in the kitchen cooking dinner because it was all I could do. My head was spinning. Peter came into the house shortly after and went into his office. A few minutes later he came into the kitchen. He was acting out of character, sheepishly asking what was for dinner. The boys were still outside and I just couldn't help myself. I asked him who the two girls were from Fort Lauderdale. He said he didn't know what I was talking about.

"You know," I said, "the two girls who sent their photo to you, the one in your inbox, who are they?" Again. he told me that he had no idea what I was talking about. I walked over to his computer and the e-mail was gone. I even went into his deleted and trash folder but it was not there either. It was clear what he had done. He forbade me to ever touch his computer again and kept it password locked from that point on which only confirmed that he had things to hide from me.

His attempt to suggest that I had not seen an e-mail with women in it was one of the most psychologically disturbing things he had tried since I had known him. Did he really think that I was going to believe that I hadn't seen it? Even though the e-mail evidence had disappeared, I continued to ask who the women were. He continued to tell me that there had been no such e-mail. He even had the audacity to tell me that I was fucked up and just looking for a reason to fight. I asked him if he was having an affair. He got angry. Not only was I furious for catching him in something involving the two women, I was concerned for my psychological safety by his increasing insistence that I had not seen the e-mail. Not only had I seen it, I'd opened it. It takes a really insane person to try to convince you that you didn't see what you know you saw. He had been caught red-handed. We would fight about this incident for several weeks until I went into the hospital. He kept his computer locked up from that day forward. He wore his phone on his belt for years afterwards. The whole ordeal had been not only been shocking to me but very sad. It was the first confirmation to me that there was more going on than just flirting. From that day on I stopped trusting him entirely. I couldn't speak with him for days after the e-mail incident. The boys didn't seem aware of the times that we spent not talking because I danced around it so well. Even though I had long stopped loving Peter from a romantic point of view, it still hurt that he was humiliating me. Each time he hurt me I went straight back to the familiar dilemma: do I stay or do I go. I cannot explain why I stayed so long considering the pain he was inflicting on me, but the right time would come.

Chapter 11

I was thrilled to be pregnant again. I had wanted this third child more than anything since having Martin and Michael. The only downside to being pregnant like the two times before was that it didn't seem to improve our relationship, even in my very vulnerable pregnant state. He worked longer hours and left me many times to take the boys out. Not once did he tend to my emotional wellbeing nor did he inquire. He just didn't seem to care about me or my third pregnancy.

By this time, as I've said, I had completely mastered the "fake image". I was good at it. I was ashamed to admit to anyone that we had little to no friendship or affection in our marriage, and how ugly and abusive things could be, and was very careful about hiding it. There were a couple of my closest friends who knew that I was not "really" happy. They saw right through my façade. I was on edge around him and nearly always wondering if everything was OK. If it was not OK, I would pay for it. And yet, as exhausting as that was to have to behave that way around him, I remained hopeful that things would be OK in the end. All I wanted was for us to be happy and free of unnecessary conflict. We had everything we needed around us...except friendship and love. We had two beautiful children and one on the way who all deserved a stable home and loving parents. I wanted a happy family at any cost; having to absorb all the emotional, physical, and psychological abuse was somehow worth it if I could continue to raise our boys and keep them close to me. Peter and I had proven that we worked well together in theory but not together in love. Therefore, if we could make it work well mechanically with our respective roles then why not physically and romantically together. My dreams of a wonderful and happy family with a promising and comfortable future was what kept me driving forward, always hoping. If only he would stop flirting with other women, if only he would stop lying to me, if only he would stop the psychological abuse...if he was just kind to me, I'd have it all.

I was around three months pregnant when Lorraine died. It was one of the saddest days of my life. She was the only friend that really meant something to me that I had ever lost. I put the ring she gave me together with her notes and cards into a safe place. I still occasionally read them.

One Saturday night, we were invited to dinner with Jody and Scott. They had invited two other couples. Jody had asked me to make an appetizer so I spent the afternoon making sausage rolls. They are a fairly easy to make but laborious in time. I put them into the oven and went to get ready. Peter and I were not really getting along that day. We had conveniently avoided each other all day. It was by no means healthy, but it was how I managed to keep things calm for the family but in particularly for the boys. I removed the appetizers from the oven and set them onto a pretty plate. We said goodnight to Martin and Michael and left in the car, neither one of us talking to each other. I had not covered my appetizers because they were still a little hot. In an effort to be spiteful and to punish me for the fact that we had not talked all day, Peter took the liberty of slamming his foot so hard on the brake that the appetizers slid from the plate onto the floor. I was livid. However, I remained calm and silent. Livid was the reaction he was looking for. I calmly picked every single one up and replaced them on the plate. I was around five months pregnant at the time and it was not the easiest thing to do but I managed it.

Without a word, I walked to the front door with the plate in both of my hands and rang the doorbell with my elbow. Just as I'd done that, Peter spit in my face. Knowing how proficient I had become at hiding and cleaning up behind his abuse, he probably hadn't expected that I was planning to do absolutely nothing about it. I left it there, slowly rolling down my cheek. As the front door handle started to turn, Peter swiftly wiped it off my face. It had been a huge feat for me to have the courage to leave the evidence of that vulgar attack. It was a silent vengeance. I was changing. It was the first time I was not prepared to hide my abuse. I was going to expose his vulgarism and expose his true self, the real person that lived behind the handsome and successful mask. When attacks like this occurred, there was always an agenda behind them. His agenda that moment was to ruin my evening. I love to socialize, meet new people and have a good time with my friends. It just comes effortlessly to me, but not after what had just happened. I felt defiled. My entire insides felt heavy and sick. I was starting to hate him on a level way too deep to be healthy for any relationship, let alone a marriage. As expected and anticipated, Peter happily sat at the dinner table and capitalized on what he thought would be my broken-spirited mood. His ability to be intensely disgusting and hateful just moments earlier and to switch so quickly and effortlessly to an engaging, and likeable guy, regardless of how fake it was, showed me one of the most prevalent traits of a narcissist, which is the cunning and impressive ability to morph into whatever person you need to be around business and social gatherings, followed by an immediate switch back to the real self once the show was over. Since he was already uncomfortable at the dinner table, the only way he was able to fit in with the intimate setting of people at the dinner table that night was to steal my energy, empower his confidence and destabilize my ability to enjoy myself. Perhaps he hoped that I would sit sullenly, silently injured, and maybe come across as unsociable that evening around some new friends that were there. I'm sure he had hoped that he had ruined my night, but not so. I was not prepared to let him do that anymore. It might seem a small thing, but it was my first emboldened step out of the image I had created, which was only proving to enable his distasteful behavior. Let them see his spit, I had thought. Time for him to be exposed.

I had hoped and prayed for years that he would improve over time, but he hadn't. That night, as devastated as I was and as violated as I felt, I found myself flourishing at the table with Jody and her guests. I was so tired of him and so ready to expose him. There was no question I was sorely hurt, but only I could allow him to continue beating me down in an effort to gain a more superior position in our relationship. My bravery at the door that night was proof that those days were coming to an end. It was the first time I had been prepared to expose him in front of friends. Try as he may, he was no longer taking me down. We were supposed to be supporting each other and bringing out the best in each other. Only a weak person feels the need to destabilize their partner in an effort to gain a social upper hand. Only a weak person void of self-esteem will try to rob another or theirs which is what he had tried to do to me since the day I met him. By the time I realized that I was married to a malignant narcissist, I was in way too long and had three of his children. My insatiable desire for a happy life and future with my husband was waning. I can honestly say that I tried as hard as I could to set the family lifestyle around him in an effort for him to enjoy it, feel safe within in, trust in me, rely on me and have faith in me. I had no choice but to give up. I had tried everything. I could finally walk away and know that there was nothing more I could have done. I had protected him for far too long. I had hidden his abuse, his cruelty, his hatred of women, and his need to feel superior over me but all I had done was empowered and enabled him. I had felt a ridiculous need to protect him and to protect the image I had created; I also had felt so incredibly sorry for him having the miserable childhood that he had had. The irony was that I was creating a similar misery for our boys in doing so.

I did not realize until I left Peter that I was dealing with a severe personally disorder and a malignant narcissist. I didn't even know what a narcissist was. I'd just thought he was really mean and cruel. I have read just about every article I can find on this sickness and it is uncanny how alike Peter is to the accounts I read. The article I read on divorcing a narcissist was identical to what would happen to me. Authors talk about the survivors who are strong enough to get away from their narcissistic partners but caution them that the narcissist will continue to try to hurt them, especially if they have children – another true fact. Writing this book is my attempt to highlight true narcissism by someone who encountered it first-hand. Many people reading this book who are in narcissistic relationships will identify with many of my stories and pain. Hopefully, I can encourage you to get out, to plan wisely, to protect your children, to be strong, because your narcissistic partner is about to put you through hell for leaving them. However, the hell you would endure by staying with them would be crippling and even worse.

Peter became more and more of a workaholic. When he came home for dinner, he would eat quickly then go back to his computer. I was always hurt by his avoidance of the family and particularly at the dinner table. I would ask him why he couldn't just sit and wait for everyone to finish. He told me many times that the boys took too long to eat and that he had sat at his computer all day and needed to get up. It was really an excuse to leave the family, especially me. He seemed to hate being there. He never spoke about his day with any of us. He could have talked about the new staff, the goals he had, silly things that happened in his day but he didn't. He was one huge mystery.

One night, soon after the spitting incident, Peter came home and told me that he was invited on a fishing trip to the Bahamas with two other men. They were going out for a long weekend. I really liked the men that invited him. They were of good character and I had no problem with him going. In fact, I was glad he was going. I spent the weekend with Martin and Michael and my friends. There was no pressure or tension when Peter and I were apart. I could actually breathe, and not worry about who I invited over and whether or not Peter would be upset about it or, worse, rude or unfriendly towards them. I had long noticed that if a person did not add any value to Peter in some way, he was not interested in them. They had to be financially successful to warrant his attention, or be able to help him succeed in business somehow. It was shallow and shameful. While he was away I could invite my friends over and enjoy them without worrying about them leaving insulted or ignored because of his sense of self-importance and his delusional sense of superiority.

99

On the day Peter was to return, I received a call from the wife of one of the men on the fishing trip. She told me that there had been very bad weather forecasted that would prevent them coming home that day. They were going to boat to a close island and sleep there for the night and return the following day. I was embarrassed and aware of my lack of concern which she had to have felt, but then only the week before he had spat in my face. I felt nothing for him for what he had done. He didn't bother to call me and tell me about the delay. That would be respectful and considerate. He was neither to me. They returned the following morning.

At the end of that week I was tidying up and was just about to throw some papers in the trash that were on the desk and noticed that one was a post office receipt for a $50 mailing of a package to the Bahamas. Naturally I wondered what he sent to the Bahamas for $50. I asked him when he came home what he had sent to the Bahamas. He told me that he had sent some paperwork for a business opportunity. I asked him what the business opportunity was. He did not like my questions and didn't answer me. I had become angry by this point because I knew he was lying. He couldn't even tell me what the business opportunity was. I was not going to let it go. I pressed him further about the secret package to the Bahamas. He refused to tell me. This went on for hours. He finally screamed at me that the box contained diapers. I asked him why he was sending diapers to the Bahamas. He was furious by this point. I asked him if he had a child in the Bahamas, which seemed like a perfectly logical question under the circumstances. My head was spinning with confusion by that point as to why this was such a big deal, a secret and now a lie. What was happening? He told me that the reason he had lied to me was because he knew I would think he had a child there. Now that he had lied I *did* wonder if he had one. I wasn't even sure if he was telling me the truth about the diapers! I asked him who the diapers were for. He was seething that he was being forced to tell me. He told me with a tone of utter disgust that they were for a woman who had served them at breakfast in the Bahamas whose child was sick and had extreme diaper rash. She was unable to buy disposable diapers in the Bahamas because she couldn't afford them so he had offered to send a box when he returned home. I left the house. His lies and betrayals made me feel physically sick. Based on his years of womanizing and our lack of any sincere friendship, intimacy or sex, my head did not know what to think anymore. Did he have a woman over there? Was it his child?

For the sake of my own sanity, I called one of the men who was on that trip. I asked him about the diapers and if what Peter had told me was true. It was. At the risk of looking like a lunatic, or a jealous and insecure wife, I made sure that I mentioned that he had initially lied to me and the story he had made up. This was another coming out moment where I had exposed him to a friend. I was not going to keep his lies private any more. If he was going to lie to me, I was going to expose it. As dangerous as it felt to stand up to him, it was liberating and freeing. I was reversing course and not lying to everyone around us anymore and, most importantly, to myself. Sending a box of diapers to a woman in need was the first kind thing that I had known Peter to do since I had met him. Why he had to ruin this act of kindness by burying it in lies was beyond my comprehension.

We had planned a trip to Italy that summer. My brother and his wife, who had just had their first child, were meeting us in Venice. I was about six months pregnant and very full around my belly. It would not prevent me from touring and seeing the beautiful towns we had lined up to visit. I was in excellent shape, extremely healthy and looking forward to seeing my brother, his wife and my new nephew. I was equally excited for them to see Martin and Michael who they hadn't seen in a while and for the boys to see them. Living so far from my family had never been an issue for me until I had children. It weighed a little heavily on me that the boys didn't get to develop a close tie with my family. They didn't have family to speak of in the U.S. since Peter refused to visit his family. I packed the suitcases for our trip, with the exception of Peter's. He never allowed me to pack for him, ever.

Being in Rome was the first time I had spent a long period of time with Peter in a very long time. Rome was beautiful. We strolled down the streets of Rome taking in the breathless sights. It tugged at me to see other families and couples walking together, some holding hands, some kissing, some taking photos and some just looking happy together. Even though we walked with our boys, we were very much apart. It had been my idea to visit Rome and if I didn't plan a summer vacation I'm not so sure we would ever take a trip. Peter was content working so it took my action to get away. I felt that Peter didn't really want to be there with me. I felt very alone. To be alone is one thing but to be with someone and still feel alone is lonelier.

Our trip went well for the first day or two, until I noticed him making contact with almost every pretty woman that passed us. He had started to behave like he was single when he was in my company. If he acted this way in front of me, I could only imagine how he was when I was not around. He had become so conceited that he had lost sight of the fact that he was doing it in front of me over and over and over again. He did not seem to care one little bit about how it made me feel. He had known for a long time how much it hurt me and yet he never stopped. He had an insatiable need for ego replenishment at any cost, which was always mine. It was beyond hurtful; it was insulting. I cannot begin to count the number of times I suggested he leave our marriage since he was clearly interested in other women. He would hurl some mean comment my way or laugh at me. Our relationship was way too convenient for him. I'd been enabling, ignoring and cleaning up behind his abuse, his narcissism, his misogynism and his womanizing for seven years! I hadn't realized that I was enabling him in the beginning, I just felt that cleaning up around him would get rid of the problem. I could easily have walked away to a better and healthier life, but that meant leaving our children in his custody post-divorce. I could not think about doing that since I found him to be cruel and unhealthy and was never going to leave our young boys unprotected around him for regular periods of time. How could I leave them in the hands of a man who did not respect women and expect anything positive to come from it. I made a sacrifice then, and for many more years I would take the brunt of the abuse if it meant that I could stay and protect our children, and raise them with morals, love and grace.

I was a great mother, a responsible and dependable wife, an amazing supporter of his desire to build a successful business. I entertained many of our business colleagues, staff and prospects over the following years. He knew I brought this great quality to the marriage and, since I tolerated the abuse, I was an ideal partner for him, one he wasn't going to get rid of. This was working out great for him.

As we walked around Rome, I refused to bring up the womanizing. There was no point. It only seemed to bring him pleasure. Broaching the subject would only ignite conflict. I psychologically removed myself from what he was doing and continued sightseeing around Rome...with Peter always two steps behind me looking for female attention. I was six months pregnant and was feeling round and plump. Seeing my husband look at other women all the time made me feel ugly and unattractive. I should have felt beautiful around him, pregnant or not. Years earlier, I had watched an interview with Lady Diana Spencer. She spoke about how she was living in a loveless marriage in front of the whole world. She talked about how miserable she felt, how alone she was and how she had had to take second place to another woman. She had stood by her husband with an insincere smile to the world as he ignored her, disrespected her and carried on like she was completely irrelevant, worthless and meaningless. I remember feeling great empathy and pity for her as she spoke about that sense of loneliness and how her marriage was just an image and not at all what it seemed. Here I was years later in that very same marriage!

We made the journey from Rome to Florence by car, stopping off for the night in the wonderful city of Siena. It was dusk when we arrived, but even so, it was very clear that the city had a medieval feel and it was absolutely gorgeous. We ate dinner in the city's famous square, the Piazza del Campo, and after letting the boys run around, we went back to the hotel. Our plans were to wake up in the morning, eat breakfast and tour the city. We both loved to walk and I was looking forward to seeing the sights. We all went to bed early that night.

The following morning when I woke, Peter was not in our room. I presumed he was downstairs in the lobby on his computer doing some work. One after the other, the boys started to wake. I opened the curtains and saw Peter's computer on the table. If he wasn't on his computer, then where was he? I got dressed and went downstairs to see if I could find him. He was not in the hotel. I went back upstairs to our room and got the boys ready for the day. Peter came back around 9am. I asked him where he had been. He told me that he had gone for a walk. I asked him why he hadn't waited for us so that we could all go together. He told me that he thought we would wake up late. We never slept late, so that was a lie. I had wondered if he had been out all night and was just coming back. It wouldn't be unlike him to wait for us to go to sleep and head out. The trouble with believing anything he said was that he was a proven, pathological liar. I had long stopped trusting him. We walked around the city after breakfast, Peter for the second time I assume, in strained silence. It was horrid. I couldn't stand it. I had started to fantasize regularly about something I thought would never happen, and that was being with someone else, someone that was kind to me.

We left from Siena for Florence and when we arrived we found out about some local attractions that we planned to visit. One was a train ride which I thought it was a great idea for Martin and Michael who didn't get to take trains rides very often. The following day we walked to the station. It was exhausting to have to pretend that everything was OK between us because it really wasn't. However, as tiring as it was, I would go through the motions of trying to look happy with Peter so that our boys didn't pick up on it. As young as they were, I wanted them to think we were a lot happier than we were, fully conscious that they were also learning from our behavior.

We had almost arrived at the train station. I was pushing Michael and Martin in their double stroller and Peter was walking behind me. As we walked under a charming arch bridge, a striking girl walked the opposite direction on the other side of the road. As she passed us, I knew it. I just knew. I turned back to look at Peter. He was looking back at her and she looking at him. It was at this moment--a moment I will never forget-- that I knew I was leaving him. He was destroying me and I was allowing it. My life was just one hurtful thing after another. He was addicted to womanizing and I was the victim of his inconsiderate and abusive behavior. I could not go on the train ride with him.

I had noticed a park on our walk and decided to turn around and go back to it. I didn't explain to Peter why I was turning back nor did he ask. He knew. He kept on walking to the station. I covered the change of plans to Martin and Michael by explaining that I had seen a great park (which is was) on the way and that we had missed the train. They were at the age where they really didn't seem to care and were just as happy once we arrived at the park. They ran off to play while I sat and wept. It was over. I wept until I saw him storm around the corner. Oh God! I thought he had gone. I almost had a heart attack as I saw him stride towards us. He looked so, so angry. I had no idea if he was going to explode right there in front of all the mothers, fathers and children in the park. My stomach was in knots. He sat down next to me and told me I had ruined the entire trip. What audacity. I told him that I was no longer going to walk by his side as he flirted with other women. I was done. He told me that he did not know what I was talking about. However, he would miraculously remember four months later in the office of marriage counselor number three. Just like the e-mail that I didn't see. Just like anything that he did that ended up being my fault somehow. Being strong natured on top of everything made me more of a target. Narcissists like to control and I was not controllable. I had used coping tools to maneuver around his bizarre and abnormal behavior, but I had never given him control over me. I had a spirit that was too advanced and strong for him and as much as he tried he was unable to break me, which ultimately intensified his efforts. It was as though I had to accept his behavior as status quo, and the minute I objected to it there was hell and it was all my fault. I had started to think about leaving Peter on a regular basis.

I wore Lorraine's ring a couple of times during the trip in Italy. Wearing her ring made me feel like I was connected with her a little. I really missed her. I had started opening up to her about our marital problems for several months before she passed. I felt she was a safe person to tell. I looked up to the sky one evening as I sat in my hotel room alone, while the boys slept and had started to sob. I had never told her that I had started to hate him while she was alive, but I told her so many times after she died. I also used to reach out to my grandmother who had passed and begged her for the strength to not fall at the hands of this evil man.

We arrived in our final city, Venice. I submerged myself into my brother, his wife, their baby and our boys. It was the best thing that happened since we arrived in Italy. I wanted to tell my brother how mean Peter was and how unhappy I was, but I couldn't. He and his wife looked so happy sitting there with their new baby, cooing and cuddling him that I couldn't bring myself to ruin that moment. He helped her and pampered her and laughed with her, it made me feel envious. Pretending to be happy with your partner when you are not is one of the hardest things to do.

I was pleased to be headed home from Italy. It would mean that I could get back into my lone routine, would see less of Peter and I could spend more of my time with the boys that I loved so dearly. We arrived home and walked through the airport to get our luggage. I had noticed a girl at the luggage carousel with a guitar strapped over her shoulder. The reason I noticed her was because Peter was staring over at her. I was sitting on a bench with Martin on one side and Michael on the other. Peter stood with his back to me but I could see her full on. He was openly flirting with her and she with him. Their ogling back and forth made me want to go to the bathroom and throw up. They played a little game together until all the cases were collected. I was so weary and exhausted I could no longer talk to him. He came back as I walked on with the boys and our cases in silence. He knew that I had seen what he was doing and was why I was ignoring him. He didn't even hide his lascivious exchanges with women any more.

A crowd started to build up as we waited for security to retrieve our customs forms. Lady guitar was close by. I was fed up. The energy between them was so obvious. I had harbored so much resentment for so long that, under my breath, I told him to take her phone number and then to do me a favor and leave me. In hindsight, I would never have said it had I have known how he would. Out of nowhere, he bellowed with rage in front of every single person in that airport. He screamed at me at the top of his lungs and told me that I was fucked up. He was completely out of control. I was horrified at how loud and aggressively he was yelling at me, not only in front of the entire wing of the airport but in front of our boys. I felt crippled at the shame he was inflicting on our family. Everyone was looking at us. I started to see everything in slow motion. I did not hear anything after that except the beating of my heart. It was like every emotion in me just shut down. I continued through security like a zombie hoping people would not think he was with me. Inside I was dying from mortification. Life literally stopped for me during those few minutes. I felt such deep hatred towards him. Looking back, I have to wonder what guitar girl thought of him after seeing that. Was she impressed? Yelling at his pregnant wife in that despicable way in front of his children. You can reach a point in life where it is easy to cut someone out mentally and emotionally so that they can no longer cause you pain. I was there. I am surprised that I didn't go into premature labor from the stress of that trip or at what happened at the airport. We drove home in complete silence. I unpacked my suitcase and all my personal belongings and noticed that Lorraine's ring had disappeared. I never saw it again.

I was around seven months pregnant and had started embracing a future without Peter. I knew that Peter would make it hell for me when he found out I was leaving him so I had to start thinking about a strategy and an income. I was going to start legal proceedings after I gave birth to our third child. Our marriage at this point was in a state of true crisis. We no longer had sex, intimacy, or friendship. I was living in hell. I had to find something that I loved that would generate an income and that I could start from home. It was the only solution that would enable me to raise my baby and be home for our boys. Being that cooking had always and continues to be a passion of mine I decided to build a catering business. I started to prepare and cook all my best appetizers and had professional pictures taken of them. In less than a week I had put together a portfolio of my work. I placed an ad in a local Junior League magazine. A week or so later, I ended up with a small job catering a Junior League fundraiser. I worked with them on a menu and landed my first job. I was close to eight months pregnant. The job went well and they were very pleased with my work. So much so that it led to job number two. It was a larger job and made me quite a bit of money. I didn't hide the money from Peter. I just put it aside and bought myself a little something for my efforts. Peter was watching this new income from a distance and, unbeknownst to me, did not plan on allowing me to keep it.

I was still meeting with my mommy and me group. We had been together for a while now. The rotation of house get-togethers was back to me. Even though I only had a few weeks left of my pregnancy it didn't stop me from hosting. I enjoyed entertaining so much that I could have been carrying triplets and I would still have hosted. I believed that it was good for the boys to be with their friends and nurture their young friendships. I had started preparing lunch the evening before so it left less for me to do the following morning. That morning I was tidying up a few things and getting ready when Martin ran to get me to tell me that the toilet had clogged up. Their toilet had been clogging up on and off since we had moved back into the house. The truth is that we should have had it professionally addressed but we didn't. For a few years, we thought it was because they were putting too much toilet paper into it. So Peter or I would plunge it and it would be fine. I had introduced a flushable wipe to the boys, which Peter believed was the new cause of the toilet clogging up. He had asked me to stop buying them. I noticed that the bag of wipes disappeared, as did anything that he did not approve of, so I bought another. I asked Peter if he would unclog the toilet before he left. It wasn't all that much to ask. He could see that I was busy and very pregnant. It sparked an angry outburst. This is what I feared about him. He stormed through the kitchen seething and spitting out angry comments about the toilet and about the "fucking wipes". He was banging doors to the garage and banging doors in the bathroom. I left him alone since I did not want to exacerbate his behavior, nor did I want the boys to get upset. I just switched myself off and continued to get things ready for lunch.

I had to run and pick up fresh bread before everyone arrived and was running a little ahead and was hoping to get ten minutes to sit down before my guests arrived. As I was getting Martin and Michael ready to leave, I could smell a bad smell coming from their wing of the house. It smelled like shit. I went into their bathroom and literally froze from what I saw. There was feces all over the bathroom. It was an incomprehensible scene. I could not believe what I was seeing. It was like Peter had sprayed feces all over the bathroom. It was everywhere. There were tiny pieces of feces on the shower curtain, all over the toilet, on the walls, on the cabinets, on the fixtures, in the bath, on the mirror, on the towels, the rugs and all over the floor. It was so meticulously even throughout the bathroom that it remains a mystery to me how he did it. He had to have plunged the toilet with such violent rage and threw the feces around the bathroom with each plunge. The bathroom and the surrounding home smelled terribly.

I only had an hour until my guests arrived so I had to get the horrible mess cleaned up. I must have been in shock because I did not react emotionally, I simply went into clean-up mode. I threw all the towels and rugs into the washing machine and sprayed everything down. I had to leave the bathroom several times to prevent myself from gagging and from breathing in the cleaning products that were definitely not good for my unborn baby. It was making my head ache. I did not allow myself a minute to think about how disturbed my husband was for committing this despicable, vicious attack on me.

I took care of everything pretty quickly which had now set me very much behind. I threw the boys into the back of my car and set out to pick up the bread. It was as we were driving that I was able to reflect what had just happened. My whole body convulsed into sobs. I tried to hide it from the boys but it was impossible. I felt completely broken. I was exhausted and I hated Peter for what he had done. How could he do that to me? I had to conclude that he did it to punish me because the toilet had overflowed due to the flushable wipes, according to him. What better way to punish me when he knew I had friends coming over and how it would most likely ruin my time with them – which it did. Even though I had cleaned up the bathroom, I could not clean up the memory of what had just happened. It was like living in psychological terror. I cried all the way to the store and back and then had to pull myself together for my friends. The irony of this account is that the toilet still clogs to this day fifteen years later. It had nothing to do with the flushable wipes. Since I had started exposing his irrational behavior, the bathroom incident would have been a perfect example of his abuse to show my friends, but it was way too severe and horrifying; I'm not so sure they could have handled it.

Two weeks after this horrific act, our third son was born. He was the most beautiful thing I had ever seen. He would turn out to be the most remarkable child I have ever met. A true crystal child. A child sent from heaven into our family with a purpose. I am aware of the purpose. We called him Alex. Martin and Michael were ecstatic. Martin was gentle and calm with him. He loved him very much in his own quiet and peaceful way. Michael wanted to feed him, bathe him, touch him, hold him; he could not get enough of him. They were both very pleased with their new brother. He was a healthy and beautiful baby boy. Peter and I were thrilled with our new son but unfortunately, not with each other.

Chapter 12

The very worst part about living with a narcissist, someone who wants to constantly hurt you on some level, is how you start to change and who you start to become. I was not just with a narcissist who was mild on the narcissist scale. I was with a strong, successful, handsome, wealthy, psychopathic, cruel and evil narcissist with a personality disorder. I was with a malignant narcissist. He didn't even know who he was, which made him more frightening. He had low self-confidence, was a self-loather, hated most women and yet had an insatiable need to inflate his ego using those same women. This is why success is so important to the narcissist since they can use this artificial sense of power and/or money to gain attention, the opposite sex and friendships though I doubt those attracted are really true friends.

When I met Peter, I did not know anything about narcissism and only learned about it towards the end on my marriage. Anyone who has left a narcissist, is currently living with a narcissist, or is going to be a victim of a narcissist will have to go through a lot of pain and suffering before they escape. The narcissist does not expose their true authentic self until there is some form of commitment and in most cases, that entails marriage and children, and then for many like myself we feel it's too late. We victims constantly remain hopeful that the man or woman we are with will grow up or change. In my case, seeing that that reality was unlikely, I stayed anyway and for way too long, since leaving my children was completely out of the question. At first, Peter seemed to like my ability to socialize; he liked my friends, he liked how I was generous not only with my money but with my time. Slowly, over the years, he started to resent it. It was as though he was resenting in me the very thing he wanted for himself. The very things that he found attractive in me were the very things he ended up hating me for and found ways to punish me for. He was incapable of being kind, loving and social like me so he attacked it. He attacked my friendship with Jose, who eventually stopped coming over, our nights out with friends, our vacations with family; anything that meant something to me he would attempt to sabotage. He was used to being in control and controlling those around him.

Since I did not allow him to control me, he would subtly or viciously punish me often. His punishment or abuse was usually cruel and having lived with it for so long I found my reactions to his behavior becoming equally cruel and verbally abusive. I knew what to say that would hurt him and I would. I am in no way suggesting I enjoyed it, but it became a defense mechanism for me. It was retaliatory. I didn't feel good after striking back at him the way I did on numerous occasions. It was affecting who I was and a sign of who I was becoming. It felt great to hurt him back and inflict pain on him through my vicious words, but it would make me feel absolutely horrible for days. It made me feel ugly. It was like I was turning into him in an effort to cope with him. Not only was I hiding an abusive and miserable marriage from everyone around us, I was now trying to hide this new mean self that had emerged that I did not like at all. I felt myself hardening and sounding harsh with others at times, since this was a new pattern of behavior adopted from my emotional and mental survival. Once in a while, by accident the boys would hear me say something unkind to Peter. It was mortifying that they would hear some of my ugly and wounding words and would kill me to think that it left them thinking that I was a mean parent. They were too young to understand that Mommy was mad with Daddy because Daddy had just done something incredibly hurtful to her – like flinging feces all over the bathroom or spitting in her face-- a couple of examples that come to mind. I was starting to change who I was in an effort to tolerate Peter, and that was not good at all.

Alex was a wonderful baby and I thank God for him even to this day. He has a warm soul and had an air of extreme kindness to him. Martin and Michael embraced him into our family with a love that made me feel incredibly grateful for all of them. There was no jealousy of any kind, just a warm, glowing relationship between the three. Michael couldn't get enough of him, he was totally in love. It was like I had given him a new toy. He was remarkably attentive to him at all times, seizing any moment he could to look into his face, make silly faces at him and kiss him over and over. Then there was Martin. The patient and calm child. He would sit with Alex for hours and watch cartoons and just play with is little finger or stroke him tenderly. Such a difference between the two of them.

I had recovered quickly from giving birth as I had the two times before. My parents were coming to stay for a month. They would be a huge help...well, kind of. My father is bi-polar so I didn't know if he would be well or not during his visit. If he was well, it was great. If not, he would spend most of the visit in bed, depressed. It turned out that Dad was well and, being that it was Christmas time, it was a nice surprise for all of us but especially for me. My father is very funny and has a remarkable sense of humor and made me laugh all the time. It felt good to laugh and be genuine with someone I trusted and who would never hurt me. When he was well, my Dad was a fun Dad. As children, he would take us swimming, camping, drive us to school, say daft things - to which we rolled our eyes but loved - show us card tricks, play board games, fix our cars when they needed it, and was the worst handy man in the home ever, but always fixed everything. He is a kind person and would never speak badly about anyone except in fun and to make us laugh. On bitterly cold mornings in the UK, ten minutes before I had to leave for work, he would de-ice my windscreen and start my car so that the heat had time to make my car cozy and warm for me. He is considerate of other people and would give you his last penny if you needed it more than him. I never once feared him and have respected and been close to him my whole life.

When my parents arrived, I was so happy for the reprieve from abuse because Peter rarely behaved poorly in front of other people. A lot of my pent-up misery was relieved around Dad because he made me laugh and feel good.

My Mother, on the other hand, was not particularly funny and very critical of people. Her conversations are usually boring and mundane. I did not trust her growing up because she was not loving or caring towards me, and had proven not to be loyal either. She was critical of many things I did in my life and of my friends. It was as though she didn't like me, which hurt me as a child but I have long stopped caring and forgiven her, since it is her loss. If my Dad was center of attention she would distract his audience and look for the attention herself. I would never give it to her because of what she did and because she bored me. Aside from her negative traits that I have accepted, she is a decent person overall, but I am not close with her.

Just before the holidays, I got a call from a lady wanting me to cater a party. She was hosting seventy people. Even though I knew this was going to make me extremely busy with two young boys, a new baby, Christmas around the corner and my parents in town, I took the job since I was looking to grow my new business and saw it as a potential financial escape. My parents would watch the boys for me. It turned out to be a lot more work than I had anticipated. I was preparing and cooking the food alone, which I probably shouldn't have done just six weeks after giving birth, but I wanted the exposure and the extra money for Christmas. I was starting to feel good about myself again since other people were complimenting my work, and more work followed as a result. I felt that my sanity depended on leaving Peter and that was the goal I kept in mind at all times.

The night before the party, I was chopping ingredients. Alex, who had a touch of colic, was crying inconsolably. I wanted so much to sit and cuddle him, nurse him into calmness and just be there for him but I had fallen a little behind. I took him from my mother here and there but kept going. I remember the pain I was feeling from having to cook for seventy people that I did not know while my little baby was crying for his mommy's touch. My mother rocked him until he settled and fell asleep. To add to that bitter pill, Michael came into the kitchen and asked me if I would read to him. I told him I would if he just gave me a little more time to finish what I was doing. He came back again later and asked again if I would read to him. I told him I would read to him in ten minutes. I probably took a little longer to finish what I was doing but cleaned myself off and went back to his room. He had fallen asleep. It made me feel horrible and weepy. It made me so upset that I went to my room and sobbed. I had started to resent the job and the fact I was not able to give my attention to my children who needed it. But most of all, I resented Peter for giving me no choice but to be in this situation. I had no choice but to prepare myself financially and mentally for our upcoming separation. I knew that, though we were making decent money at the time, Peter would fight me financially-- he had warned me of that; he would find a way to make sure that I received very little of it. My busyness and my parenting were exhausting during that holiday but the sense of empowerment that came with seeing a young business grow so steadily only continued to build my strength.

I worked all day the following day so that I could finish the work and get the food delivered on time. Martin had not been well and woke up feeling warm. Around dinner time I noticed that he had a slight fever. I gave him some ibuprofen. I hated to leave him while he was sick, but I needed to deliver the food. Around thirty minutes before I had to leave, Martin's face started to swell and ten minutes later he was wheezing. The timing was terrible. I was on the phone with his doctor who told me to give him Benadryl. Peter seemed very unhappy about what was going on but I wasn't sure if he was more upset about our home smelling of food that was about to go to someone else, or because I had given Martin the Ibuprofen that sent him into an allergic state. There was nothing I could have done to prevent either and up until that day had not known he was allergic to Ibuprofen. Martin recovered quickly and my mother – unaware of the magnitude of the stress between Peter and I – urged us to go and have a drink with some friends who had included us in their company party that night and relax. We delivered the food to my new client who was very happy and rewarded me with a handsome check. I was starting to see how my new venture could flourish since I was seeing a pattern of happy clients and an increase of money.

Peter didn't speak to me once during that holiday party. I danced with the other girls and tried to have a good time but I was finding it harder and harder to have a good time when I was around him. Many times, I wanted to expose how things really were and tell all my friends that he was really not a nice husband to me, especially when we were alone but our society is not ready for that kind of brutal honesty and neither was I. It had been a very stressful week. Yearning for my newborn and not having time for him, delaying reading time with Michael only for him to fall asleep, and watching my child suffer an allergy attack and putting a delivery deadline before him had simply been too much. Nothing seemed to be going well except for the handsome check which gave me hope.

Peter had worked out a monthly budget for our newly renovated home shortly after we moved back in. It covered the general running of the home, the boys and food. Our company was in its infancy stage and, though it was doing relatively well, our monthly budget was quite tight. I figured that my new income would help subsidize nice things over the Christmas holidays. If I continued to grow at that nice rate, I could see a promising future and financial independence. My financial daydreaming came to a screeching halt when I opened the monthly budget only to find the amount was reduced by the amount of money I had earned from the Christmas party event I had catered. It took me only one second to realize what he had done. He had taken it from me. There had been no discussion about how my monies would be spent and I must have missed the one where he told me that the money I had just earned was his. He had taken it cunningly and deceivingly by reducing that months' monthly budget by the amount I had earned. He had interfered in my finances, the very same area that he kept intensely private from me, and not only prevented my ability to keep or spend some of my income, but to suppress the spirit that fired the willingness to continue.

I knew he meant every word of removing and controlling my future income and I decided that I would not continue any further business until we had separated. Though I regret it today, since I could have taken these catering skills and the business to a completely different level, establishing financial independence and success, I never took on another catering job and there were many that I turned down.

I asked Peter why he had taken the money from me the way he did. I had not planned on hiding it. Quite the contrary, I was going to spend it on the family. He told me that I had to start contributing. The financial profit I had made had been good but was a mere fraction of the profit that the company was making. He didn't need my money at all. It was all about controlling it. We had got into quite a heated argument over it. He was enjoying watching me squirm and softly beg for my money back. It was typical behavior of and was the brutal cruelty of a misogynist. Another classic trait spinning off the narcissist.

I spent the rest of that Christmas with such a heavy heart. Instead of supporting my business efforts I felt like he had punished them. Had he just been kind and supported my efforts, we could have been very happy and content today relishing in our different and yet successful marital businesses. I will never know if it was desire driven to prevent me attaining success, or if it was just desire to keep me trodden down so he could feel superior, which was very important to him. Our new technology company was doing quite well financially and he did not need my meager monies to help with anything financially pressing.

Peter was not always respectful to my parents during their stay. He would often laugh at my mother behind her back for being overweight though she was always as nice as she could be to him. He couldn't seem to get my Dad and his humor and would criticize him more than enjoy him. He liked to deride my parents at any opportunity. It became clear to me that he had had no family love, loyalty or respect ingrained in him whatsoever. I had seen this very early on but had not realized how it would impact us as a couple around my family. Having missed the opportunity to have a normal family and having endured an extremely dysfunctional family dynamic in his childhood and adulthood, I would have thought he might have embraced and appreciated my family with more respect than he did. If he couldn't show me any love or respect, there was no chance he was showing them any. Many years later and after many years of being around Peter, my family told me that they couldn't put their finger on who he was. They were unable to connect with him. They took the words right out of my mouth. How sad, and how sadly enlightening it was

I suspected that when I next saw my parents I would no longer be with Peter. My brother, his wife and their son came to visit with us over the remainder of the Christmas holiday. It felt so good to have them around that holiday, especially since they were such good energy and nice people. I needed it more than ever after resigning to the fact I would be filing for divorce shortly after their departure. I managed to keep anything negative away from them and, by switching Peter off emotionally, I actually had a good time with them. It had been a great relief knowing I was going to leave Peter and that upcoming reality made me feel somewhat elated for the rest of their stay with us. I felt empowered by my secret and anything that Peter did around that time no longer bothered or hurt me. I'm sure they had to have noticed our lack of intimacy. We weren't tender to each other, we didn't touch or go near each other for most of their stay. I felt so happy and emotionally safe while they were staying with us and was dreading their departure.

I started to prepare myself mentally for the courage to file for divorce. This man did not deserve me. He was cold, emotionless, empty, mechanical, abusive and cruel. I started to ask my friends about divorce attorneys. I told them that a friend of mine was getting a divorce and asked if they knew anyone who was good. I ended up with the name of a female attorney who had a wonderful reputation of being fair and getting good results for her clients. I had her name but did not quite have the courage to call her. That call would be the beginning of the end and was not the easiest call to make especially since there was a period of time that we had been getting along and that always made it harder for me.

When things between Peter and I were good, the pressure to leave always subsided. There had been a few months that were good and it was those times that played with my emotions more than ever. I knew that getting a divorce would completely and forever change the lives of our three young boys. During periods of time when things were going better between us, the thought of divorce dissipated and a new surge of hopefulness would creep in... perhaps we could survive and things would get better between us over time. I am not a person who quits too easily and am extremely loyal by nature. I also fight harder than most when I believe in something and I truly believe in marriage and the family. Having to face the harsh reality that Peter was not a healthy partner for me, and perhaps me for him any longer, was becoming a daily burden. I struggled constantly with the fact that the one life I had been given to live on earth was with a person hell-bent on making it miserable for me. The only one who could change this mission to destroy me...was me. Living with a narcissist endures a lot of emotional push and pull which is not healthy and can change from month to month, week to week, day to day and in some cases from one moment to another. Many times, I wanted to leave for all the horrible reasons I have mentioned, and yet, many times I wanted to stay and fight to keep our family together and capitalize on the better times. I wanted to find love somewhere in us. I wanted to love and be loved. I did not want to give up and simply walk away and become a divorcee. Even though every ounce of me knew that I was with an unpredictable man in an abusive and unhealthy marriage, I still wanted it to work on some level for the sake of our boys and for their future. I wanted to remain married for the sake of all of us.

The lack of cruelty and outbursts made it a tolerable time, but far from content. My mind was consumed with what a divorce would bring and how it would affect our boys and their upcoming milestones, their teen years, their prom nights and their graduations. The thought of a major disruption during these years made me feel physically sick, and yet there was always an unconscious understanding that it was inevitable. I was looking forward to their futures, their graduations, their first girlfriends, their proms, their eighteen-year-old birthdays, their college applications, their college choices, Christmases, Thanksgivings, weddings and families. I knew these occasions would be greatly impacted by divorce but also realized that they would be equally impacted by the memory of unhappy parents. As our boys were getting older there was no question that they would see we had a loveless and miserable relationship. I didn't want that for them. What kind of example was I setting for them? I felt that Peter and I were setting them up for their own marital failures.

Many couples stay together until their children leave for college. I commend those parents, and if my marriage was simply flat and loveless I might have been able to hang on too, but mine was abusive. I have a friend who had parents in a loveless marriage; she spent her childhood wishing her parents had separated. She told me that she had experienced many problems in her own marriage because of her parents. Her parents' lack of love or respect for each other had taught her to go on and find difficulty in loving her own husband, which ultimately led to her own marital problems. I did not want our relationship to impact our boys' marital futures, and I knew it would if we or I did not change it. My boys were not going to learn anything healthy from my relationship with Peter and this very fact haunted me nearly every day for years. I loved our boys unconditionally and invested as much as I possibly could into them and believed that our healthy mother/son relationship would give them an advantage with their wives. I was firm with them when I needed to be, helped educate them, enhanced their social skills endlessly, respected them and their space, allowed them to make mistakes and encouraged them to get back up and learn from them, cooked them their favorite meals, hugged, kissed and adored them.

121

I pray that my emotional, mental and physical investments will pay off for them in their adulthoods.

Sometimes when our boys talked rudely to me, Peter did not correct them. I had talked with him about showing some united front and correcting their disrespectful attitude. Instead of agreeing with me, he would get upset with me. I couldn't understand why he wouldn't want to reprimand them since I thought it was a goal for both of us that they learned the difference between being respectful and disrespectful. He would eventually go back to their rooms and have them come and apologize, which I appreciated but then he would later tell me he could only imagine the hell he'd have to go through if he hadn't done it. What absurdity. I wouldn't have been at all surprised if he went back and told them the very same thing. Self-victimization would help him have our boys feel sorry for him instead of respecting him and his authority to apologize to their mother. It was a way to devaluate my importance in their life. I had spent their entire childhood building a relationship that was solid, loving and respectful in an effort to send three successful, loving and respectful gentlemen out into the world. It was hurtful when he grumbled about having to address them to respect me. Hurtful, but not surprising, since he was a misogynist.

I felt like I was living in a cloud. All I had in front of me was a wall of pending divorce. I decided to discuss it with a therapist. I did not discuss our major problems with my friends back then and I desperately needed to talk to someone. It felt like my situation was choking me. I found a female therapist in my community. I felt very comfortable with her and consequently told her as much as I could fit into that first visit. I cannot begin to tell you what a complete relieving it was to share my private pain and suffering with another person. It felt a little scary for me; it made me feel vulnerable after revealing the truth behind our marital façade, and yet it felt exhilarating at the same time. I told her how I had learned to ignore him, tune him out, and emotionally shut down around him, all in an effort to cope. I also told her that I wanted to leave him but I was afraid for our boys and afraid of losing time with them. She told me that she was extremely familiar with his type of personality and that I needed to prepare myself for the inevitable if I should leave. She told me that once I left him, he would project his cruelty onto the boys since he could no longer get to me. This in turn would hurt me greatly, which would be the point. I had found it hard to digest what she was telling me; I could not comprehend the idea of him being that cruel to them. She made me look at her straight in the eyes and repeated what she had said, "He *will* start on the children, trust me." I left her office feeling very uncomfortable with what she had just told me. I went to see her a few more times, mostly to get things off my chest. She had been right, though. Years later, he did abuse our boys with a level of psychological abuse and lies that I would liken to psychological terrorism.

It was a medical scare that pushed me over the edge and led me to sign a retainer with my second divorce attorney, Susan Greenberg.

I was in bed watching T.V. one night while Peter was sleeping. It was a part of the routine at this point. I would wake up in the morning and Peter had already left for work or the gym. I would give the boys breakfast and get them ready for school. I would collect the boys from school, come home and have them do homework, let them play and prepare dinner. Peter would come home, get changed and go straight back to his computer. He would eat dinner with us and go back to his work. I would get the boys ready for bed, read to them and, usually by the time I returned to my bedroom, Peter was asleep. He rarely made any time for me. As I was watching T.V. that night, my eyesight suddenly started to blur. I blinked a couple of times but I was unable to see the T.V. In a split second, I started to shake. I thought I had food poisoning at first, due to the shaking and the groggy feeling in my head. I got out of bed and walked around the room for a minute but the shaking was getting worse and it felt really, really strange. I woke Peter and told him that I didn't feel right. He told me that I would be OK and to go back to sleep. I got out of bed again. My heart was beating so rapidly that I started to panic. I woke Peter again and asked him to call 911. This time he woke up. I started crying uncontrollably and, since I seldom cried, he knew it was serious. He called 911 immediately.

I thought I was dying. Spiritually speaking I was. With tears streaming down my face, I walked across our home to the boys' bedrooms. My body would not stop shaking and I was starting to have trouble breathing. My vision was blurred and I could barely see. My heart felt like it was about to explode. There was no way I was going to die without saying goodbye to my boys. I went to Martin's room first and told him in his sleep how much I loved him and that I would always watch over him and through hysterical tears I kissed him goodbye. Then I went to Michael and did the same thing. I left his face wet from my tears. Lastly, I went to Alex's crib and leaned over and kissed him too. I told him that I was about to leave and how sorry I was to go too early and that I loved him. Though I was in an extreme state of distress, I remember feeling gratified that I had said goodbye to all three of my babies.

Moments later I was surrounded by a medical team. It turned out that I had had a massive anxiety attack. There is no question whatsoever that this attack had been brought on from months and years of silent anxiety living in a contentious and hellacious relationship. The disease in our marriage had finally crept around from behind and attacked me physically. I had spent years ignoring red flags and had accepted on some level that this was just the way it was going to be. However, the red flag that I was not prepared to ignore was my health. I had three young boys to raise and my determination to be around for them superseded my need to be with Peter any longer. My health warning had come from a higher power and it was time to listen. After a few days of recovery, I called Susan Greenberg. I was not going to let this marriage kill me. I was done, I was out.

I told Susan in my first appointment that I needed to get out my marriage because it was abusive. We had been to see three marriage counselors and had exhausted all efforts. It just wasn't working for us. I had just suffered from an extreme and frightening anxiety attack unquestionably brought on by the unhealthy relationship that we shared. It was like breathing poison and slowly dying from the toxic fumes. I told her that she had to file immediately. I needed to get away from him. She scheduled the divorce papers to be delivered the following Monday morning to his office.

I was not happy with my decision to get divorced at all. I did not want to be divorced and I did not want to put our children through a divorce, but I now felt it was leave or die. I could not stand how he behaved around me any longer. The lustful ogling at women, the lies, the capricious and unpredictable behavior, the lack of any romance, love, affection or emotion of any kind. I was sick and tired of living in a fake place with him. We looked so good from the outside and we were so very despondently broken. I just wanted to feel at peace with myself and our boys; this was not obtainable with a clandestine monster at your side.

It had been a very long time since I'd felt as empowered as the way I felt when I walked out of Susan's office that day. I was back in control of my life. It felt exciting, liberating and scary, very scary.

That weekend I stayed out of his way. I had nothing to say to him. It was over. He had not only ruined what should have been our most treasured life together, he had taken great pleasure in it. He had long stopped going to therapy. He told me that it was a waste of money, his time, and that most therapists are more screwed up than their clients. What he was really saying was that he didn't want to work on himself or us. My avoidance of him that weekend angered him. I just didn't have anything left to say. He was no longer worth my time or energy. I do not recall what happened that following Monday morning before Peter left for work but he was upset. It may very well have had to do with my avoiding him and saying practically nothing to him most of the weekend. I was sitting at my computer, as I did most mornings. As he passed me he turned and spat on the floor right beside me. He walked out of our home and slammed the front door behind him. For the first time ever, I didn't care. It was vulgar and abusive, and a reflection of his own self-hatred; it had nothing to do with me. I got past that disgusting moment rather quickly knowing what lay ahead for him that morning. Shamefully, it made me feel happy.

I received a call late that morning from Susan's office to say that Peter had been served and that he was in receipt of the divorce papers.

That afternoon Peter came home early from work. I had wondered if he had reflected on his spit attack as he read the notice of divorce proceedings. He slumped himself onto the floor by my desk. He told me that he could not believe what I was doing. I ignored him for quite some time before telling him that I had filed for divorce because of all the cruel things he had done to me over the years and because of the emotional and intimate void. He was in utter disbelief. He sat on the floor with his head in his hands and started to cry. I was shocked and taken aback by his tears and started to feel uncomfortable. I had to remind myself that his tears, while real, were only a part of his act. He was going to do whatever it took to make me change my mind and tears were step 1. He walked around our home as somber as one could be and did not go to work for almost a week. I was so used to the emotional push followed by the emotional pull game that this time I refused to allow his strategy to impede me or my decision. He was no longer in control and it was freaking him out. I had never seen this side of him before. It was refreshing to see a vulnerable side to him however I suspected that it was not sincere or authentic. It was the classic behavior of the narcissist to manipulate back what he wants or needs and he was a master manipulator. He was doing whatever he thought it would take for me to drop my suit and I saw right through it. He apologized for all the things he had done and they included all the things that he had accused me of not seeing. Even the ones he said I was making up because I was insecure and deranged. Now he was apologizing for them.

I told him that I felt that he had severe childhood trauma, specifically with his mother, that was never addressed; it clearly was impacting our relationship. Issues that would continue to manifest and feed the intensity of his anger if he didn't do something to heal the wounded boy within. He told me that he would go to therapy and work on himself intensely if I dropped the divorce proceedings. He started therapy immediately. This is not at all what I had expected or wanted. I had been mentally and emotionally preparing for this day for a long time and now it had taken on a whole new twist. I had never seen him so upset and genuinely terrified of my leaving him.

I went back to Susan and told her what was happening and how Peter was behaving. He had reassured me over and over that he was going to get help and change. He acknowledged that he had not been treating me well and admitted that he was looking at women. His confession had been somewhat relieving, but it sickened me further to hear his excuse. He said he looked at women out of habit because he had been single for so long before being with me. That was one hell of an insult since we had been together 7 years by that point.

Peter had been seeing his therapist for a few weeks, going twice a week to show me commitment. His therapist had wanted to meet with both of us, which I agreed to. I am not sure why I went really because it was our fourth therapist by this point and I no longer really liked or trusted Peter so it seemed like a waste of time to me. I ended up going out of curiosity after the therapist requested a second time that I join Peter. I could tell, after reciting the incidents that had happened over the years that the therapist was unaware of most of them. I know they addressed a lot of his childhood issues but he would never understand my hurt and pain if he did not know how Peter had been treating me. For the first time Peter confessed that he did flirt with other women. The reasons he gave him were the same pathetic ones that he had given me. Single for so long and out of habit. He admitted he knew he was doing it and that he knew it hurt me. Sadly, this behavior would go on for 9 more years.

The therapist told Peter that he did not appear to be happy or enjoying his life. He suggested that Peter consider taking a mild anti-depressant. I was over the moon to hear his diagnosis, since I had long suspected that he suffered with depression. However, when I brought it up a few days later, Peter adamantly refused to accept he was depressed and claimed that he would never take an anti-depressant. I was optimistic about his suggestion because for years I had not only suspected that depression was responsible for exacerbating his mood swings which directly affected our marriage. Actually, the root of his depression, which spilled over to our marriage was from what happened to him as a child; until he faced and resolved that personal trauma, he would remain depressed and that depression would affect everything in his life, everything except control, his business and making money.

My fleeting glimmer of hope and change was quenched by his inconsiderate and stubborn decision to refuse medication. I say inconsiderate because he had nothing to lose by trying and everything to gain if it worked, including me. He was controlled by the narcissist within him who rejected all possibility that he had a problem of any kind, especially one that required medical attention. The narcissist doesn't believe there is anything wrong with him. He is superior, he is successful, he is important, he is powerful, he is handsome, there in NOTHING wrong with him so why should he change.

After seeing his new therapist regularly and after visiting him together for a few weeks, our marriage started to improve. There were calm and respectful conversations, I felt that I was being treated nicely, I felt a little more empowered and less of a victim. Since there were signs of improvement, I felt less willing to leave the marriage. He was showing signs of the very hope that I had been chasing for years and it seemed like my patience might not have been in vain, that we might, just might have discovered a little foundation to build on.

While there was much relief about this change, I remained acutely cautious. I was never really convinced of the authenticity of his new behavior but each day that I saw improvement I felt was a win. Susan eyed me dubiously when I told her that we were going to try to make it work. I told her about him going to therapy and later with me. I shared that I had seen improvement and was optimistic about us resolving some of our chronic issues. The irony was that I was trying to convince her that the monster that I had described to her just weeks earlier was now a teddy bear. No wonder she was not convinced. I suspect the stories I had shared with her were enough for her to know the personality that I was dealing with and that I'd be back. She told me so too. She told me that she admired my efforts to keep the marriage working for the sake of keeping the family together, but felt that she would be seeing me again. Peter had convinced me that he was truly going to change and was going to do whatever he could to improve our relationship. Because of this apparent sincerity at that time, I dropped the lawsuit. I had just taken the most courageous and frightening leap off the top of the cliff into the waters below and all I had left was to swim to shore and I would be free. Yet I had foolishly decided to climb back up the cliff. I wanted out of my marriage as much as I wanted to stay in it for the sake of keeping our family together, and there lay my internal conflict.

However, Susan had been right, I would be back. I had vowed that my ferocious anxiety attack was the final straw and yet it wasn't. What the hell was wrong with me? Seeing Peter in such a vulnerable state and spending hours in therapy to improve himself and our family dynamic had blindsided me. Since I had not expected this kind of reaction it threw a wrench into my plans to start a new life without him. I went back to the hope and change dream that I had been pursuing since early in our relationship. Maybe if he changed enough or, at least stopped being cruel and unkind, I could tolerate the rest if it meant not breaking up our family.

Peter continued in therapy for at least six more months, or at least that is what he told me. I don't think he went for nearly enough time and I am certain he deemed it a waste of time and precious work hours. He most likely only continued for that short time to appease me and to make his point. I went with him a few more times. He hated going and complained about how much work time he had just lost from being there and how our money would be better spent elsewhere. It was extremely sad for me to hear him because of his promise to resolve his childhood traumas and issues stemming from them in an effort to save our family was contingent on my dropping the lawsuit. I admit that I could never love Peter after what had occurred over the years, but I could stay with him if he stopped the abuse for the sake of raising our boys. Maybe then I could reassess. I was mentally, emotionally and spiritually divorced from him anyway.

Shortly after, Peter stopped going to family therapy. From that day on, I miserably existed with a man I did not love and who most certainly did not love me and yet we somehow managed to get away with it in front of our family and friends for nine more years. I was able to survive this long period of time for a few reasons. Peter became a full-time workaholic. It was an escape from us and if there was no us, there was no conflict. In addition, I started working from home for our company. My efforts came with significant reward and I was able to add a vast amount of value to the company through sales, marketing, hiring, conventions and hosting prospects and clients. This was a flourishing time for me because of the social aspect to my work which I loved. The work day really left very little time to look at what we were or what we were not. I did everything I could over those years to protect the boys from our toxic relationship which slowly started to deteriorate over time. We could only keep busy for so long. Immense distraction is what got us through those next nine years.

For several years after therapy stopped I submerged myself into raising our boys, taking the majority role in their education, well-being and health while Peter worked around the clock at our company. My courage to file for divorce had gone in my favor somewhat since it did turn things around. There were fewer blow ups and Peter managed to contain his anger around me. It was always there, however, just controlled. He knew he had to be careful around me since I had shown I was prepared to leave him, but he was not as careful around the children. Michael had started to show signs of anxiety, especially during the night. On many, many nights after we were asleep, he would come into our bedroom extremely scared. This is quite common with young children, and when it occurs your parental instinct should be to address the fear and make them feel safe. When Michael came into our room at night he not only woke me but, unfortunately, also woke Peter. Peter would go into an instant state of rage. He would bellow loudly at Michael for waking him. Michael would turn and run out the bedroom more afraid than when he came in with Peter yelling behind him that he had just ruined a day of work because he would not be able to go back to sleep.

I cannot begin to explain how it made me feel to hear that type of abuse and selfish guilt spewed at our scared son in the middle of the night. I hated Peter to the very core for doing it to him. It happened multiple times over his younger years. Michael was obviously afraid, else he wouldn't be coming to our room scared and needing comfort. He was being punished for waking the monster. I used to sneak him in bed next to me so many times as long as he didn't wake Peter. If I was to accidentally touch Peter during the night and wake him it would be fine. If I was to accidentally touch Peter during the night and wake him due to Michael being in the bed with us, he would explode. It made no sense. His son was afraid and all he cared about was himself, as usual. Displaying this kind of rage towards Michael during the night was like sticking a knife in my heart. For each time he yelled at him which only exacerbated his fear, I would not speak to him for days. There were times that I did not speak to Peter for weeks for hurting Michael at night. It was so dysfunctional. It was not who I was, but it was who I was becoming. My silence must have been brutal for Peter because I was good at it. I could have kept it going for months, only I was embarrassed at how it must have appeared to the boys. I was worried about looking like the bad guy. I hated behaving that way and yet I felt I needed to punish him as much as I possibly could for hurting my child. It was another sign that I was behaving abusively to cope around Peter and his hurtful abuse. I would solve this issue by taking Michael back to bed and sleeping in his room with him. This seemed to bring him the comfort that he was looking for. It went on for a long time.

His sensitivities and vulnerabilities would be severely attacked again years later when Peter launched a daily crusade of alienation to turn this pure and anxious child against the only person he trusted the most in his life, his mother.

It was during the nighttime rages at Michael that I recalled what my old therapist had told me, "He will start on the children next, trust me." Those chilling words had become a reality and new conflict started over how he spoke to and how he treated the boys. My nights became stressful for many years hoping that Michael would not come into our room. Peter would warn Michael every night to not come into our room until the morning. It turned out that Michael was suffering from the onset of anxiety that would morph in his teen years into major depression.

I started taking our boys every Sunday to Calvary Chapel. I wanted them to have faith in their lives. I wanted them to start a relationship with God. Calvary Chapel is a Christian church which has a modern day and simple approach to life. They taught simple principle values through humor and kindness. I absolutely loved going. Peter refused to go with us and I didn't care one little bit. It became my refuge, my safe haven. I believe in faith but I had not been very good about practicing it, especially when I had really needed it. However, when I did, it brought me much comfort and peace. I wanted our boys to share this same faith and to believe there was a higher power--other than the human power of their father--one that would never let them down, one that would bring them comfort, one they could trust and one that would bring them peace. It was a loving and safe place for us every Sunday and I felt good about all of us being there. We would stay after church for lunch and the boys would play all afternoon on the enormous campus's playground and fields. I never wanted to go home. I felt emotionally, mentally, and spiritually strong while I was there. It felt so refreshing to be around so many nice people. I would stretch the day out as long as I could and then head home.

Peter didn't seem to care that we were gone all day. It meant that he could keep working. One day we came home and he asked Martin what God had said to him at church. He was asking this in an attempt to intimidate and humiliate him, to make a mockery out of church. He would later go on to convince our boys that church had no relevance or value in their lives.

Attending Calvary helped me to keep my focus on my strength and spiritual wellness. I felt like I was David fighting Goliath. My unwavering and increasing spiritual strength kept me from being defeated at the hands of an angry, cruel and emotionally abusive husband. That was real power. Something he did not have. It was the kind of power I needed to face what was waiting for me down the road. My spiritual strength would be what kept me from crumbling at the hands of a man that was going to punish me for leaving him. The pain I was about to endure for leaving Peter was two unjust years of alienation where Martin and Michael left my home after being psychologically tortured for months with ugly lies. The emotional distress and strain that it put on Michael, the most sensitive of the three boys, caused him to spiral into a state of depression so severe that he was later hospitalized and is still on a slow and long road to recovery.

Chapter 13

We managed to get through the next few years by keeping out of each other's way. It seemed to be the only way that worked for us. I was so grateful for our three boys because they really helped distract me from what I did not have with their father. We had become adept by this point at behaving like a relatively normal and happy couple when we were around other people. I had engineered a social life for our family that included dinner parties, meals out with friends, and anything that precluded us from having to be alone together, even as a family. I tried to fill the emptiness and loneliness by surrounding us with certain friends, buffers really, ones that had proven helpful in our presence and had not only prevented us from conflict, but distracted us from each other. It was nearly always the same few people we were around since making new friends seemed senseless to me. In essence, I had developed another coping tool which helped us get through weekends, social events, and evenings out. The main friends we kept at the time were not much happier themselves. However, it appeased my need for socializing and, as long as Peter was comfortable with the people we were with, things would be copacetic.

The irony was that I loved meeting new people and flourished around large groups, but I could not be that same person when I was with Peter. He would either ruin that occasion for me by flaunting his insatiable need for attention from other women, or would punish me at some point, especially if he was not enjoying himself or felt uncomfortable, which he often did. It was so much easier to visit with the same group when socializing, especially since I had weeded out those who bothered Peter.

We used to see Richard and Sarah often throughout our marriage since their boys were the same age as ours, and because they were clearly as unhappy as we were. It was probably what caused us to be drawn to them; they had the same miserable energy between them and were a perfect couple to be around in the sense that we didn't need to pretend so much. I didn't feel that Peter and Richard treated Sarah and I nicely when they were together.

Sarah was a troublemaker and had caused marital trouble for me several times over the years. She would purposely sting me with comments about Peter and other women, or instigate between Peter and I by saying something that caused us to argue after we left. She was a snake. She complained about how Richard treated her for years, but was not brave enough to demand the respect that a woman, a wife, or any human being deserved. The two of them were not healthy to be around but typical of people we were attracting.

One of the social challenges of our marriage was that I stayed away from nice couples. I felt like we would be cheating them. I also felt that we would be transparent to happier and healthier couples. I did not want to risk meeting and investing with new people, specifically nice couples, and then have to lose them or drag them through the inevitable breakup. The peripheral friends we had were mostly mine, girls that I had been friends with when I was single and now their husbands. We had newer friends through the children, but I did not let them get too close.

Unless it was business or unless Peter was looking for something advantageous from of one of my friends' husbands, he seldom had an interest. He was the closest to Richard and that did not surprise me knowing how utterly disrespectful and disparaging he was towards his own wife. Peter was happiest when he was close to someone like himself. He didn't have many guy friends and rarely kept in touch with anyone. Peter and I survived on coping tools and on rare or strained times together during the week and social distractions on the weekend. Once again, our marriage was one big fat lie. We were fooling ourselves and cheating each other out of a happier relationship and, sadly, Peter seemed OK with it. As long as it appeared great on the outside, and I left him alone, he didn't seem to care about anything else that involved him and me. He was only about his image and making more money.

When Alex entered preschool, I found myself with hours of free time and asked Peter if I could work on sales in an effort to sell our technology, get myself back in business, prove my worth and help grow our company. He vehemently objected to it initially, but since I had recently filed for divorce and I pressed the issue, he had become more lenient; after a day or two he agreed. I worked diligently for 2 weeks calling one institution after another, utilizing my tele-marketing experience and engaged an institution looking for a new vendor. That company ended up becoming my first account, a huge feat in our industry for a two-week stint. Not only did it show my husband that I was good at what I did, it gave me a euphoric sense of accomplishment. Peter needed to step in to close the deal, but there was no denying that I brought it to him. Our new clients praised my sales approach, manners and dedication to Peter, which they said had ultimately led to the agreement.

I did not see Peter too much at the office. I knew he was busy and knew it was best to respectfully give him his space. Peter didn't seem to mind my being at the company, especially after engaging a new client. He was receiving great feedback about me from other clients of ours and most likely was starting to see me as a valuable business asset. A narcissist's nature is to use people who he can gain advantage from, even a wife. A narcissist uses people for social status, a business opportunity, sexual favors, financial advantage or anything that builds them in some way. All in the name of ego. I continued to work diligently, making up to a hundred calls a morning trying to get our company name into the industry and e-mailing as many people as possible with information introducing our company and, most importantly, our technology. Shortly after signing our new client, however, Peter took me off sales calls. I was confused as to why he would want to halt my progress and complained to him that it made no sense. He claimed that we didn't want to grow too fast. A baffling concept, considering we had the foundation to support the growth. If I had to guess, he was envious at my fast success and of the relationships I was forming in the industry, which he deemed were *his*.

Instead I segued into marketing our technology via social media companies and was solely responsible for exposing us to the industry by making sure I registered our company and attended all conventions that were relevant to our growth. Being a people person to my very core, the conventions were by far my favorite thing in the company. Since Peter had given me some free reign in this area, I was able to register our booth at conventions, sometimes minutes after open registration. Since it was based on a first come first served basis we would be one of the first booths through the main doors. For years, this gave us great exposure. It felt liberating to be given (mostly) unilateral control over our entire convention program, including breakfast, lunch and dinner arrangements, meetings with prospects, and full permission to start sponsorship opportunities. As long as I continued to attract attention to our company, and Peter flourished as a result, he allowed me to do as I pleased most of the time.

I had mentioned one day to Peter that our increasing growth in business was not being reflected well with our website and suggested that we revamp the entire website to reflect this new and upcoming success. He agreed and told me to go ahead and work on it. He did not micromanage my work, which was a sign that he was starting to appreciate and trust in my input and efforts. I spent the next four months building our new site. It included new logos for three of our new services, a new company logo that would encompass the new logos, descriptions of our technology and how it worked, management bios, product information, company information, news, press releases, convention dates, and a short video animation that showed how our technology worked and how it would increase profits. It was wonderful, and I was extremely pleased. To complete our new image, I recorded the company voice mail, not only because of my British accent, but also because of the feedback Peter was getting from clients/prospects who told him that I had a beautiful telephone voice. Our management team seemed very pleased with it too. I used to run a lot of my ideas past Penny, who was our operations manager. It was important to me that she be on board with my ideas, especially since she was an integral part of the team and I very much valued her opinions.

Shortly after our new site was up and running Peter placed me in charge of getting our website translated into Spanish. It was a fun learning how this process worked. Working at our company gave me a priceless look into how business ran from the bottom up. Utilizing my own skills, in addition to Peter's technical and programming insight and skills, we collectively took our company from a handful of employees to over 100 employees.

I had segued from one area of the company to another, fully absorbing the experience and knowledge. I went from sales to hiring to marketing and conventions. It had all happened very fast and was very exciting to me. After some rapid growth, I suggested to Peter that we keep our name active in the industry by sending out press releases to our client base, prospects and across the wire, in an attempt to reach any and all persons in our industry. Through this process, I was able to collect data and information about who was reading our press release, which service they were reading about and where the press release was opened. It was remarkable data which I shared with our management team during our monthly meetings and, consequently, with our salesman so he could call them. I was finding everything incredibly fascinating. I got along beautifully with our management team, our clients and our business colleagues.

One of my many accomplishments within the company was securing a lifetime sponsorship for our company logo to be used on every napkin used throughout the convention that included breakfast, refreshments, snacks, lunch, dinner, cocktails, beer, water, etc. The sponsorship was for one of the main annual conventions that most of our prospects attended. Our company name was everywhere. Even our competitors were impressed.

Before conventions I would scour the attendee list looking for our clients to make sure we touched base with them for breakfast, lunch, dinner or just a coffee. Prospecting was essential, therefore, if we had an interested prospect we would arrange a meeting in an effort to connect and establish a stronger relationship. I have an ability to engage with anyone, so my personality was a good fit for working at the booth during the events. I didn't push our services when I met with people initially. It was more important to me that we engaged respectfully, that we left a good impression, that we represented our company by being friendly, polite, well dressed and memorable. The relationship was more important. Things were going well at the conventions. We were getting plenty of exposure and the industry was starting to know who we were.

It was during my last convention with Peter that the penny finally dropped regarding the current and future situation of my marriage. Typically, at conventions Peter and I spent more time around each other than any other time. During our last convention, I observed that Peter was still flirting with other women, but with one in particular. He kept leaving the booth to walk around the room, but was really leaving so he could walk by, talk to, or flirt with her. Minutes after he returned, she would walk by a couple of times, ever so slowly, and play eyes games with him in a very suggestive way, grinning at him the entire time. She did not realize that I was his wife, and that was why she did nothing to hide it. It was blatant and so hurtful that I felt I was being choked. When Peter flirted with women in the early days of our marriage it hurt me to the point that we would argue constantly about it. When it continued years later, I had become quite insecure about myself. When I filed for divorce and saw a vulnerable side to him, one full of sincere remorse and regret for how his behavior had impacted me, I thought things would change. Perhaps he had just hid it better, because here we were five years on and it was obvious that he was never going to change.

I actually didn't care about him and his women any longer, I only cared about the disrespect, embarrassment and humiliation it caused me. I yearned for a partner that I could feel comfortable with. One that I could love and one who would love me. A man who would be kind and treat me with respect. At the end of the day, I brought up the woman, mostly because of the effrontery of the performance. He immediately denied it, as he always did, but this time we didn't fight, instead I broke down and sobbed for hours. The tears came with a deep sense of sadness, I was mourning the death of our relationship. I was too tired to fight for us any longer. That was the last convention I attended.

I was exhausted from the emotional pain and humiliation of what he put me through at that convention. I cried for days afterwards while I was alone, but the tears were no longer for us. The anguish I was facing was the reality of what lay ahead for our family. I was now left in the very same situation with the very same decision to make from where I was five years earlier. I needed to prepare and build the emotional strength that I knew I was going to need to get through it. I knew that it was not going to be easy, but I had no idea just how bad it was going to get. I sincerely believed that after we divorced and everything was settled that Peter and I would make better friends for the sake of our children than we could at being husband and wife. It was a very bitter decision for me to have to end our marriage, especially since we had everything going for us. We had three wonderful and healthy boys, a beautiful home, a successful company, financial independence, glorious vacations and yet we were very unhappy and had no relationship. I really had a hard time wrapping my head around all that we had but didn't really have. I was truly fed up of pretending that we were success, we were far from it.

Things in life don't just happen coincidentally. Everything has a purpose and always comes for a reason. Often unexpectedly, but always when the time is right. Life throws us lifelines when we least expect them, and if you are paying attention and don't miss the opportunity, you will be lifted from your pain and suffering and become free of it. My lifeline was coming.

The mere thought of breaking up our family tore at my heart, however, I needed to get away from him to set an example and show our boys that this type of abusive relationship was unacceptable, wrong and unhealthy. No more lessons about dysfunctional relationships, just lessons on how to get away from them. One day they would learn why I had to do what I had to do. I wanted to be free from the nothingness, be free to love and to be loved. I wanted to teach our boys through a healthier relationship, how to respect one another and, most importantly, how to respect women. It was impossible to do with Peter. I was constantly concerned that they might treat their girlfriends or wives with the same level of disrespect, or worse, with some kind of abuse. If I did not leave, then I would be to blame since Peter did not recognize or own his abuse.

Chapter 14

We made plans to spend five weeks in California that summer to escape the brutally hot summer where we live. We had been taking long summer trips for at least eight years. Peter would continue to work most of the time during our trips. The boys were getting older and Martin decided to bring two of his friends for the first two weeks. Before we booked our trip, Peter and I had bickered terribly about where we would stay. I was usually the one who planned activities for the duration of our long stays, and after researching where Peter wanted to stay, I was concerned about there being enough for us to do outside of going to the beach. It was a very small town with expensive shopping, restaurants, and a beach. We typically took trips to places where we could walk, bike, take train rides, visit city attractions, hike, go to movies, visit markets, and all the other things that a city on the coast offers that we could not do where we lived. Peter couldn't care less if my argument had merit because he placed no value on anything I said, unless it involved something advantageous for him. There were no bike paths, no walking areas from the home, and a very busy highway outside the front of the house. The home was absolutely beautiful, but was isolated to a beach. I am fair-skinned and not good in the sun and because of that rarely go to the beach. Peter didn't care. He was just determined to go. The home was perfect for Peter since he worked most of the day. I reminded him over and over of the endless things to do in our favorite spot further north but he would not budge. I had no idea what I was going to do every day for five weeks. This was a town where people vacationed to go to the beach. We already had this lifestyle at home. Even though I knew it was far from ideal, for the sake of peace I reluctantly agreed. Little did either of us know as we bickered about the location, not only would it be our last trip, but it would be the trip that ended our marriage.

Before that fateful trip, Peter and I attended the wedding of our friend's daughter. It was a small intimate wedding on the beach and it was beautiful. It tugged on my heart a little to see two young people so incredibly in love with each other. You could see and feel their love by the way they looked into each other's eyes. I knew that Peter and I had never looked at each other that way. I was not only feeling envy as I watched them but was starting to yearn that love for myself. As I stood among the guests in the ceremony, my body took a slight jolt when I caught someone staring over at me. Unbeknown to me at the time, it was my lifeline.

Up until the wedding, Peter and I had been going through the motions for years. I had long been checked out and he had long stopped caring about me or my feelings. I think we had most people fooled. When I had filed for divorce eight years earlier, I had let my guard down regarding my secret life. I had told a couple of my friends and family what was really going on. After succumbing to Peter's masterful manipulation and staying in our marriage, I felt ashamed because they knew my darkest secrets, and felt embarrassed when I went on to have another child with him. I was miserable being back facing the same painful decision. I was so tired of pretending. We were not good together. We were alienated from each other and had been for a very long time. I was denying myself a healthy and meaningful relationship not only with someone else but with myself.

For five or six years prior to that wedding we had not been intimate or sexual on any level. We didn't kiss, hug, dance, hold hands, tell each other how we felt about each other, enjoy meals together, make time for each other, or anything that would involve an intimate setting. I couldn't even convince him to drink a cup of coffee with me in the morning.

After the beautiful wedding ceremony was over I found myself discretely looking for the guy who had been staring at me. I had found his stare to be intriguing, exhilarating and exciting considering the emptiness I had endured for so long. I saw him and confidently introduced myself. His name was Rob and he was the brother of my friend and the uncle of the bride. We had a short conversation which was when he told me that he lived in California.

We were ushered into the restaurant by our hosts and as dinner was served the music started. We were all encouraged to get up and dance, something Peter and I rarely did together. He was engaged in a business conversation with a man sitting next to him and had no desire to talk to me, or to be with me on that dance floor. So, when Rob came over and asked Peter if he could dance with me and Peter said yes, I was over the moon. It felt so good to have someone interested in wanting to dance with me at such a fun event instead of talking pointlessly about business all night. Rob was a lot of fun on the dance floor and as I danced with him I realized, as I had many times before, how much I yearned for this kind of partner that I could enjoy life with. He was complimentary of how I looked, of my dress, and the way I talked. My dress looked lovely on me, but Peter hadn't even noticed. I had stopped caring that he didn't compliment how I looked; I shamefully don't even remember if he ever did. It felt really good to be complimented.

That night was Day One of my spiritual pass-over into my new life. It would be the start of the old me becoming the new me. The one that would walk with unwavering self-respect, self-esteem and be shielded with the light and an abundance of spiritual strength. A woman who would never allow herself to succumb to any more abuse in any form ever again.

As we left the dance floor Peter was still talking business, and I was laughing and enjoying the light banter and humor of this stranger from California. The music stopped and the groom came out on stage with his groomsmen. They surprised everyone and sang a cappella to the new bride, with the groom taking the lead spot. She had had no idea he was going to sing to her. She was elated with surprise and was beaming with adoration. That moment also cemented my decision. I had to leave Peter. If I had a fraction of their love, I might have been able to stay. Before we left the wedding, Rob gave me his number and told me to call him when we arrived in California. We had briefly discussed my favorite things about LA and he kindly offered to drive us around his home town of Hollywood and take us on some local hikes and local markets that he thought we would enjoy. I thought it would be a great day out for us and suspected I would be driving into LA often.

A few weeks later we arrived on the West Coast. The house we rented was amazing. It was located right in the middle of the bluffs overlooking the beautiful Pacific. The view from the home was so impressive that the home was used for movie shoots - that gives you an idea how stunning the place was. We were steps up from the beach. Yet the beautiful view and home was clouded with our unhappy reality. It could have been a wonderful stay filled with love, happiness and great memories if we enjoyed each other, but we didn't. Peter set up his workspace upstairs and that was where he stayed for most of our trip. We had brought Martin's friends with us for two weeks, which I suspected would help buffer the unhealthy parental dynamic.

I knew that I would not be spending much time in the sun so I immediately started researching things to do in the area. Aside from the beach, beach shops and restaurants, there was really little to do there, aside from taking the trolley into the small town for the beach shops and restaurants. It was a cute little town but I was now even more concerned that there was not going to be enough to do for five weeks. If Peter and I were friends, it would work itself out, even with little to do. Five weeks was going to be very long and very challenging. Vacationing with friends would have been a buffer, but since Peter worked all day it would have been difficult to have friends stay with us.

Alex was too young to leave alone at the beach because of the ocean. He was a very sensible child but still too young to leave around water without me being there. Peter was upstairs working most of the time so I was compelled to sit watching them play. As beautiful as it was to be blessed with the time to watch our boys surfing and playing in the water, sadly my mind was very far away.

Closer to the weekend I had begun to get excited about our trip to visit Rob and tour parts of LA. I really didn't like where we were located and was already feeling a little bored. I was as alone as you could possibly imagine. I was looking forward to taking the hike that Rob described with spectacular views of LA and being shown around the Hollywood farmers market and being around the more active hustle bustle of the city. I reminded my family the day before about our hike and, to my surprise, they did not want to go. I tried several times to encourage them, including Peter, but they all wanted to go surfing. I felt a little hurt that they didn't want to join me since we had all agreed to go and that they had surfed on and off most of the week. I was the most disappointed with Peter. I felt that he should have gone, even if he had wanted to surf again, to show the boys the importance of doing something for their mother instead of always being about themselves. Disappointment had become commonplace in our marriage, but it dissipated quickly and turned into elated excitement when it sunk in that I had the whole day to myself, in my favorite city, without Peter.

That night we all took the trolley into town for dinner. I had hoped that Peter might stand next to us or close at least like the other men with their families, but he went all the way to the very back of the trolley and stood alone. It was another painful acknowledgement to me that he did not want to be with me. When we arrived in town we went to a restaurant. It was a charming and lively little place, and with the right energy could have been wonderful... except Peter and I were not talking. I was not sure why either. It was exhausting that night pretending everything was good when it wasn't. As often as he behaved that way, and as often as I tried not to feel hurt, it still hurt. I had to force a façade in front of our boys – again - and in front of the guests at the restaurant, which always left me feeling completely drained. At one point during the meal Peter spoke to me unkindly in front of our boys and their friends. I cringed inside from the humiliation I felt and tears started rolling uncontrollably down my cheeks. I literally could not stop them. It was so obvious I was crying that I got up and went to the bathroom to pull myself together. I wasn't just crying from humiliation, but from the long mourning process of the death of our marriage and of our family.

The following day I made my way up to Hollywood. I remember feeling refreshed, free, happy and excited as I drove each mile further away from Laguna. I had music playing, I was singing, the windows were open, the weather was cool and I felt like I hadn't felt for years--alive. Through courage and strength, I had finally taken a step out and away from a man who, filled with rage, vindictiveness and spite, would later morph into a human monster. Rob met me outside a farmer's market which was our first stop. The fruits, vegetables, oils, breads, foods, flowers, and local musicians were so interesting to me, I was truly happy to be there. I had mixed emotions about our boys missing out on the experience, but also knew that Peter would only have brought poor energy and most likely have been rude to Rob.

Rob and I got along very well that day. He was incredibly open and completely comfortable to talk with, unlike Peter, which felt a little strange to me at first but I really loved it. Communication had been a huge component of what was missing in my marriage for seventeen years. We sat on the sidewalk to eat since there were no market tables available. It felt so easy to be with him. We ate and watched the beautiful women and men of the Hollywood market walk by. We talked for ages about everything. I found him to be extremely knowledgeable and interesting. He showed a sincere interest in me and that interest reignited a feeling of self-value that had long been suppressed. I felt healthy being around him. After the market, we took a hike up into Hollywood hills. Rob pointed out all the buildings, famous homes, restaurants, theatres and anything of interest along the way to the hike. He really knew the area well. It was flattering to have someone care enough to want to show and educate me on the geography and attractions of the city. I felt incredibly liberated, which seemed wrong considering I was spending time with this new friend, but my soul disputed any wrongdoing. It was my soul that led me there. The trip was, in fact, the beginning of my new life away from Peter. At the time, I was upset that he didn't join me but, spiritually speaking, he was not supposed to. Rob had crossed paths with me for a purpose, and that was to help push me away from what was suffocating me and what I was afraid to leave. He was my savior.

When I met Peter, I was so determined to be with him that I ignored, to my detriment, many early signs of narcissism. However, spiritually speaking, I had stayed with him because I had a lot to learn about myself and my own childhood. I had chosen a man that would keep me as void of love, attention and a relationship as my own mother had. I realize now that I had to forgive and heal this void, but not go through it again before doing so. Through years of pain and suffering I had grown strong and insightful, and this would be to *his* detriment. It takes immense strength and courage to break up your family and it took me a long time to do it. However, I eventually did it for the sake of my health and happiness, but mostly so that our boys could have a glimmer of a chance to see their mother (or father) in a loving, respectful and healthy relationship. This would be the kind of relationship I would want them to emulate when they started their own relationships. I was going to pay dearly for leaving Peter. I thought the abuse would stop right there, but sadly it would continue for years, long after our divorce and to this day.

I believed our boys would be OK once the dust of the divorce settled. There is no good divorce since there is an upheaval within the family, but the trauma could be minimalized in the best interest of the children if that was the desire of both parents. They had a mother who adored them and who would protect them as much as possible and continue to parent them well. They had a father who would look out for their best interests and continue our basic family morals – or so I thought. I was wrong.

148

hen it was time to leave LA that day, I felt like I was headed back to the lion's den. I felt sullen, weary and miserable. There was no question I had a horrible chapter lying ahead of me, and I was not looking forward to it at all. In fact, it was going to be really bad. When I arrived back at the house everything seemed quite normal and the same as I had left it. Peter was on his computer and the boys were doing their own thing. However, I was no longer the same. Marriage was not supposed to feel this miserable and our loved ones are not supposed to hurt us. I started fantasizing about a relationship with a man that I could respect and one who would respect me. A man who I loved and who loved me. A man who I could trust, who I could laugh with, who enjoyed being with me and me with him. One that would always support me and always be in my corner and me in his. It wouldn't be for a while, but that man was coming.

Rob asked me a few days later if I would like to go back to LA to go biking along the coast. He asked me to bring Peter and the boys too. Peter did not want to go. The following morning the boys and I headed up to Marina Del Rey, rented bikes and met Rob. The boys wanted to go off on their own for a little while and meet with us for lunch. We had been relocating to Marina Del Rey for years and they knew the area well. The four older boys were all in high school and had phones, including Alex and it was safe for them to go since they were not going into the ocean. It had been a nice break for me. Rob and I biked all over west LA. He showed me all the beautiful little spots in the area. It was like having a personal tour guide on a bike. He asked me a lot of questions that day and continued to show great interest in me. I was very comfortable talking with him and did not mind his questions.

We met the boys for lunch and we all continued biking to various places until it was time to leave. It tugged at my core to leave. It wasn't just about leaving Rob, whom I was growing extremely comfortable with and fond of, it was about leaving a place that I loved and heading back to place that I didn't and facing the reality that lay there. I could not believe how fast things were changing. I felt like a bird released from its cage. I was not going back. I had already flown too far.

Chapter 15

Every day was painfully long for me during that five-week trip once I had finally and mentally checked out. I had been treading water for years and I was fed up with wasting any more of my valuable time with a narcissist. I don't believe that anybody should have to be subjected to an unhappy and unhealthy relationship in the short life that we all have. I didn't think that Peter should have to either, only he seemed to be quite happy in our unhappy relationship. He claimed he worked hard to support our lifestyle we lived but clearly that was not true. We already had more than enough at this point to live well for the duration of our lives. He worked so many hours as he wanted to. He had an insatiable desire to make more money because it was money that defined him as a person – or so he believed. The more money he made, the more powerful he felt. The company's rapidly rising success led to adulation and praise, two things that fed his ego and fueled his desire for more.

A long week after our day out with Rob I wanted to go back to LA. Staying in a home with a husband I no longer wanted to be with, one who sat at his computer all day knowing his marriage was in shambles and doing nothing about it, in a town that was designed for lovers and weekend getaways was making me feel like I was being choked. I was in the wrong place at the wrong time. I decided to take the boys back to LA with me and to stay at the beach for the night. Peter agreed and had no problem with me going since all he did was work anyway. My heart jumped for joy. I was so happy that he was not coming. That feeling of elation was further confirmation to me that the relationship was irretrievably over.

As I made plans with Rob for another bike ride, I felt absolutely no guilt, no regret, and no remorse about leaving my husband to meet another man. As happy as I felt, I was also aware that I was swimming in dangerous waters. I knew that Peter was not going to tolerate my new liberated behavior much longer. As much as he had ignored and neglected me for most of our marriage, he was highly intelligent and it would not take him long to realize what I was doing. I was behaving like a free woman and had absolutely no remorse about it. There was a scary thrill emerging when I made plans to visit Rob because of my disregard of my husband both morally and spiritually. Yet it would not stop me. I was not just walking away from Peter, I was running. My husband had had seventeen years to show me that he cared for me and he hadn't. He only cared about himself. He was in search of some self-superiority and would stop at nothing, not even his failing marriage, to get there.

We went on our overnight trip to LA. We rented bikes, went to the movies, to the carnival at the pier and just enjoyed the endless things to do in the Santa Monica area. Rob spent most of those two days with us. He had a boyish way about that him so much fun to be around. He took us to off-the-beaten-path restaurants known mostly by the locals, where we ate the best meals, we played Frisbee in the park, we checked out the street artists and musicians and everything we did seemed so easy, uncomplicated and interesting. It was getting harder to say goodbye since I was thoroughly enjoying my time with him and very much disliking my time with Peter – or lack of it. It was at the end of this day that I shared with Rob that I did not love my husband and I was filing for divorce when I got home. I had not shared this with anybody up to that point and the relief I felt from saying it was overwhelming.

I was never dishonest with Peter about what I did during my days in LA and was always forthcoming that I was meeting up with Rob. Peter was invited on all three trips and refused each invite. Not wanting to spend time with me was not uncommon. It was nearly always the case because we were irreparably broken. I noticed that there was some change in Peter after I spent the night with the boys in LA. He had started to pay attention to me. Not in a loving way but a concerned kind of way. He would eye me suspiciously. I did not like the attention, or how it made me feel, it felt uncomfortable. I found myself texting Rob a lot during the day and Peter knew it. Rob had become my path to peace, and the more we spoke the safer and freer I felt. There is no doubt that Peter checked my phone bill and knew I was texting and speaking with Rob constantly. I am sure it not only hurt him but infuriated him; I didn't care. Most of my communication with Rob was about why I was leaving Peter and all the hurtful and abusive things I had endured while married to him.

On my second to last week of our trip I told Peter that I was going back to Santa Monica for the day. He told me that he wanted to go with me. I refused to let him join me and went upstairs to take a bath before heading out. I considered us 100% over. I also felt empowered by my new reality and did not want him with me. He had had seventeen years to be with me and had chosen not to most of the time. Now it was too late. The trauma of events that had taken place between us over the years had finally manifested and I was looking into the face of a very unkind and mean person; I wanted to get as far away from him as possible. As I bathed in a hot tub overlooking the beautiful Pacific Ocean on a crisp clear morning, Peter appeared and sat on the edge of the tub. I was slightly afraid because I knew how angry and rageful he could become and was not sure of his true agenda. He looked at me with an eerie stare that made me very uncomfortable. He asked again if he could come with me. I told him that I had already made plans. This would have been the ideal time to tell him I wanted a divorce but I was afraid of his rage. This time I was filing for divorce, and it would be forever. Then he said something to me that I found creepy and disturbing. Peter had found himself in a situation outside of his control, and the narcissist in him had to change his personality to achieve his desired goal. He needed to get me back in his control since it was quite clear he was losing me, and imminently. He looked in my eyes and told me that in all the years of being married to me he had not realized how beautiful I was. Yikes and yuk. I couldn't believe he said it. He would have been better off not saying anything at all. It was manipulative and insulting, considering he didn't mean a word of it. He was feeling threatened. He probably figured that if he complimented me, told me what I had been waiting for years to hear, that maybe I would be swooned and ditch Rob. However, it was too late. They were insincere and foreign words coming from the mouth of manipulation, and ones that had tricked me into staying once before. Not again.

He sat on the side of the bath with a sinister look on his face masked with an unfamiliar smile. I still felt a little afraid of him. I could tell he was panicking. Apologizing for not telling me for seventeen years would have been a more effective line. He also told me that he really loved me. That was the first time he had ever said that to me and that is why it meant absolutely nothing to me. The manipulator was not successful that day. I knew what he had been trying to do and I was not going to succumb to it. His behavior was classic Narcissist 101. He treats me with utter disdain, and when I have had enough and I attempt to leave, he says and does whatever it takes to pull me back. It works a little like Stockholm syndrome. I put up with years of abuse on and off, mostly for the sake of keeping our family together and me in the life of our boys. Each time I reached my tipping point and started proceedings to leave, Peter would buy me something valuable or show immense vulnerability and remorse to the point that I felt sorry for him and for wanting to leave him. I felt sorry for his childhood trauma which I blamed for the majority of our problems. I became a victim feeling sorry for my abuser. He was adept at manipulation, as pointed out later by one of the finest psycho-therapists in Florida who labeled him as a dangerous and very intelligent master manipulator.

I no longer felt sorry for him, I needed to take care of me. He was an extremely damaged little boy living inside a financially successful adult who had become a powerful and destructive narcissist. When that damaged little boy was angry he lashed out at me and subsequently the boys. He had never healed. Many people were fooled by Peter because of how convincing, how successful, how impressive, how striking and how devious he was. Since I was the primary recipient of his volatile projections and abuse, Peter got

154

away with being an abuser around our family, friends and clients. A couple of my closest friends knew, my therapists knew, perhaps a few suspected, but the majority of the people that knew us had no idea.

It was exhilarating and extremely frightening as I began to take back, take over and reconnect with my own life. I knew it was not going to go smoothly but even though there was going to be upset along the way, it would be good for both of us in the end –at least that is what I thought.

When he started telling me how beautiful I was I had been concerned because it was not typical of his normal behavior and was highlighting how afraid he seemed to have become. Martin and Michael were teenagers at this point and, in an effort to protect them and allow them to enjoy the remainder of their summer trip, it meant that I had to tread very carefully around Peter to prevent them witnessing and being affected by any fighting or anger outbursts. I had to do whatever it took to get through the remainder of our trip in California without provoking or awakening the monster in him. Even though my soul sensed a great deal of turmoil in what lay ahead, it was not going to prevent me from leaving.

He continued to stare at me with a strange look, which I believe was an attempt at feigned adoration and lust. It turned out that Peter's pantomime of adoration for me was actually fake and was a staged set-up to make me feel loved because he did not want me to suspect for one minute that he was having me followed that day by a private investigator. He had not made me feel loved, he had made me feel sick. If anything, he had risked giving his own game away because what he was doing was uncharacteristic of him and it was clear to me he was scheming. He wasn't having me followed because he wanted to know where I was going, or who I was with because I had been transparent with him all along. He was having me followed so that he could pre-emptively accuse me of having an affair since the photographs would show Rob and me together. The irony was that he was invited to every trip with Rob, with the exception of the last trip.

Peter would manufacture an elaborate plot that included me having an affair and would be why *he* had no choice but to file for divorce ahead of me. That ploy was intended to bring him sympathy from those who knew us and, moreover, from our three boys. Rob was not the reason for our divorce at all, Peter was. I had become physically ill during my years with him. My nervous system was continually in fight or flight mode, instead of a relaxed and calm mode. One ugly scene after another over the years had psychologically wounded my heart and tore at my soul. He made sure the word "affair" was used over and over again in front of our boys. It spilled over to our friends, our clients, our management team, and to some of the parents at school. The insinuation hung around my neck like an albatross. Any intelligent person knows full well that by the time a person leaves a marriage, or actually has an affair, the marriage has most likely been on life support for a very long period of time.

Peter wasn't going to tell our boys or friends that we split up because he had intense rage issues, that I was afraid of him, that he had spat in my face many times, that he had lied to me continually throughout our marriage, that he had physically hurt me, had tried to strangle me, had insatiable desires for other women, had disturbing sexual addictions and that we had absolutely no emotional connection on any level. Why would he do that when he could show them photographs of their mother and Rob and tell them that I broke up the family because I had an affair - which is exactly what he did. That lie turned him into the victim, as he had intended. That lie would entice people to feel sorry for him, and they did. He would later lure our boys into one of the most horrific cases of alienation I have ever heard of – and I was the recipient of that alienation. He used our boys as retaliation. His cruelty, and what it did to me, and our children, is what prompted me to write this book. I want to help women and men dating or married to a narcissist that

156

are living in hell. I want you to see the miserable life I led and would still be living if I had stayed. I hope my story will encourage you to escape--which is literally what you have to do. Your partner is a narcissist and will never change because they don't think there is anything wrong with them; they have you convinced that all the problems are because of you.

The narcissist will eventually destroy you, starting with your self-esteem, your self-worth, your spirit and eventually your health. In many cases, they will physically hurt you and in rarer cases, kill you. My narcissist specialized in psychological, emotional and mental abuse, especially after I put an end to the physical abuse once I involved the police. Your narcissist partner is self-loathing and hates himself and will take out his inner hatred on you whenever possible. They will leave you feeling depleted, empty and weak for as long as you allow. However, unfortunately, when you fight back they will intensify their efforts. That is why you have to leave.

I commend and admire any woman or man who has escaped their narcissist partner or family member and had the courage to leave them for the sake of their sanity. I suspect that those who haven't made the same decision that I did, which was to stay for the sake of staying close to their children, or because they are too weakened and/or afraid to leave. I don't blame you for staying with your children but it will not alter your partner's behavior, so you have to choose how long you are prepared to put up with it or how long you want your children to learn from it, which is not healthy for them either. I pray that you do leave your abusive partner and I caution you strongly that when you do, they will most likely attempt to turn your children against you as punishment for leaving them and for exposing their not-so-perfect world. They don't really want the children, necessarily, they just want to hurt you. The pain felt from the alienation inflicted on me was worse than seventeen years of marital pain and suffering combined.

Peter got away with his evasive ways and abuse not only because I kept it a secret and hid it for so long, but because he is tall, handsome, and very successful which, sadly, is what our society seems to be impressed with. I had never forgotten Peter's words years earlier warning me that if I ever left him I would never take our children and that he would fight me for them. That fear was the very fear that kept me from leaving him. I cannot believe the control that I had allowed him to have. I spent ten more years with him, protecting and hiding our loveless marriage from our boys and everyone else to prevent them growing up and modeling it. I was kidding myself, they saw everything.

I drove back to LA that morning unaware I was being followed. I met with Rob and we went on our long bike ride. He talked with me most of the time asking me many questions about what went wrong in my marriage. Describing a narcissist or narcissistic behavior to someone who has not had experience with one is hard, but I tried. We turned around at the end of the eighteen-mile bike path and ate lunch together on the beach. Then we headed back. We stopped halfway back and took a water break when Rob surprised me by asking if he could kiss me. Perhaps he felt sorry for me. He knew that I had been through hell and was terribly unhappy and lonely in my marriage. To my surprise, I said yes and he kissed me. It was a simple kiss on the lips and as morally wrong as I knew it was, I did not care. It made me feel wonderful and alive.

After the bike ride we spent the rest of the day walking around stores, being silly, telling funny stories, laughing, drinking coffee and feeling completely youthful; something I hadn't felt in a very long time. I am not sure how many photos were taken that day or of what, but I was later told by our eldest son that his dad was going to show them to him on his eighteenth birthday. Great gift, dad.

When we left California to return home that summer, I felt like my heart was being ripped out. Not only was I leaving my favorite place, I was leaving my savior and new trusted friend to face my upcoming reality alone. Rob and I had had so many long talks about the state of my marriage that I felt an insatiable sense of therapeutic relief and, because of it, I felt that I needed him. I would end up sharing practically everything that happened from that day on with him, which unquestionably helped me get through the turbulent times that lay ahead.

The war with Peter caused me to miss Rob terribly. He had become my new and trusted friend, one who knew everything and someone who brought me comfort. I cried constantly on the plane going home, I must have cried for at least an hour. I stared out the window and watched the lights of LA disappear and sobbed. Peter knew I was crying and said nothing.

Chapter 16

Even though I had made up my mind to leave Peter, and had told him so, he continued as usual once we returned home. It was as though nothing out of the ordinary had happened during that last summer trip. Yet so much had happened. I had awakened to and fully grasped the fact that I was married to a narcissist, something I had not known until the very end of our marriage. After visiting privately with a couple of therapists and revealing what was taking place in our life and in our home, they had introduced me to the word, "narcissist". I had not known the definition of a narcissist since I had not known what one was. When I started researching everything started making sense. It seemed as though every single article I read was written about him. The personality that I was so familiar with was a malignant narcissist, one that was more hurtful and lacked any conscience, which differed somewhat from the common narcissist. The personality that I read about was identical to my husband. Cruel, mean, absent of conscience, psychological need for power, sense of importance, aggressive, and sadistic. He had shown me his true self for most of our marriage and, I am fairly sure, to his mother and sister also.

I read everything I could find. There was just no doubt in my mind, this is what he was. One area I did not think to research was "divorcing a narcissist". Perhaps if I had, I may have been more prepared for what was coming.

It was very difficult for me to live in our home and pretend that there was no pending divorce on the horizon. I spoke to Rob every day about it and truly do not know what I would have done without him during that period. I made an appointment with the same divorce attorney who I had met with when I first filed for divorce. She didn't seem particularly surprised to see me again. I gave her a retainer and signed an agreement with her that day. I had to move quickly for there was no going back.

Peter seemed like he was in major denial about what was going on. He went back to his old ways which was to buy me something of value. Something he felt that would make me happy to forgive the situation and stay with him. He bought me a new car for more than $80,000. I had needed a new car since my last car was creeping up in miles, but did not ask for it. His manipulation had become way too transparent. Through his lack of concern for my well-being on any level, he had finally pushed me away for good. I was not going to be the recipient of his inner raging self-hatred and loathing any longer.

The car was amazing and I loved driving it but it was symbolic of deep emotional pain and suffering just like the flowers he sometimes bought me after a fight. I didn't want valuable gifts from him, I wanted him to be my friend. I wanted to love and be loved. All the things he bought me were temporary pleasures, yet all I wanted was someone in my corner and one that would treat me with respect.

One day Peter came home and was angry with me for texting and talking so much with Rob. He told me that I had talked more with Rob in one month than I ever had with him. You could have knocked me over with a feather. He rarely wanted to talk to me about anything. All he wanted to do was get back to his computer.

Rob turned out to be my support system during the divorce, during the upcoming alienation and during the endless months of a contentious and unnecessary divorce. It was a divorce filled with obscure nonsense driven by Peter to avoid giving me half of anything that was ours. Obviously, Peter had started checking my phone records and censoring my calls. I did not hide my new friendship with Rob since that is all it was at the time. I was filing for divorce so I no longer cared if he knew or not. Living so far away, Rob seemed like a safe friend to have. Tension was beginning to build in our home and I felt that it was time for one of us to move out.

Around this time, there was a weekend bike race taking place in LA which Rob invited me to. I needed to go, not only because I loved LA and biking in LA, but because I wanted to see the man that was propping me up, keeping me from falling and going insane, and because it was starting to become ugly in our home. I felt that I needed to get away. Peter had lost all control of me and, since his manipulation was no longer effective, he had stepped up his game and unbeknown to me at the time, was preparing an all-out war against me.

Rob provided a lot of comfort at a time when I needed it most. I decided to ask Peter if he minded me going to the bike event; to my complete surprise he told me that he didn't mind. I would never have left him with our three boys if he had said no, but he gave me his permission. Not only that, he drove me to the airport. Before I left the car, he told me to go to California and "get it out of my system". I assumed he meant to get Rob out of my system, have my fling and come back, perhaps, but the irony was that he was the one I was trying to get out of my system. California was special to me, especially the Marina Del Rey area which is where I stayed most trips and had been doing so for over fifteen years at the time. I loved every time I was there. We had spent many summers in the Marina when the boys were young. There was something about being there that made me feel alive, free and peaceful. Being in California that weekend allowed me to think clearly about what I needed to do during the next few months.

Rob was a great listener. I felt healthy when I was around him. I loved how much he cared about my situation and how he endured all the gloomy aspects of what I was going through and facing. I was not used to that. It felt like I hadn't been heard in years. He made me feel completely supported which is what I needed so dearly at the time. I am convinced he was sent from the divine power to help me. I had a fantastic time riding around L.A. that weekend. The distraction from the looming divorce was good for me. I missed the boys terribly while I was gone, but the short break allowed me to come home a more refreshed person and a stronger mother; it gave me some time to recharge and I had really needed it.

I had started getting frequent headaches for the first few months at the beginning of our divorce. I knew it was from the stress, and from worrying about what Peter was telling our friends, our business associates, school parents, and our boys.

I had asked my attorney to serve the divorce papers to Peter's office to avoid our boys having to witness anything upsetting. He was being served that week. I cannot begin to tell you how taken aback I was when my attorney called me the day before he was served to tell me that Peter's attorney had just served papers to her office, on Peter's behalf, filing for divorce. I was perplexed by this news since Peter had maintained that he did not want to get divorced for weeks, and I had not been aware he had retained an attorney. I wonder to this day if he just wanted to beat me to it so that public records would show that he filed for divorce from me.

Life in our home was quickly becoming very uncomfortable. Peter started to accuse me of cheating on him. It was as though that if he said it enough that I might actually believe it and confess to it. Rob and I had never started out as an affair, but there was no question that we had become very close. Many might argue that until you sign divorce papers you are not divorced, and you are cheating. On that note, he had psychologically and abusively beaten me down for seventeen years and I don't fucking care if what I did is deemed as an affair, I only see it as a God-sent escape.

Our divorce was taking way too long, and we were nowhere close to a resolution on any level. I had wanted a quick divorce but my attorney didn't seem to be on her game; each time we went to court it was her paralegal that showed up. My attorney had a great reputation as a strong and well-respected divorce attorney but I was getting extremely frustrated with her lack of attention. Both our mediation times ended in a stalemate and seemed like a waste of time and money. Peter refused to agree to every fair deal I offered. I had offered a deal that would end up being more favorable to him than me, and was prepared to do so just to get it over with and move on. He dug his heels in and did not think I deserved half of everything we had acquired during our marriage. He once leaned over and whispered to me that I had better plan on being nice to him since I would be asking him for money for a very long time. Of course, that would be over my dead body. It was when he made the claim through his attorney that our company was not a marital asset that I knew I was in for trouble. That is when I changed my attorney to Palm Beach's top divorce attorney and things started to change very quickly. It was the best decision I had ever made, because a year later my first attorney died from cancer.

It was not healthy for us to live together any longer. Peter was becoming angrier by the day and starting to involve our boys. I asked Peter if he would find a place to stay until we were able to resolve our situation. He told me to get the fuck out of his house since it was me who wanted to leave. It felt so weird to me that we were sleeping in the same bed and in the same home while he was at war with me. I knew if I left that he would never let me back in and I was never going to abandon my children. I had also been given legal advice not to.

It led to persistent bickering late at night in bed. I was so tired of it. I was always worried that the boys could hear us and it turned out that they could. I pleaded with him one night to stop. He became angry and went on for hours until I finally left the room. I decided to sleep with Martin in his room that night. I was hoping he would calm down if I left. It was very late and I was exhausted. I was just falling asleep when the door flew open with a loud bang and there he stood with visible fury. He was completely naked. He demanded to know where I was on a certain date and with who. That particular date was the night I had stayed over in Santa Monica. He kept asking the same question over and over and over again in front of Martin. He must have asked at least twenty-five times. It was like he had gone crazy. He became so loud that Michael and Alex woke up. Alex started crying when he saw how Peter was behaving. It was a horrible scene. Michael ushered Alex back into his bedroom and closed the door. I kept telling the boys that everything was going to be OK but it wasn't. I can only imagine the impact it had on our boys to see their father naked, acting like a lunatic and completely out of control. Martin continually asked Peter to calm down. Martin felt the need to take on a parent role which at the time was his only option and seemed sensible. However, this role (which he played often) may have defined his future as "a son of a narcissistic father" and I suspect will come with some emotional and mental setbacks and self-esteem issues in his adulthood. I realized the only way to stop him scaring our boys was to go back to my room. I left the boys crying and afraid which caused me more pain than anything Peter could have done to me that night. Once back in my bed, he continued with the same question over and over again like a madman. It was exhausting. It was this episode and others like it that led my new attorney to file in court to have Peter immediately removed from our home. The judge agreed. I was horrified that he had subjected our boys to such a chaotic and frightening scene. His behavior that night was perplexing, considering he usually attacked me independently of them. He was manipulating them and building a case in an attempt to portray himself as the victim of mom's poor decision. Mom hurt dad and broke up the family. It was classic narcissistic behavior. Manipulation at its finest. He was sowing seeds in preparation to lure our boys away from me just for retaliation, hurting me to my very core but inevitably hurting them more.

When Peter moved out he packed all his clothes, his toiletries and left everything else behind. I figured that when he settled he would ask for other items in the home but he never did. In fact, he did not ask for one single thing except photos and videos of the boys, which I gave to him. It stung me pretty hard when a friend revealed that Peter had told him that I had kept everything in the house and he got nothing. I can only imagine how I might feel as an outsider if I heard that story. I would naturally feel a lot of sympathy for him and would view the wife as a rapacious villain. He was attempting to make me look horrible to anyone who cared to listen to him. It was all that he could do to control the damage and, most of all, his image.

I spent time with my new attorney going over numbers that I felt were fair. The biggest challenge I faced was not knowing the current market value of our company. I wanted to get divorced as quickly as possible so that we could both move on, raise our boys, and end our relationship as husband and wife with some dignity. In an effort to keep our attorney fees and billable hours to a minimum, I called Peter and asked him if we could meet and discuss a solution to our finances. I hated seeing our monies unnecessarily wasted on attorneys. Unfortunately, some attorneys tend to instigate and fuel a divorce in an effort to increase their billable hours. I felt that both our attorneys were involved in this and was hoping Peter would agree to a number. It might not have been an ideal number for either one of us, but at least we could protect our money from wasteful fees and move on.

Peter had stopped on the way to pick up sushi for us and we met at a local park. When I opened the bag, I was stunned when I saw that he had selected my two favorite rolls. I could not grasp how he knew that they were my favorite since I had not eaten these particular rolls with him before. Evidently, he called the restaurant to ask what I ordered when I went there. Why he had to wait until the end to do something so thoughtful is a mystery. For a moment the kind gesture had made me feel good. It made me wonder if I was doing the right thing, as I often wondered when Peter did out-of-the-way kind things for me. My past experiences with his manipulation brought me back to reality. He wasn't looking to regain his image with me, I already knew who he was, nor did he care about my palette either. He was looking for something else. I would find that out as I ate my last bite and he offered me pennies on the dollar for my half of our company. The lunch that started out so nicely

166

ended cruelly and abruptly. He had been there to try to screw me, plain and simple. His goal had been to offer me scraps just to get rid of me and to move on with the majority of everything that we had built together. I was not going to let that happen.

It had been the first time I had ever heard that the business was his and not ours. Peter had also talked about our home being his and not ours. My attorney told me that he had the right to make any claim he wanted, but that we would have to prove otherwise. That didn't seem like such a big deal to me considering I knew everything we owned was a marital asset. He would end up driving our divorce costs up to well over a million dollars from making one bogus claim after another. It was as though he was enjoying the fight and was determined to hurt me at any cost, both financially and with our boys. He just wanted to win and that meant taking almost everything away from me. I just wanted what was fair.

Growing up I had believed that evil was physically ugly. I perceived evil as people who hurt other people, like a pedophile, a murderer or a rapist. These people always seemed to be depicted as physically unattractive. As I became an adult and paid more attention to news, I became cognizant that some evil people were actually attractive. Evil is dangerous when it masks itself in an attractive package. Then, there was my attractive package. The narcissist whose abuse went mostly unnoticed by others. Abuse is easy to spot when you are physically hurt, bruised, cut, unconscious or even dead. However, the astute abuse of the powerful narcissist, my husband, was secretive and destructive and attacked the very core of my being. One intentional strike after another, causing me years of grief had shown me that he too was evil.

When it became abundantly clear that Peter was not planning on playing fair during our divorce, in fact trying every dirty trick, my attorney had to start working aggressively to dispute and refute all Peter's phony claims about non-marital assets. The billable hours were the very thing I was dreading and they were being driven by

Peter's list of lies. It was the very nonsense I was hoping to avoid. A narcissist considers everything they have in their life as theirs and theirs only. He had told me several times that I was not getting any money from him and to get a job. Things shifted legally when my attorney told me that Peter had retained a new attorney. And the war started.

He decided to go after my throat because I wouldn't agree to his pennies-on-the-dollar offer and because I was standing up for my rights. That meant we had to spend significantly more money on attorneys due to his reluctance to settle fairly. He was being ridiculous, but he was a narcissist and he was not going to let me have anything that he felt belonged to him. He made a false claim that the company was non-marital. It was true that he had opened a corporation before we were married which had held some stock, but that stock was sold soon after. He was entitled to all that money and I agreed. However, the company we had at the time of filing had been started five years into our marriage. Even though I knew it to be 100% marital, I had to spend a lot of money, time and effort to prove it. A tip to anyone about to marry a narcissist. Watch to see what assets they purchase just before you get married. This is an intentional purchase and an asset you will never have claim to. It is a preparatory and strategic move that should clue you in to his or her doubts about your marriage surviving. In fact, Peter would get married again shortly after our divorce and conveniently bought a home close to a million dollars one month before the wedding.

During this time, our boys were going back and forth between Peter's new apartment and our home. This was a new reality for all of us and it must have been as difficult for them as it was for me. I had never spent more than a day or two away from our boys, especially Alex who was only eight years old. The pressure of the contentious divorce was overwhelming but not being allowed anywhere near our boys for four days felt like torture. Peter had made it very clear that I was not to have any physical contact with the boys during his time with them. That had seemed unconscionable to me and my only reasoning with this demand was that he was very angry. When they came home after their stays with Peter, they would tell me stories about how they had free rein the entire time and that there were no rules. One night shortly after they went to stay with Peter, Michael and Alex had found themselves lost on the beach after it had turned dark. I would never have placed them in that type of situation. This would be the beginning of the 'Disney Dad' lifestyle that he would create to make our boys feel that staying with him was more fun than being with mom. Manipulation and control. That would later backfire but it still didn't stop him allowing them to do whatever they wanted to, which completely went against our former parenting morals.

In an effort to watch over our boys I installed an app on their phones. If something should happen to them or I needed to know they were safe I could check on them. There was another option that sent a standard message to them via the app asking them if they were OK; each of them knowing it was me could let me know they were safe. The app worked beautifully for a couple of weeks and then I noticed that their phones were not responding. Peter had deleted all three apps from their phones and had the disgraceful audacity to tell them that the only reason I had them download the app was so that I would know where Peter was. It couldn't have been further from the truth; I couldn't have cared less where he was but they had believed him. One of them mentioned to me that I did not need to know what Peter was doing or where he was anymore. That comment told me everything.

Thank God for Rob because he was one of a handful of people at that time keeping me from going insane. Through intense emotional support, he brought me great comfort over and over again. There was no question whatsoever that he was placed in my life to help me get through the process of divorcing a narcissist. Each time our boys stayed for long weekends with Peter, I felt like they were being held hostage from me. I was not allowed to contact them, or see them. He repeatedly told me to stay away and not to interfere with his time while he was with *his* boys. The irony was that he spent little of that time with them, but as long as I didn't get to see them, that was all that mattered to Peter. When our boys were with him, he behaved like I did not exist. Since I could not have any contact with the boys when they were with him during, the only way I could get through those long weekends and stay well was to leave and visit with Rob in California. I ended up going there once every three weeks or so, for over two years. Every time I arrived in LA I was instantly able to shut out the pain of what I was going through. It felt like Florida was another life far, far away. I was able to distract from my reality by going on hikes and going to outdoor events, farmer's markets, art fairs, food festivals, music shows, movies and bike rides along the coast. Rob and I did everything together and there wasn't one dull moment that would allow my mind to wander back to Florida. The trips eased the struggle of having to watch our boys go into the home of a man who had declared war on me. It was healthier and safer at that time for me to detach from it than deal with it. There was a new danger approaching and it sadly involved Martin and Michael.

Our divorce had become costly. The first few invoices I received had actually made me physically sick. The last three months of invoices prior to our final dissolution were invoices I couldn't bring myself to open. They still remain unopened. I resented even looking at the unopened envelope knowing that the costs inside were driven by Peter's cruel determination to fight me. For the first few months after Peter moved out, I would receive offers to settle our finances that were truly insulting. Each one refused to acknowledge my ownership of or involvement in our company. They kept referring to it a non-marital asset. One letter suggested that Peter would relinquish more time with the boys if I accepted his terms. The fact that both he and his attorney would consider using our boys as pawns for financial gain was not only disgusting but an ugly and inhuman strategy. I thank God for the strength I endured to turn down one insulting offer after another even the one that offered me more time with my boys because he was planning on taking them from me anyway.

Chapter 17

Looking back, there were so many things that I missed...or chose to perhaps. I had completely given all of myself to Peter during our first couple of years yet he was unable to give back of himself our whole marriage. It was very early into our marriage when I started pulling back in an effort to protect myself from his abuse. Just seeing how he treated his mother and sister alone should have been the loudest warning sign. Clearly, he wanted to hurt them and it was in retaliation for something that I would never be privy to. He ended up speaking with her only a few times a year or so during my marriage to him and they were calls made to him. Even those calls ended with him being mean and aloof with her and his sister.

My attorney called me and told me that we had a court date set to determine the status of our company. He had collected enough evidence to prove that it was a marital asset. We had always known it was a marital asset but any phony claim can be made in the state of Florida and the opposing counsel has to contradict it to prove otherwise. It was Peter's bogus claim about our company that drove us to spend hundreds of thousands of dollars just to get to that day in court. Our day in court went in my favor and the company was ruled a marital asset. Peter immediately hired a second attorney to represent our company.

For the majority of their childhood, all three of our boys had been well-behaved and respectful. I had been an attentive mother and felt that not only did I love them unconditionally but that I had done a good job in how I had raised them. I had been respectful of their space and their ability to grow and learn without my hovering over them. I had stayed home and raised all three of them until they went to school. I nurtured their social lives, their emotional lives and had protected their physical lives. I knew them inside out and consequently was horrified when they started to say certain things to me that were completely unacceptable and uncharacteristic of who they were. I understood that they were going through a tough time seeing their parents separate, but I could not stop being a good parent and allow them to start becoming abusive and disrespectful. I continued parenting the boys the same way I always had to maintain a healthy continuity that they needed, especially at that time in their lives. It was challenging for me since their behavior had rapidly deteriorated, but it did not prevent me from standing my ground regarding unacceptable and hurtful behavior.

It was tough watching the boys marvel at their Dad's home with no rules and no consequences as I upheld my principal parenting values. I knew what he was doing. He was trying to coax them to his home via fantasy living in a ploy to lure them away from me. But more dangerously than that, he was brainwashing them against me. I learned that he had taken Martin and Michael out onto his patio night after night and invested hours of his time turning them against me with despicable and untrue stories. I heard that he had told them that I had an affair which led to our family breaking up, that I had spent their college money during the divorce on frivolous items such as bags and shoes, that I had lied to them during their childhood, that I was trying to sabotage *his* company, that I was trying to steal *his* money from him, that I had had our judge throw him out of *his* home, that I was trying to get them removed from their private school, that I was trying to get our judge to remove them from him, that I would be throwing them out next, that I was a bad mother and the worst one, that they had been afraid of me when they were young. These were just a few of the things that came out in therapy sessions mandated by our judge shortly after the alienation and other factors led to Michael being hospitalized after having a severe emotional breakdown.

I was terrified of losing them at the hands of an angry, malicious, vindictive and revengeful father. He was brainwashing them. His intention was to alienate them from me so he could viciously hurt me, and it did. That sleazy manipulation played out in my home.

173

They became rude, verbally abusive and harbored immense anger towards me. He wanted them to hate me as much as he did. He didn't care that he was hurting them more than he was hurting me. He hated me more than he loved his own children.

It had taken a lot of effort for me to stay upbeat around the boys during that time. They had no idea of the stress that I was under during the day in the legal system and how much pressure it had put on me. I had to stay mindful at all times not to take it out on the boys, and that had proved difficult since they had started to act out in my home. Some of their poor behavior was inevitable and due to the trauma of the divorce, but the majority of it was because they were being brainwashed by their father. I found myself having to reprimand them often due to their new and very unacceptable behavior. It felt like they hated me and it made no sense whatsoever. At the time, I had had no idea they were being abused by Peter and just thought they were angry at the situation and taking it out on me since they knew I would never turn away from them and I was the safe parent, emotionally speaking. Everything started falling into place little by little, especially when Martin told me that he never wanted to get married. When I asked him why he told me that he didn't want to work hard his whole life and have some woman take everything from him. And there it was. I challenged him further on this topic and told him that perhaps the wife was rightfully entitled to half of everything both legally and morally. I told him that a woman had the same equality in a marriage as a man and that while her role might be different than her husband's, their combined efforts were what contributed to the value of everything that they acquired in their marriage. He objected to every sensible point that I tried to make. I felt total heartbreak for him that he was being taught that the woman had no value in a marriage and felt equally heartbroken since I knew he was referring to me. He was being told continuously that I had no value in their family and worse, that I had no value in his life either. I would learn this with everything that came out of the boys' mouths for the next two years. What was coming out was what Peter was putting in.

One evening I had some friends for dinner. As I always did, I set the table beautifully and prepared a meal during the day. Michael came home from school that day and saw the table set and the food in the kitchen. He told me that the meal my friends were eating that night was being paid for by his dad and asked me why his dad should have to continue buying meals for my friends. Peter knew that I would continue having dinner parties, and to this day I still do. He had wanted to trigger upset in the boys each time they saw me entertain and it had worked. He was attempting to ruin my evenings in his absence through our boys, which it did. They even fought with me several times about my money not being mine because I was forcing a judge to make their dad give it to me. It was such a terrible time.

After living with me for almost ten, fifteen and sixteen years, which is how old the boys were shortly after Peter and I separated, they knew exactly who I was. They knew I was loving, fun, respectful, giving, caring, and firm. They knew my sad moments, my happy ones and, also, when I was annoyed. *But they knew me.* During the alienation, they were being told things that were not only untrue but were 100% contradictory of what they knew of me. I could only imagine how confusing and agonizing that must have been for them at that already difficult time. The fact that they were being forced to listen to such treacherous lies in an effort to turn them against me was no different than psychological warfare. It must have been incredibly perplexing for them to comprehend and reason with the fake stories they were being told about me especially since they knew the authentic me. Peter had been extremely convincing and manipulative and his tactics had paid off well for him since their behavior towards me continued to deteriorate. As hurt and completely broken as I had felt, I kept faith in the fact that I had spent years giving them love, care, values, and my time and that it would not go forgotten forever. What I hadn't counted on was how bad it would get. It was the beginning of several years of hell facing a man that was not only out to destroy me financially but also to sabotage my relationship with my own children. Although this was the worst time of my life, the boys would eventually see through his evil and destructive agenda. His rotten and cruel attempt to alienate his own children from their mother because of his own anger would highlight the fact he was absent of a conscience, spirit or soul. He was empty and consequently dangerous.

Peter paid an out-of-state appraiser to claim that our company was worth a fraction of its value. Since he had made this claim, my attorney told me that I had no choice but to dispute it and get the company appraised by a different appraiser if I was to get a true value. The value Peter's appraisers were claiming was based on what Peter was telling them it was worth. It was the most unfair appraisal you could imagine. Upon learning that I was going to get it appraised, Peter then followed up with another claim that the company had no value if he was not the CEO. I had absolutely no intention of sabotaging our company nor did I want it. I respected all of our management team and staff and would never dream of jeopardizing their jobs and income.

My attorney advised me that the only way to prove the appraisal was a fraud was to professionally analyze our company which meant having to depose some of the management team. Since Peter was the only one that hosted all of our company information and was not forthcoming, deposing staff was the first step in determining its true value. That had not been good news to me. The last people in the world I wanted to involve in our divorce was our staff. I respected all of them and did not want to put them in the middle of our mess. In reality, it had been Peter and his pathological dishonesty who put them there, not me. He was the one who was giving me no choice. Peter thought he was being clever by delivering court ordered documents to my attorney in the form of a huge document dump. This deceitful and defiant delivery dump would take months to go through and would cost us hundreds of hours and hundreds of thousands of dollars to boot. It was indicative of a narcissistic tantrum. Our divorce process was starting to feel surreal to me. This was not what I had wanted or had expected. I was copied on

176

deposition notices to four of our female and two of our male management team employees who I had grown very fond of. I spoke with most of the girls regularly and one of them daily. I felt that we had developed a very nice working relationship, especially with Penny, our operations manager. The notices had made me feel nauseous. It suddenly made our war seem real now that they had been deposed. I could not believe that Peter was actually going to allow the staff to become involved. He could have stopped it by being honest.

Penny was a stellar employee. She was responsible, kind, and honest, and over time had become more of a friend and confidant to me than an employee. She was a devout and very faithful Christian. She prayed with me many times over the phone for support, guidance, and safety for various things. We had spent time together at conventions, at company parties and in management meetings. I spoke with her regarding business issues at least once a day and sometimes several times a day. She had not spoken with me or taken my calls since Peter had moved out of our home and was most likely warned not to. I was mortified that she was being summoned to Florida from her home for a deposition, yet a little happy that I would get to see her. I had missed her. I had wanted her to know that I had not wanted to involve her and that Peter's dishonesty had brought her and other management team employees into our mess. A year before the deposition she had suffered a serious medical situation that put her in a coma for several days. I prayed for her every day. I called to check on her several times a day during her hospitalization and was deeply grateful to the higher spirit for bringing her back to us. I had not shared our personal problems with her over the years and was not sure if she had picked up on it or if she was as completely unprepared for the shock of it as many others were. I wanted to tell Penny that Peter and I were getting divorced myself since I knew that she would most likely hear a different version from Peter. I spared her most of the real details and basically told her that we were very unhappy and had been for a very long time. She had sounded very sorry for us and had begged me to keep my boys in their faith since she believed it would help them get through the difficult time. That was Penny, always leaning on and believing in her faith. It was what I loved about her. Little did she know that her own boss was the one who had ridiculed and diminished faith to our boys and how he proudly boasted about being an atheist.

When I found out that Penny was one of the employees that my attorney had to depose my heart sank. I hadn't wanted her involved at all and I really didn't want her to be stressed about it since she had been hospitalized not that long before. I'm certain she was told that I ordered the deposition. I wouldn't be at all surprised if Peter told her that I was trying to sabotage the company and ultimately her career and job security to boot. It would explain why she had stopped talking to me overnight. That suspicion became evident when I saw her the morning of her deposition. She was nice but also very cautious like she had been coached to treat me like I was the enemy. This was not the Penny I knew. She had to have been deceived about why she was attending the deposition. I would have hoped that she was wise enough to know that I would never do anything to harm her, her family or her career. She should never have been involved in our divorce. Peter must have been ecstatic at how this was playing out, especially knowing how much I liked Penny and how crushed I would feel when she no longer treated me the way she once did. The irony was that she had had no idea what I had lived through. If she did, I cannot imagine her Christian heart turning from me the way it did. She was either afraid of talking to me for fear of being fired or, sadly, she had decided to ignore the work of the devil regardless of his wrongdoing to keep her position in the company. I have long forgiven her because I know that not only did Penny need her job but enjoyed her work.

Ironically the next management employee that arrived for a deposition was also a devout Christian and a former pastor. We had a good working relationship and, like Penny, we had spent time together at company functions and over the phone multiple times.

She was a true sweetheart who was also divorced. Her husband had been so abusive that she literally left her home one day with her children and never went back. She told me that she had run to another man, a kind man, she had told me. She not only was still with him but had told me that she was very happy and felt emotionally and physically safe too. When I saw her, I went to hug her and she too was cold, guarded and a little unfriendly. It really hurt me to see her behave that way towards me. It hurt more in her case since she had been in this same situation herself. I would hope that people, especially another woman in my case would admire my quest for fairness and equality. How could both these women that I had believed to be strong in spirit, character and in Christian morals repudiate my fight for justice and fairness? Perhaps she too was afraid of her career and her future with Peter. It was painful for me to watch how these two women who I had grown to trust and respect could cut me off so abrasively. I have had to resign myself to forgive both of them for it. I suppose they were both afraid of losing their jobs if they had continued contact with me but, worse than that, since I don't feel that was the only reason, I suspect he lied to them about me that led them to fear me on some level.

I was notified by my attorney that the entire management team were given a nice raise during that period of time. The payoff. How devious of him and incredibly generous all at my expense. The sickening part of hearing that news was that for years I had encouraged Peter to give more perks to our staff, especially around the holidays; his answer was always no. He claimed that no employer had ever given him anything for Christmas and therefore he was not going to give either. The irony was that they were in fact financially rewarded, for turning on me. He had played them like a fiddle.

That is how the narcissist operates. Divide and conquer. Lie, deceive, manipulate and control. Once you are under the control of a narcissist you are going to be psychologically pummeled unless you have the courage to fight and get out, especially if you are an immediate family member. The narcissist can oppress you mentally, physically, emotionally and psychologically and then shower you with gifts when looking for forgiveness for their sins or for you to stay with them. That happened frequently during my marriage with Peter. His primary abuse started out as physical until my second call to the police. He knew that physical attacks were far too risky since I had showed the courage to pick up the phone and ask for help. That is when he moved solely to mental, emotional and psychological abuse which intensified as I started to fight back. These are the types of abuse that people can't see or prove. After hurtful behavior he would switch and become humble and the degree of that humbleness depended on the severity of the hurtful or abusive behavior. He might laugh a little around me feeling me out, or buy me a gift of some kind. In a narcissistic relationship, you are constantly on edge and tormented by the push/pull behavior. When the push happens, it hurts and when the pull occurs I found myself forgiving my narcissist because of the beautiful gift of forgiveness that I received, or from the tears that he mustered to manipulate me back, or from the overwhelming empathy that I felt for him due to his lonely and traumatic childhood I wanted to believe that his pull stage was an attempt to show me that he loved me, but he really didn't. He didn't even love himself. It had astounded me to see that same pattern of manipulation take place with my former colleagues and friends and how they too had been rewarded for his psychological and deceitful abuse.

After the humiliation of seeing my former friends and colleagues at our depositions and how they had reacted to me, it confirmed my belief that he was saying things to them that were dishonest and, sadly, they appeared to have believed him. I strongly suspect he told them that I was trying to sabotage our company, and consequently they were in fear of their jobs, career, finances and future. I didn't blame them for that fear; I blamed him for putting it there. My spiritual and mental strength that had re-blossomed over the latter abusive years is what kept me grounded at a time when I could very easily have crumbled at the continuous torture being inflicted on me by this monster through my children, our friends and the community we lived in. I knew the truth and that ended up being all that really mattered.

My attorney had to depose Peter's appraiser. It was the most torturous grilling I have ever seen a man get in my whole life. My attorney went after him with a vengeance knowing full well that he had provided us with a phony appraisal of our company's value. Part of me felt sorry for him since he was being brutally annihilated on every point. Towards the end of the six grueling hours of torture he had started sweating and whimpering like a child. My attorney made him look pathetic and like the liar he was. The other part of me felt immense satisfaction that he was being exposed as another lying piece of the puzzle and to my credit, in front of our judge. It turned out that he had presented a fake company evaluation value based only on what Peter had told him. What a joke!

When Peter made the claim that our company was non-marital, he was lying. Tens of thousands of dollars later we were able to prove that it was marital. Peter provided an appraisal of the company that was completely undervalued and was a farce. Thousands more dollars later, we were able to prove its true value. Peter made the claim that without him the company was worth nothing. He was lying again. Thousands more dollars later, we were able to prove that the software held the value with or without Peter. These lies were what made our divorce drag on so long and become so painfully costly. We could have put ten teenagers through private college with the monies we spent on our divorce, so you can only imagine how gutted I was to hear that Peter had told our boys that I had spent their college money on frivolous items.

Things between me and the older boys were getting worse. I went to see a therapist who specialized in divorcing narcissists, the effect it had on the children and how to manage them during the divorce. She really was amazing and through a few of my accounts knew exactly what I was dealing with and what I was facing. She told me that during divorces, and especially one from a narcissist, the narcissistic parent gives the children whatever they want void of any rules and consequences in an effort to draw the children away from the other parent. She urged me to continue parenting them as I always had since children actually yearn for and still need the parent who gives them rules, structure and a foundation that they are familiar with. I had no problem with continuing my parenting style because I am not fickle, nor was I trying to pull our boys from their father.

One evening Martin and I started bickering about how he was talking to me and it escalated into an argument. I started crying and asked him why he had started to talk to me so badly and what I had done to him to deserve the way he was treating me. He starting crying too. He went from crying to sobbing at which time I embraced him and held him for a long while. He told me that Peter had told him that I would be throwing him out next. I felt like a fist was in my throat. I couldn't feel anything except an intense feeling of hatred towards Peter, the father of my children whose intent was to lure these beautiful boys away from me at any cost, even if it was a deep poisonous penetration of their souls that would wound them on an unconscionable level. Peter knew that I was a caring, protective and loving mother. Not perfect, but unconditionally theirs on every motherly level.

Since Peter was losing his battle to prevent me from receiving my fair share of marital assets, he turned to the only place left that he could hurt me. Our children. He chose a destructive and pitiful path indicative of the anger and meanness within him. The psychological damage he was inflicting on our boys was beyond criminal and a cruel game to play with innocent children. There is no doubt in my mind that he will face retribution from all three boys at some point as they mature and reflect on his actions, words and treatment of their mother. If Peter had managed somehow to take every marital asset from me, which he could have done if I hadn't had such a proficient attorney, he still would have alienated our children. I had been wise and shrewd not to fall for his earlier offer of receiving less in assets to get more time with the boys. I knew him too well.

Chapter 18

The boys went to Hawaii for two weeks with Peter during the first summer that we were separated. I spent those weeks with Rob in Los Angeles which had been such a comfort and relief for me because of my awareness of the alienation and not being able to do anything about it. Rob enjoyed a very active lifestyle and we kept busy the entire time. He was an amazing support system for me as I was going through the worst time of my life with one severe heartbreak after another, especially with my children. I really don't know what I would have done without him and will be forever grateful to him for being there for me. Not only was he there for me emotionally and mentally, he distracted me from my pain by introducing me to every little part of Los Angeles. During our times together we covered all of LA on our bikes which really helped me get through what was going on. That period of time was nurturing to my soul since all the experiences were able to take me away from my pain and give my soul a chance to breath and heal.

Our relationship had morphed into a romantic relationship over the months with talk about a future together. We ended up spending many weekends together over two years and there was no question that he had become an unwavering loyal and supportive person in my life. Sadly, we would end up separating over fundamental differences. However, my time with him was valuable, memorable and crucial. It hadn't helped that Peter had immediately poisoned our boys against Rob. He had told them that Rob was the reason that our family split up and that he had had an affair with their mother. Martin harbored much hate towards Rob and showed him great disdain every time he saw him, which only taught Martin to harbor hatred. This might be a trait that Martin struggles with in his adulthood.

I met the boys in Los Angeles on their way back from Hawaii where they vacationed with me for two more weeks. My brother and my nephew flew over from the UK to join us. I had been very excited to see the boys and had missed them terribly. Pretty much from the time they arrived until the time we left California, Martin and Michael's behavior was despicable. I had never seen them behave so poorly in their lives. They were not only rude to me but to my brother and my nephew also. Martin's behavior was the worst. He was defiant, hostile, critical and unacceptably rude to Rob when he was with us. They were never the same since they went on that trip to Hawaii. I had lost any and all control over them as their mother and was mortified by how they were treating me in front of my family and Rob. I will never know what was said to them during that two-week period, but they do. Peter had taken the older boys out onto his patio at home and had long conversations with them about me and I'm sure those conversations continued in Hawaii, hence their despicable behavior. It must have been very important to Peter to kill the mother-son relationship quickly so he could stay in control of them. His callous behavior and motive was evidence that he did not care about the mental and emotional well-being of his own boys. Incidentally, this very type of taught alienation behavior from parent to child can elevate the inception of the narcissistic personality disorder, causing children great disappointments later in life when this disorder interferes with their future relationships – and it will. I trust and pray that I have invested enough of myself and my values into our children to prevent the narcissist cycle continuing. I hope that showing them that I was not prepared to stay in an abusive relationship will be a crucial life lesson for them as they start their healing process and futures.

Alex was not allowed outside with Martin and Michael during the late-night patio alienation. I suspect it was because he was too young, and perhaps Peter feared that he would tell me what was being said. He could not inform me on the content but did inform me many times about the patio meetings. It kills me to think of the purpose of those late-night talks. Michael had struggled the most with us separating and was by nature a sensitive child. Why would any parent want to torture an innocent and sensitive child? Peter's callousness and insensitivity towards Michael highlighted that he didn't care about his well-being as long as he could get him to disconnect and become alienated from his mother. Alex remained loyal to both Peter and I, which is typical of his spiritually heightened personality. He was not and is still not a child who can be corrupted since he is very strong in his foundation and in his soul. He was acutely aware of everything going on around him and was fully aware of what was happening in our family.

The mother-son disconnect from Martin and Michael had been rapid and unexpected which had left me feeling emotionally distressed and frantic. I had no idea how to cope or deal with the alienation. Alex spoke up for me many times when Martin was being rude or blaming me because he was being rude. I felt like I was living in a nightmare. Martin didn't mean to say most of the horrible things he was saying and doing in my home, but having been wound up so tightly from Peter, he was like a pressure cooker and the tiniest thing I did made him explode. None of us liked the situation but since Peter had refused in writing to allow any of the boys to go to therapy, I was left trying to sort everything out myself. Michael would go back and forth being angry with me and then being upset for being angry with me. He had not wanted to be angry with me, but he was being brainwashed to be angry with me. He was being emotionally pulled back and forth between wanting to please his father's wishes and not wanting to hurt his mother. I felt so sorry for him.

As Peter was losing ground in court with our marital assets, he started an e-mail war with me. His e-mails became so abusive and hurtful that I eventually had to stop reading them or replying to them. I realized, after way too long, that the only person who could stop this abuser from attacking me was me. He would write emails accusing me of causing the boys "emotional distress" and that they would be better off living with him. I couldn't believe what I was reading since *he* was the one causing the distress. He spoke about the harmony in his home and how they laughed and danced when they were there. Well, I almost choked from laughter and anger when I read that, knowing how completely untrue it was. He was either delusional or was laying the groundwork via the e-mails to legally take them from me. I asked him many times to allow the boys, then minors, to go to therapy, and each time he vehemently refused. I warned him that I would petition the court for them to receive the therapy that I felt that they all needed under the circumstances. He told our boys that I was taking him to court to force them into therapy so that I could take them away from him. Not only was he deceitfully claiming victimhood again, but he succeeded with his phony fear tactic since Martin and Michael vehemently refused to ever set foot in a therapist's office. Peter was afraid that his alienation would be revealed and of the legal ramifications. The fear of his own wrongdoing was preventing them from getting the psychological help that they so desperately needed.

During the e-mail barrage, Peter accused me of not creating a peaceful environment for our boys and that they did not like the way I was treating them. For the seventeen years we had lived together I had created a very functional and loving home for our boys and he knew damn well that it was still the same, but took relish in the accusation anyway. He continued his hurtful e-mail accusations for several months.

One day I went to talk to Martin and he told me to get the fuck out of his room. He had never spoken to me like that before and had never cursed in front of me either. When I told him that he was not allowed to speak to me that way he slammed the door. The following day I got an e-mail from Peter telling me that I had upset Martin, that he was unable to do his homework and that I needed to consider allowing Martin and Michael to live with him full time. He knew I would never agree to voluntarily give up any parenting time with them, therefore the only way he could accomplish his goal to hurt me to my core was to work on them to leave me.

187

When a parent brainwashes a child, what they are really doing is implanting stories or memories into their minds that never happened or even existed. One example that comes to mind is when Michael said to me one day during an angry outrage, "No wonder I was afraid of you as a child." I was flabbergasted when he said it. I could not believe it. I went into my room and cried. Then both he and Martin asked me why the hell I was crying and to stop acting like a selfish mother! I thought I was going to choke. My boys had never been afraid of me as children, nor had they ever talked to me with that kind of insensitivity. He hadn't feared me at all but he had been told that he had by the only man a son trusts in his childhood, his father. And he had believed him. Not only did he believe him, he acted out on the memory that had been implanted that never existed. It's the power and danger of brainwashing. He was upset with me for being afraid of me as a child. It's the danger of brainwashing.

I had started to feel unhappy when I was around Martin and Michael. I was walking on eggshells; if I said anything that they perceived as unfair in any way, I would receive an e-mail from Peter accusing me of wrongdoing and poor parenting. I felt like I had my hands tied and that I was being monitored. He was preventing me from appropriately parenting them by siding with them instead of supporting me. He really hated me. I was already suffering tremendously fighting for my rights but to have a second fight to try to save my relationship with my own children was overwhelming and causing deep anguish.

I had started to cough regularly which, over the months, had intensified to a chronic cough that woke me up during the night. I thought I had triggered a dormant genetic asthma from all the emotional trauma. It was not asthma, as I would later find out, but the asthma-type symptoms were definitely driven from emotional trauma. I was on one medicine after another during that period in an effort to calm the symptoms.

I was tormented with unkind feelings towards my own children whom I loved unconditionally yet hated how they were behaving towards me. I had to remind myself constantly that they were victims, and to not take it so personally, but it was hard for me not to. They were the victims of alienation and what they were saying to me was a result of what Peter was telling them. I continued to show them love them regardless of their words and actions. The rotten behavior was not theirs, it was extension of Peter through them.

I was paying dearly for having the courage to leave Peter. I had made him look bad in front of everyone who knew us. I had shattered his image and his ego; his response to that was to become dangerous, bitter and retaliatory. He was going to punish me and that started by making sure that everyone who knew us would be told that I left for another man. He failed to tell those same people about his inability to love me and the years of abuse and cruelty that I endured being married to him.

It had become challenging for me to allow the boys to continue speaking to me the way they did in fear of e-mail reprisals from Peter. Whenever I firmly addressed their unacceptable behavior they would threaten to go and live with their dad, which was my biggest fear and what Peter was deviously orchestrating. I was under immense pressure with the divorce and having to deal with two hurt and angry teenage boys by myself was horrible. From time to time I found myself getting into conflict with one or the other regarding things they were saying about me that were untrue. In hindsight, I should have walked away and left it alone, still, I felt the need to defend myself against the false allegations. The conflict would escalate and then the e-mail would arrive the next morning. It was unfairly exhausting. In therapy, I had discussed that it didn't seem fair for Alex to have to live with contention within the home and that I was concerned about him.

My therapist told me that the next time there was an upsetting outburst in the home that I should calmly and lovingly tell that child that they were no longer allowed to speak to me that way in my home. She added that when that child could come into my home and speak to me with respect then they could stay. I was also to explain that my allowing their abusive behavior would only enable them to treat women in their future the same way and that I did not want to be responsible for it. She suggested that I ask them to pack an overnight bag and come home when they felt that they could treat me with respect. I was so afraid to ask either one of them to leave, yet, sadly, I had known that it was coming. Something had to change and it had to be me. It felt unfair for Alex to have to witness this type of abusive behavior from his older brothers.

One evening shortly after talking with my therapist, Martin spoke rudely and horribly to me. He had done it in front of guests in my home. I used that opportunity to have "the discussion" with him. I sat on the edge of his bed and calmly and tenderly told him that while I loved him unconditionally, he was no longer allowed to talk to me the way he had been, including that evening. I told him that I would no longer enable his verbal abuse since I did not want to be responsible for him moving on into his own relationships and talking that way to other women. I asked that he speak more respectfully to me; if he wouldn't it might be good idea to take an overnight bag and come home whenever he felt he could. I made it abundantly clear that I was not asking him to leave but, I *was* asking him to change. He angrily told me that I absolutely disgusted him. With that comment, I suggested that he pack an overnight bag, think about how he was talking to me and come home whenever he could talk respectfully to me. He took a bag and starting filling it with school work and clothes, and left my home slamming the door behind him.

I had been so afraid to lose him, but my conversation with him left me feeling back in control and empowered. As a parent, it was very difficult to do what I did, but once it was done, I immediately started to feel better about myself. I was back to being the parent in charge.

The next morning, I received an e-mail from Peter. He accused me of throwing Martin out of my home while he was trying to do his homework. He relished in telling me how detrimental my actions and words were and how it impacted him as a student. He went on to say that I was an unfit mother and that *my* behavior was leading the children to reject me. Martin, he wrote, would be living full time with him, now that I had "thrown him out". It tortured me to read that e-mail since at that time I was so raw, so hurt, and so vulnerable and was such an easy target for him to impact. However, he was wrong and what he was saying was not true, he was not there, Martin was not thrown out, and I felt that I had dealt with the situation and its escalation maturely with calmness and great inner strength. I was back in the driver's seat. With therapeutic support I had started parenting them again with more confidence and without the fear of constant threatening e-mail reprisals that were getting repetitive and ridiculous. I was going to receive e-mails no matter what I did, so I had nothing to lose by regaining my parenting role. He had no idea how much he was setting them up for failure and, even if he did, he didn't care as long as I was suffering.

I didn't speak to Martin for several days after he left my home and he would not return my texts. Even so, I made sure I reached out to him every few days. I was NEVER going to give up on my children. A few weeks passed and I still hadn't heard a word from him. The longer I didn't hear from him, the more concerned I became about him being deeply alienated. I didn't mind if Martin needed time, but I very much minded if it was due to Peter's manipulation. My closest friend lives four doors down from Peter. One day while I was there I saw Martin in Peter's driveway. Peter's car was not there so I walked over to talk to him. At first, he was aloof and spoke a little harshly to me, but he softened after a while. I had carried him around in my arms lovingly for years and I don't think you can take that connection away from any loving mother and her child for long. We spoke for at least fifteen minutes about what had happened the night he left. I reminded him that he had not been thrown out like his dad suggested, but that he was asked to come back when he could be nicer to me. I told him how much I missed him and how much his brothers missed him being with us and asked him to consider coming home for a fresh start. He told me that he might come home the next day. I noticed Peter's car coming from the top of the street and respectfully left and told him how much I loved and missed him. I believe that he very much wanted to come home but was conflicted by the unnecessary and ugly dynamics that he was being forced to live under.

To my surprise, he came home after school the following day. I was thrilled. The following morning, I received an e-mail from Peter. He'd seen me in his driveway the day before and said that if I stepped foot on his driveway again, he would call the police and have me charged with trespassing. The truth is that he was livid that Martin had come home. He was hoping to isolate him from me and hadn't succeeded – yet.

A few weeks after Martin came home he called me a vulgar name one day in front of his brothers so I decided to take his car keys. I had leased a modest new car to surprise him on Christmas Eve well before the verbal abuse got out of control. I had wanted to do something nice for him considering he had been through such a tough time. Before Christmas he'd been excited because Peter was going to get him a car. He was devastated to learn he was not getting one because he had to get straight A's in school and he had just missed it by getting one B. I had felt so sorry for him and thought that his grades were amazing considering the family dynamic he was dealing with. It had not seemed right to punish him for the one B so I surprised him with the car on Christmas Eve. He was so happy that told me it was "the best day of his life". I was over the moon to hear him say that and had hoped that his new gift and new independence would help relieve some of the recent struggles that we had been having.

Taking the keys from him was not what I wanted to do but was what I had to do to teach him that verbal abuse was completely unacceptable. I had presumed that he would miss his car and come to me with a sincere apology, which is all I had wanted. He refused to apologize for almost a month. It surprised and disappointed me that he would prefer to go without his car than apologize. But. Peter bought him a larger and more prestigious car. It was a gigantic *fuck you* to me. Peter's merciless purchase made me detest him. He deliberately sabotaged my efforts to teach Martin the consequences of verbal abuse. He had also told Martin that he did not need to apologize to me. I was very disappointed and upset with Martin for accepting the car, knowing it was wrong. Yet, I knew he was the victim of his father's hatred towards his mother and I had to forgive him for not knowing any better at the time.

Michael is a sensitive boy. All the patio alienation conversations had filled him with turmoil. All the conflict was emotionally overwhelming for him and he was unable to cope with the lies he was being told about me. He had, unfortunately, taken some hallucinogenic mushrooms from a school friend; they had an adverse effect on his mind, exacerbating his emotional distress. His emotional state was deteriorating rapidly and he was showing disturbing signs of deep emotional stress, and this prompted me to reach out to Peter via e-mail. I told him how worried I was about Michael, that he was struggling, and that I felt that we should push our differences aside and take him to a doctor. The reply I received was utterly despicable. His lengthy e-mail only blamed Michael's emotional state on me. He wrote that I was a very unhealthy person in Michael's life. He forbade me to take Michael to a doctor and warned that he would take legal action if I did. Not once in his replies did he inquire into Michael's symptoms, my concerns about Michael, or Michael's escalating anxiety, nor did he offer or show an interest in helping him. His response was focused only on attacking me. I sent another e-mail days later after seeing a steady decline in Michaels's mental and emotional state, and I received yet another mean and condescending response. Not once did he care to ask about Michael and how we could help him.

193

I took Michael to see a psychotherapist, regardless of Peter's threat. When Peter found out about the appointment he wrote an e-mail to the doctor threatening her with legal action if she were to see Michael again. Her diagnosis had been as I suspected. "Significant psychiatric issues that need to be addressed by a trained professional." Instead of listening to the doctor, Peter challenged her diagnosis. Meanwhile, Michael was hospitalized one week later for a severe psychiatric breakdown. Peter's intimidation towards me, the doctor, and subsequently the ER doctor ended when a judge granted me an emergency court hearing.

Prior to Michaels's hospitalization, I had started legal action to get a court order so that Michael could visit with a doctor and a therapist. Each appointment I scheduled for Michael regarding his escalating anxiety or other issues was cancelled because Peter would call the doctor and threaten them. One time he sent an overnight FedEx threatening a doctor with a lawsuit if he saw Michael without his consent, which he had no intention of giving. I knew the court would rule in my favor; he had already been diagnosed as needing this help. Unfortunately, I was unable to get the ruling in time. I was, however, granted an emergency hearing the day he was hospitalized. In a state of panic, Michael called Peter on our way to the hospital. He was terrified because I was taking him to the hospital without Peter's knowledge. That is how much he feared the wrath of his father.

The ER doctor told me that Michael was a very sick young man and that it had been negligent not to bring him in sooner. I explained my situation and how Peter had prevented me from getting help, and how I was in the midst of getting a court order to get Michael that help. Peter had legally threatened three doctors even after one cautioned him about how mentally frail Michael was and how she had observed some "deeply disturbing emotional issues". I was terrified that Peter was going to walk into the ER, cause a huge scene and remove Michael. Michael was curled up in a fetal position sobbing and reaching out to me like a terrified infant. The ER doctor decided to transfer him to another hospital that specialized in the type of help he needed. She told me that Peter had just called and spoken to her and that she had made a unilateral decision to have hospital security guard our room for the rest of the day until the ambulance arrived. Whatever he said to her had not only supported my account of Peter, but had caused her to deem him a threat. I could only imagine how much it infuriated him for any doctor-- particularly a female doctor-- to refuse to discharge his son that day at his command. That beautiful woman was the turning point in Michael's recovery. Peter did not visit with Michael for the eight hours we were in the ER waiting for transportation.

An emergency motion was filed in court the day after Michael's hospitalization requesting uninterrupted mental health treatment for Michael and for him to stay with me until he was well enough to attend school, as per the recommendation of two doctors. He was not well enough to go back and forth between our two homes, especially under the circumstances. Peter didn't fight the court order. I had copies of all the e-mails that he had sent to me diminishing my concerns for Michael's health and his subsequent attacks with no regard to Michael's health. I also had copies of the written threats that he had made to three different doctors. The court order was good for Michael since he would be able to get the help he needed. Sadly it would turn out very badly for me because this minor win to get Michael medical help infuriated Peter and would cause him to intensify his efforts to remove Michael from me.

You would think Peter would be have been overly sensitive around Michael moving forward and conscious of his fragility. Unfortunately, he continued the alienation and attempts to remove him from me even after our judge ruled it "in his best interest to stay in one home with his mother until well enough for school". Peter told Michael that if he took the medication that the doctors had prescribed for him that they would ruin his future, make him sterile, prevent him from entering certain careers and make him addicted to them. I am not a fan of medicating children myself, however, he needed them at that time. Using scare tactics to prevent him taking medication was just absurd. He had just experienced the most severe emotional breakdown that I have ever witnessed and needed medication at that time. It had seemed Peter was trying to interfere in his recovery process and I could not for the life of me figure out why. I e-mailed Peter and asked him to stop interfering with the doctors and their plan of action to help Michael recover. I should have known better. He told me in some of those last e--mails I ever read from him, that Michael had suffered a medical setback because my behavior and what I had done to our family...and on and on and on. He was and still is the most abusive, hurtful and cruel person I have ever met. He had the audacity to tell Michael that the doctors were giving him "really bad meds" and, just to scare him further, e-mailed him a list of all their side effects. Michael's need for the medicine was far greater at the time than any potential side effects. It was the most ominous behavior that I had ever been witness to, and to see it happening to my own son by his father was alarming. Soon after Michael became afraid to take his medicine and stopped taking it. The results were horrific. He told me that the doctors were only giving him medication so that they could make money. Not something the average fifteen-year-old would say; obviously that kind of thought process had been fed to him. Michael stopped trusting in all his doctors and eventually refused to see them.

The doctors were aware that Peter was the primary cause of strife for Michael and that his scare tactics were interfering with and preventing his recovery but were legally unable to do anything about it unless I took him to court. I could very easily have done that and won with all the professionals in my corner only I knew that Peter would involve our boys. I begrudgingly opted not to take the issue to our judge, mainly to save the boys from the aftermath. When Michael stopped taking his medicine his health deteriorated and he became afraid of everything. He had started to become afraid of me too. Peter had convinced him, in his vulnerable and impressionable state, that I was in cahoots with his doctors and medicating him so I could control him, and that eventually he would become dependent on them and me. It just couldn't get more disgusting and abusive. If you have cancer you get help. If you have asthma you get help. If you have diabetes you get help. If you have a severe anxiety attack and depression you also get help. He made me sound like I suffered from Munchausen Syndrome, and against the advice of all the doctors, convinced Michael to stop taking his medicines. This left Michael unstable, unwell and in Peter's favor, impressionable and vulnerable.

I discussed Michael's issues with Martin one night; I felt that he was old enough to understand and comprehend his issues. Martin told me that Michael hadn't suffered from anxiety issues in his childhood and denied that he was suffering with depression; he went on to say that Michael had become sick because of me. I hated him for saying that but hated Peter more for feeding it to him. Michael ended up with me for four months to recover, and the entire time Peter continued to interfere with his convalescing time and continued attempts to lure him from my calm, loving home to his. Peter had daily access to him at my home but most of the visits did not go well with Peter saying something ugly to me each time he left. One time he beckoned Michael to his car and drove off going completely against the wishes of his professionals and took him to the beach. Michael was so upset that Peter had gone against all rules that he proceeded to have another anxiety attack that prompted Peter to bring him home.

All Peter wanted was to lure our boys to his home, not because he wanted to be with them, but because he wanted to hurt me by taking them away from me. He was travelling a lot at the time and had no right luring a sick child to his home only to leave him alone. It was ludicrous to think Michael would be better off at his home. However, that had not stopped his dad from continuing to scare him as he sat on my patio almost every night for his one hour visit as per our court agreement. His nightly visits were always disruptive. He continued to try to convince Michael that I did not know what I was doing regarding his recovery or his medication. It was an attempt to break him down further and put nonsense into his mind to suggest I was an evil mother.

The most valuable thing that came from Michael's very unfortunate breakdown was the court order for him to receive mental health visits, doctors and psychotherapy. I had found an excellent therapist who was the one who had originally highlighted his deeply disturbing emotional issues. He liked her very much and felt safe with her. Peter, of course, did not like her at all. She did not like him either, especially after he had legally threatened her. I felt like I could breathe for a while knowing Michael was receiving the right help under the watchful eyes of the professionals and the court. It wasn't long before we found out that Michael was suffering specifically as a result of the alienation. He could not emotionally cope with having to choose between his mother and his father. He wanted both his parents in his life, but his father was trying to make him choose him over me.

Michael invited me to join him in one of his therapy sessions, which I did. He was not able to hold onto what Peter was telling him and needed to let it out. He wanted to tell me what had been said about me. It was the beginning of his recovery. I cried as he told me what had been said. He had been told that I had stolen their college money, that he had been shown e-mails that I had sent to Peter, that he and Martin had been forced to watch me in my video deposition talk about them attending a public school (taken completely out of context), that I was trying to ruin *his* company, that I had taken all of *his* money, how I had had an affair, that I was not a good influence in their lives, and that they would be better off being away from me for the sake of their mental health. Anything to make me or my family look bad. Literally anything. As much as that session hurt me to my core, it not only confirmed most of what I already knew, but helped me understand why my boys were so angry with me. It also had given me a starting point to help him recover and heal. I had done everything in my power to keep our boys out of the divorce. Finding out that he had sat our boys down to watch a specific part of a court-ordered video to substantiate his alienation to make their mother appear bad was a disgrace. Only a monster could go to such lengths.

Michael's psychiatrist suggested a family meeting to help alleviate the pressure on Michael due to the family dynamics. He knew that Peter was the primary reason Michael was struggling and wanted to host the therapy session himself since he knew what the problems were after lengthy discussions with Michael and Michael's psychotherapist. To everyone's surprise, Peter wanted a contract drafted before agreeing to the session. He vehemently refused to attend until his attorney had the contract signed by all parties. The contract basically read that nothing brought up in any session could be used against him in court. Only a paranoid and guilty person would request such verbiage in a contract. It took three weeks to receive the contract and everyone signed it. It seemed superfluous and ridiculous but made a sick kind of sense since Peter knew he was guilty of psychological crimes. After making us all dance around his contractual bullshit and making every effort for him to attend family therapy for the sake of Michael and our other boys, Peter never went.

I had misread and misunderstood the intensity of the danger in our family dynamics. I knew our boys were angry with me, but always thought they would settle down and continue living with both parents throughout their high school years. It was our job to promote their relationship with their mother and their father, but Peter had been destroying it on a level I hadn't anticipated. The dexterity of Peter's manipulation, along with their conscious or unconscious fear of him, resulted in their leaving my home to live with Peter full-time. Everything suddenly felt surreal. I'd lost them. The only thing that kept me afloat was Alex and Greg's unwavering loyalty and support, and my spiritual strength. Greg is my current partner of four years who I met a few months after ending my relationship with Rob. He was the man that my soul had been yearning for. He was the person that I had reached out to the universe to meet. He is not only a true gentleman but the kindest person I could have ever asked for, which is not surprising since I had been asking to meet him for a very long time.

Their departure was swift, unfair and unjust. I felt that Martin had been completely oppressed and very much bought into the deceit and, because of it, I couldn't seem to do anything right by him. I also believe that Michael followed since he was in a sensitive and vulnerable state and was the perfect victim for a master manipulator's great timing. I was devastated. Every day that I was not with them felt like a year. I was broken.

I plan to continue writing about our family dynamics in a sequel to this book. It will be an insight into the aftermath of the damage caused to all of us by Peter. I will be interested to see how the trauma affected all the boys, particularly Martin and Michael, and specifically in their relationships with women. Martin still doesn't acknowledge his father's wrongdoing, which I find bizarre since it is brazenly transparent to everyone. Michael, who now has clarity on the matter and, unlike Martin, acknowledges what his dad had done and what he continues to do, will hopefully be able to expel any remnants of the poison over time. Hopefully, as he matures he will heal further.

I will continue to love and care for all my boys and hope my unconditional affection, along with Greg's unwavering support of all three of them, will help undo and unwind the negative restraints of brainwashing.

Chapter 19

During the two years that it took me to get divorced I was physically sick nearly the entire time. Watching my children drift away affected my physical health. My headaches became so severe that I was convinced that I had a brain tumor and went for a brain scan. I did not have a tumor. They went on for well over a year. My cough had become worse and had left me coughing constantly and, on many nights, gasping to breathe. I was afraid that I would choke during my sleep. I was on one antibiotic after another and had convinced myself that I must have throat or lung cancer. I investigated that possibility and was told that I was fine. The coughing continued which, after a process of elimination, led me to believe that I had triggered the onset of the asthma that runs in my family. Whatever I had was not going away. I went to see a doctor who specialized in chest conditions. He asked me about my life and what was going on. He convinced me that if I could relax my symptoms would go away. He told me that my symptoms were all stress related. It really should have been obvious to me that the stress was causing my physical symptoms, but at the time my mind was so full with divorce clutter it had not allowed me to consider it. It was me who was allowing the power of Peter's cruelty to infiltrate my physical wellness. I had to continue my personal growth and strengthen further so that I could reject his cruel attacks and not allow the unhealthy and dysfunctional energy to penetrate me. I had spent way too many years getting sick and hurt while I was married to him, and over my dead body was I going to allow it any more. That crossroad led me to a man who would be the beginning of the end of Peter in my life physically, emotionally, mentally and spiritually.

I was very fortunate to be introduced to that amazing spiritual man, called Shantam Nityama, by an influential friend of mine. He travels around the world specifically helping women and children to heal. He had studied under a man called Osho (Chandra Mohan Jain) who lived in India. Osho was a world-renowned professor of philosophy, was a mystic, a guru and a spiritual teacher. I was struck by Nityama's appearance when I met him. He had the kindest eyes and the warmest smile. He sat a few feet across from me and asked me how he could help me. I told him about all of my anguish, my pain and my fears of losing my boys. He did not say one word, he just watched and listened. He did not take his gaze off me for one single moment. It felt like he was looking beyond my eyes and into my soul, and most likely he was.

When he finally spoke, he told me that I had to let my boys go. Not just physically, but mentally and emotionally. He said that I had to let them go and live with Peter so that they could find out for themselves who he really was and why I had had to leave him. He told me that an unauthentic person uses an abundance of energy pretending to be a person that they are not but that even the best of them tires eventually and their true self becomes exposed. He asked me if I had chased Peter in the beginning of our relationship. I told him that I had. He put it quite simply and asked me to visualize the scenario. Spiritually speaking, I had had to chase him because he was running from me. He was running from me because I was not supposed to be with him. He was not the right spiritual match for me. That was the spirit telling me that Peter was not for me and to stop chasing him, yet I had ignored it. I was not accustomed to listening to the spirit back then and had not paid attention to or understood the caution that lay beyond his running from me. I must have been very determined because I had chased him for some time and that determination had led to severe consequences. Nityama told me that when people are spiritually compatible they meet naturally without effort, especially effort from the woman. He likened it to the animal kingdom and reminded me that you never see a female animal chase the male. It is always the male chasing the female, since instinctively he senses who his right partner is. He told me that this same instinct exists in humans, only we have ignored and manipulated it due to social pressure and man-made rules of who we think we should be with. Those requirements are shallow and the ones that I had been attracted to in Peter. People choose appearance, money, power, fame, status, prestige, cars, homes, and style as prerequisites to dating, which sets a somber precedent. He warned me against ever chasing a man again unless I was looking for more hardship. He told me that the right man would find me and would chase me and not vice versa.

Nityama told me that Peter was a psychopath based on my accounts of his treatment of me over the years. He emphasized that I had given birth to three of *his* children and that he had absolutely no excuse to treat me with disdain of any kind. He spoke quietly and methodically with such profound wisdom and did not break his eye contact with me once. He explained that Martin and Michael had decided to walk down a road that had a very lonely and unhappy dead end like that of their dad's. When they realized how lonely and miserable it was down that road, either they would stay there with him and wallow in his same emptiness, or they would turn around and walk back and have to pass me along the way. He told me that would be the day they would come back to me since I would always be there for them with open arms and an abundance of unconditional love.

He was firm that under no circumstance should any of our boys treat me poorly, and commended my asking Martin to leave when he had been verbally abusive. It was a very hard decision for any mother to make, Nityama said, and that I had shown great strength and had taught him a valuable lesson by doing so. After spending hours with Nityama that day, I left feeling an intense sense of empowerment like never before. The fog had lifted and everything had become clear. After leaving Nityama, I felt mentally and emotionally strong enough to let Martin and Michael go to Peter without further distress. I realized that I could do absolutely nothing to protect our boys any longer. They had chosen their path and they were on their own. It was their turn to learn who their dad was. He was not going to change. He would expose his true self soon enough. And he did.

I had to let the boys go but I would not give up on them nor give them up. I kept in touch every few days via text and calls. I didn't hear back from either of them for weeks. It broke my heart knowing Michael was still in recovery and how I felt that I needed to be there for him. Each day that I didn't hear from either of the boys felt like an eternity to me. In any other situation it would not have been so bad, but since I was faced with the reality that they were living full-time with a man on a mission to permanently destroy our relationship it very much felt like an eternity. I wanted to knock on Peter's front door to see them from time to time but I had been warned about trespassing and I knew he would follow through with his threat. I continued to reach out to them every few days with absolutely no intention of ever giving up on them. I told them how much I loved them and how much I missed them. On occasion, they would take my call and were usually short and aloof. I knew that was healthy and productive since only weeks earlier they refused to talk to me at all. I was also fully aware that they were psychologically being held hostage.

I struggled to wrap my head around the fact that we were going to court for five days to get divorced. Murderers, pedophiles, rapists and terrorists sometimes don't get a five-day trial and here we were wasting everyone's time, our monies, the taxpayer's monies and my health dragging a divorce into this arena, all because Peter didn't want me to have half of our marital success and assets. It was ludicrous and telling of how greedy, mean and spiteful he was. I could not have been more grateful to the prudent and intelligent decision I had made to retain my new, powerful attorney since without him I suspect Peter would have stopped at nothing to cheat me of everything he could. Now he had a bigger problem, and that was my new attorney. He was stronger, more experienced, was proficient in exposing Peter's many lies made under oath and was arguably better than all Peter's attorneys combined. We started on Monday morning with my attorney putting the company appraiser on the stand and attacking every part of his appraisal to the point that the man was left sweating and babbling. Our judge fully understood what was going on but, due to Peter's legal persistence, he had to go through the process.

The following day, Peter's attorney produced three witnesses to vouch for Peter's parenting. It was an attempt, I presume, to ask for more parenting time post-divorce. A joke considering the lack of time he spent with them during the temporary situation and considering how often he left to go out of town when he had them. He only wanted more time with them to hurt me. He also knew that he could use this threat as leverage to get me to settle for less money. It was a clever, and calculated, but sick, move. One witness didn't show up. I was relieved since this man was a friend to both of us and I was surprised that Peter would want to put him in the middle, though he would have not been unfavorable to me at all. Richard was the second witness. Not surprising since he was Peter's only known friend who knew him as a father and me as a mother too. He spoke favorably about both of us as parents. Either he lied for Peter or had absolutely no idea what Peter was doing to our boys during that time. The last was a strange woman who neither of us really knew. All we knew of her was that she had been married to a drug dealer who had died; I had long ago distanced myself from her because I thought she was odd. My attorney started out by asking her the names of our three boys. She only knew two of the three names and he immediately dismissed her and told the judge he had no further questions for her.

By Thursday morning it must have been clear to Peter and his attorneys that he had lost his fight to wring me dry; he had his attorney stall the court proceedings and make me an offer. My attorney and his attorney went back and forth for over two hours and settled. Peter must have realized that he was swimming in dangerous waters and most likely was warned that he could lose a lot more that he had hoped to by continuing to lie to the judge under oath. He reluctantly decided to take the right road-- which he should have taken from day one. It was evident to me that I had originally made him a very fair offer based on what the judge awarded me.

Had Peter have taken the higher road earlier it would have also saved us almost $1.5 million dollars in attorney's fees. In court that day Peter sat with a perpetual smile on his face. I found it disturbing since I knew how angry he really was. His desire to take everything away from me had just slipped away and common sense told me that this loss did not match his happy appearance. That outward smile did not fool me. It was a feigned smile that told me that I was going to pay for the decision made in court that day for a very long time, and I still am. That day, after years of misery and suffering behind the scenes, we were finally divorced.

As a side note, after watching the Steve Jobs movie I found a striking resemblance to both he and Peter, starting with their early adoptions just after birth. They were both dropouts although Peter went on to further his education. They both had terrible sexist attitudes towards women and not only found them to be inferior but treated them as such. Steve Jobs' treatment of the mother of his child was cold and cruel. He refused to help her, instead focusing on his own life and success. His reluctance to give her financial help to support their child is indicative of superiority, power control, and cruelness, something that Peter fought desperately to achieve in our divorce. It turns out that Jobs gave the mother of his child a meager and pathetic sum of money relative to the millions he was making, which is exactly what Peter told me to expect. I was very fortunate that I had found a top-notch attorney who prevented that very same financially insulting outcome from happening to me. They both focused on building power and wealth which they deemed as the only successful thing in life.

Neither one of them were able to express sympathy or empathy on any level. They share similarities in the pain they inflicted on their children. One denied being the father for years, causing feelings of rejection, abandonment and emotional pain; the other inflicted emotional, mental and psychological pain through alienation and control. I leaned over to Greg during the movie and told him that I felt I was watching a movie about Peter. The only thing that mattered to both Jobs and Peter was themselves.

Martin and Michael had slowly started to communicate with me again a few months after they left my home. One day Michael called me and told me that Peter had gone out of town and left them alone for a week without food and had forbidden Martin to use his car because of some poor grades. He told me that he could not believe a dad could do that to his children. They could call in food if they needed it. It was disgraceful to me that after finally luring them away from me he would leave them alone with absolutely no regard for their needs. Leaving the boys alone for a week at the time had been irresponsible considering they were both in high school and needed some level of supervision, especially since Michael was still recovering. He used to tell the boys that he was away on business which is hard to dispute but he was really flying to the UK to date – because that was more important.

It was so obvious that he didn't really want them full-time, he just wanted to inflict pain on me. They started to call me that week to bring them food, which I took to them every night, never mind that I was trespassing. Martin's car privileges were removed regularly for the duration of his high school years, which is ironic since his bad grades were due to lack of supervision and post-divorce stress and not from poor behavior. He needed to be helped, not punished. *Let them go to him so they can find out for themselves...* They weren't sounding so happy anymore to me. They were used to cooked breakfasts, responsible parenting, dinner at night, accountability for homework, and a parent at home most of their lives. In the beginning, I'm sure it was great for them living with their dad. On many occasions, Martin told me that there were no rules at dad's house and I have to admit if I were a teenager I would most likely find the home of the parent with no rules very appealing. What killed me though was that Michael had just taken a long medical absence from school and was still unstable and far from well.

I had heard from girls in school that Peter was dating several women, which was proof that the cycle had started again, especially since none of them knew about each other. When I asked Martin how he felt about his dad dating three women at the same time, he told me that he thought it was cool and that his dad could do whatever he wanted since he was single. Martin and I were in a very fragile place at the time so I decided not to venture into the morals and poor character of what his dad was doing and what he was teaching them. It infuriated me to be aware that he was teaching our boys that the women didn't deserve the respect to know about each other and of the deviousness that was being displayed. A typical narcissist behavior trait. It had saddened me to hear Martin's answer to my question but I think he was still angry with me and did not mean it, since his lowly opinion on Peter's treatment of women is not indicative of the morals that he was raised with. Not too long after this incident I was introduced to a wonderful man who would end up setting a fine example to all three boys on how to treat a woman with respect coupled with rich traits of a true gentleman.

Throughout the whole awful experience of my divorce, the one person that stayed solid and unknowingly helped me through so much was my youngest son, Alex. He was aware of everything that was taking place and watched as his brothers fought their way out of my home into Peter's. Alex was completely in control at all times and remained loyal to me from his birth to this day. He treats me with the upmost respect and was my rock through those years. I will be forever grateful to him for his support and more grateful that he was not targeted in the alienation. I am also relieved that Peter and I did not live together long enough for him to learn the narcissistic marital abuse traits that he could have very easily been taken into his own future relationships.

Peter didn't only use our children to hurt me, he used our dog Kobe too. Shortly after Peter and I separated my boys begged to take Kobe with them when they went to stay with Peter. I came up with a plan to have our dog go back and forth to the home where the boys were. I thought it was a good idea and in the best interest of the boys for comfort and familiarity. One night after Kobe returned to my home, he woke me up in the middle of the night. He had bad diarrhea. I thought he was sick because he was also bleeding. It took me a long time to clean the mess and remove the smell along with tending to Kobe. I e-mailed Peter the next day and asked him what kind of food he was giving Kobe. No reply. Two weeks later, on Kobe's first night back in my home, he woke me in the early hours of the morning for the same reason. He had gone all over my carpet again and was bleeding. What a coincidence. I remembered that he had that reaction to bacon when he was younger and wrote an e-mail to Peter to ask him if he was feeding him bacon and if so, to please stop. It was making our dog sick. No reply. I asked the boys if Kobe was getting diarrhea in their dad's house and they told me that he was not. Two weeks later, the same thing happened. Not only was I furious that he was deliberately making Kobe sick, I was just as mad that I had to spend an hour cleaning my carpet every time he came home from Peter's house. I knew Peter was giving him bacon on purpose knowing the outcome and told the boys that if their dad didn't stop giving Kobe bacon and making him sick then he could no longer go there. I was afraid to enforce this rule since I did not want to upset my boys any more than they already were, but when it happened a sixth time I was done. No more trips for Kobe to Peter's house. That had a huge impact on the boys and they became pretty hostile about it.

Martin and Michael had slowly started coming home more to see me but sadly it seemed that each time they came, something minute would trigger them to leave upset. I was mindful that their recovery with me was going to be very slow. The fact that they were even coming back to me was positive considering that six months earlier they refused to talk to me at all. Martin and Michael asked me one evening if they could take Kobe home with them and I refused and told them why. They immediately became hostile and abusive and accused me of trying to take everything away from their dad, including his dog. It took all the power that I could muster to stay firm with my decision as I watched them leave angrily. They left shouting unkind things at me. It upset me, but I was proud of myself for remaining firm and for doing the right thing, not only for me, but for Kobe too. Peter denied for months that he was giving Kobe bacon and making him sick on purpose until one of the boys accidentally mentioned it and turned white when he realized what he had said. I ignored the comment since I already knew anyway. I did not want my boys walking in fear from anything they ever shared with me. Kobe has not been sick once since I have forbidden for him to go there.

A friend called me one day and told me to click on a video clip posted on my former company's homepage. I felt sick as I watched his deceit. The clip showed him at a charity event handing over a hefty check for teenage children in foster care that had been abused and neglected. It was very generous, don't get me wrong, and was intended for a good cause, but so insincere. The irony was that he was abusing his own teenage children. He spoke very impressively about the importance of the boys in the foster care system and about his desire to personally help them and support their futures, especially educationally. To attempt to remove the mother from the life of her son is no different to an attempt to mentally kill her off and is abusive. He made his speech with a smile from ear to ear and from start to finish. His attempt to create a fake image to those around him seemed to be effortless, which I found disturbing. Only a true master manipulator could pull it off. He might have looked and sounded convincing to those around him at that charity, but not to me.

Martin had started cross country at school. It was wonderful to watch him race, even though it was always shadowed by Peter's angry and threatening presence. I found it disturbing over and over again to watch the father of my children walk past me and completely ignore me. I felt vulnerable when I was there alone, especially since Martin was living full-time with Peter but it did not deter me from going to every race. The first race I went to watch was by far the most hurtful and painful experience for me regarding all our boys and their sports. After the race, I went to congratulate Martin, despite the fact that if I was going to say hi and congratulate him before he left I would have to approach him with Peter there. As I approached, Peter purposely stood between me and Martin and blocked my attempt to talk to him. He was filled with rage, and I could feel it. However, I would not leave. Martin was visibly uncomfortable and had no idea what to do. I moved around Peter and hugged him regardless of Peter's attempts. Seconds later, Peter marched away with Martin dutifully by his side. I cannot begin to explain how that made me feel. Peter made me feel like I was a threat to Martin. Obviously, Martin had feared Peter, or else he would have gladly embraced me as he always had. It was pitiful, painful and heart-wrenching to watch my son obey his father the way he did that day. I felt like he was suffering with Stockholm Syndrome.

One day Martin came over to my home. Although the visit was short and tense, I had wanted to address a couple of things that I had learned about in therapy with Michael. I felt that every lie he had been told deserved an explanation and the truth. I told him that I was aware he had been told that I had spent all of his college fund on expensive accessories. I wanted him to see his 529 savings account, in his name, on my online banking page as proof that it was not true. He refused to look at it and asked me why I was trying to pull him into marital fights. There was no fight intended, just the facts and the truth. I asked him again if I could show him his full college fund and again he refused to look. Seeing his college money in a 529 account in his name would mean that he would have to accept the one thing he was unable to cope with at the time, and that was that his dad was lying to him. He left angrily which is usually how it went when I was starting to make sense.

A few months before Michael left to live with Peter, our school reached out and asked if we could host some international students. I had been hosting international students for a few years and the boys always seemed to enjoy their stay, so I accepted three students. I believed that it was a wonderful experience for our boys to get a firsthand look at cultural differences with children their own age from India, South America and Eastern Europe. I wanted to show our boys the value of opening their home and welcoming children from overseas and the value of the relationships that are formed from doing so. I should have known Peter would attempt to ruin their visit somehow, causing me some humiliation and embarrassment and I had not known that Michael would move in with Peter before their arrival. Michael was incredibly impressionable during his recovery and had been played well by Peter. Michael had voluntarily signed up for the host exchange program in school which meant that he would greet and chaperone the visiting international students until they left. We had three boys who were staying in our home for one week.

I suspected that Michael might need reminding about his commitment to the school and phoned him about their imminent arrival. As it was, he had forgotten and told me that he was out to dinner with Peter. I told him to ask Peter if he would drop him off at school after dinner. After all, he had signed up to greet them and he was expected. I heard him ask Peter and he came back on the phone and told me that he was not allowed to go. It felt like my son was in a hostage-like situation. It was nauseating that Peter was prepared to make him miss out on this opportunity just to spite me. In fact, there would be a perpetual attempt to ruin anything that had my fingerprint on it. I greeted the international boys alone and apologized for Michael's absence.

The following morning my attorney forwarded an e-mail to me from Peter. He claimed that I had "disrupted their meal twice and had left Michael very upset". In that same e-mail he demanded that I "stop harassing the boys when they are with him" and told my attorney to "tell his client to stop interfering with his time-sharing time with his boys". Need I say more about this complaint? Michael was not upset about my call, he was upset because his dad refused to take him to school after dinner. This spiteful decision prevented Michael participating in the school assignment that he had signed up for.

That was not the only time he interfered with the student exchange program that year. The students were kept so busy during their stay that there was only one evening that they would eat dinner together with their host families. Michael had wanted to join us for that dinner since he had become close to the boys in school. I arranged dinner at a fun restaurant on the beach with other host families and their students. Michael had a scheduled basketball game that night so a basketball parent said she would drop Michael off after the game. Shortly after we arrived for dinner I received a call from the player's mother. She told me that Peter had refused to allow Michael to go with her. Not ten minutes later Michael called and asked me to pick him up. If I had, everyone would be finished by the time I got back to the restaurant; Peter knew that and it was why he did what he did. Michael was upset with me for not going to get him and now I was perceived as the bad guy. Martin got on the phone and had the audacity to tell me that I was making the whole evening about me and not them!

The entire episode was orchestrated by Peter the minute he saw that I was not at the basketball game and had learned that we were meeting at the beach. He intentionally ruined our evening and skillfully turned his own actions around by blaming me for what happened. Typical narcissist, blame me for his own evil deed. He was playing a very sick game with their minds. *Let them go to him so they can find out for themselves...*

Once I had surrendered and followed the advice of professionals, I stopped getting sick. Their advice and help had left me feeling empowered and physically well again. I was reminded all the time to hang in there and give the boys the time they needed to learn who their dad was. Any professional I have ever spoken to or any article or book I have ever read on being married to a narcissist describes a person identical to Peter. The numerous articles that I have read on

213

divorcing a narcissist were accurate too. The common traits they all had was that they were going to turn the children against you and they were going to make you pay for leaving them. Many people unfamiliar with the narcissist tell me that Peter will eventually change and start talking to me over time, but they have no idea of the depth of his hatred or his disorder. I have accepted that he will most likely never talk to me again and, after everything he put me and our family through, I prefer it that way. He is fifty-two years old and there is no chance of him changing at this point, primarily because he doesn't think there is anything wrong with him.

Michael started to share stories with me that indicated things weren't so great at dad's house. Michael was not feeling any emotional connection to Peter at all and was not living in a nurturing environment. Peter left them regularly without food or supervision. They were left completely unsupervised for weeks during their last few years in high school. Michael indicated one day that he was being mentally and emotionally abused. After Michael returned to school from his medical leave his grades had not been great. He was still not 100%. His grades had nothing to do with his ability, just his mental state. Not only was he struggling with his academics but, due to his heightened anxiety and medical setback, he did not get onto his school basketball team which had completely devastated him. Prior to the escalation of his anxiety, Michael was one of the strongest players on his school team. He was destined for varsity throughout high school. He had the height, the skills and the determination to stand a good chance at playing college basketball. He told me that when he had spoken with Peter about his not making the team that Peter had coldly blamed *him* for it. There had been no compassion whatsoever. It had been a hurtful and cruel thing to say to a devastated young man recovering from an emotional breakdown due to this very kind of abuse. To this day, Michael struggles to forget that insensitive comment and struggles to understand how Peter could be so ruthless for saying it when he was at such a low point in his life. He was looking for support and a father who could show him love and empathy during that weak moment but instead he was attacked and made to feel inferior, useless and an embarrassment. It was like Peter had given up on him. *Let them go to him so they can find out for themselves...*

I understood the emotional coldness and hurtfulness of Peter only too well since I had lived with it for so long. Our boys were just starting to get a more concentrated taste of it. They would never receive empathy from him since he was unable to feel empathy himself. He was good about making those around him feel inferior.

After getting through a two-and-a-half-year contentious divorce, overcoming all my physical health issues, succumbing to my boys living unjustly with their father, having no further hurtful communication with Peter, saying goodbye to Rob, confirming that I wasn't a lunatic and forgiving myself for believing some of Peter's accusations, I felt that I was finally able to breathe and embrace some peace. And that is when things started to turn around. Martin and Michael started coming home more often, and a few months later I was introduced to the most wonderful man that I have ever met.

There were some rough moments during that new peaceful period while Martin was finishing up in high school. One was Martin's graduation and the other was Martin's college process. Both were hurtful times with Peter at the reins. Martin had informed me that Peter did not think it was a good idea for us all to sit together for his graduation. Even if there was one brother either side of Martin to keep Peter and I away from each other he told me that his dad did not want to sit anywhere close to me. Childish and selfish. I agreed since there was no point putting unnecessary pressure on Martin; it was *his* day, after all. Peter beamed proudly with Martin and Michael by his side in the chapel but I knew that his smug smile was not sincere. He was gloating because I did not get to sit with our son on his graduation day or with Michael, just as he had planned it. As I looked down from the upstairs seating I noticed many divorced parents sitting with their child on their special day. When I had looked down at Martin and Michael sitting with Peter without me and Alex, I had felt so emotionally overwhelmed and hurt that we left early. Michael looked up at me at one point. He looked hurt by the dynamics also. He didn't smile once. He knew how wrong it was that I was not sitting with them and I could feel it in his look as I looked and smiled at him. For a brief second, Peter looked up at Alex and me and gave a smug look. I bet he was very happy with himself. The image must have been exactly what he wanted.

The other thing Peter did in Martin's last year of high school that was an attempt to diminish my role in his life in any way was overseeing all of the college choices for Martin and refusing to discuss, involve or update me on anything that they were doing. One day when Martin was home I asked him about his college choices. He asked me what the hell I knew about colleges. On one hand, I wanted to ask him to leave since I had made it abundantly clear that he was not allowed to talk to me that way any longer, yet he was my son, the victim of a very manipulative and strong narcissist who was only talking to me as he had been instructed. I'm sure he expected a harsh retort to his rudeness but instead I agreed that I didn't know much about American colleges. I asked if he would explain them to me. My reply must have taken him off guard since he proceeded in telling me about his choices and about various colleges. Peter had told both of our older boys over and over that I had not gone to a good college and that I added absolutely no value into their lives. He was reaching at anything and was starting to look pathetic and desperate. It was also orchestrated so that Martin would not value any input of mine into his future.

Greg was very sweet when I first met him. He seemed kind, open and honest. A friend of mine had made the introduction and had told me that he was a really nice guy and a righteous person. I met him for an hour or so where he told me all about himself, his two children, his family and his business. It felt like I knew more about Greg in that first hour than I knew about Peter in seventeen years. Greg told me that he was a sports agent which I found fascinating

216

though I knew absolutely nothing about it. It just sounded interesting and different. Weeks later he encouraged me to watch *Jerry McGuire,* which is when I got an insight into what he did for a living. He texted me shortly after I left and thanked me for meeting him and told me that he had had a nice time. I was impressed at how gracious he was and what a gentleman he seemed to be. I had shown up in jeans, boots and a t-shirt. I figured if he didn't like me for who I was then I was not interested. He showed up in a nice shirt and pants. He was pretty serious and intense, however, which were not the kind of traits that I felt were compatible for me. A day later I received a text from him inviting me to dinner. *"The right man would find me and would chase me."*

Every part of me was looking for an excuse not to go, but after not being able to come up with one I said yes. If it didn't feel right then perhaps we could be friends. I was so happy that I decided to go. He picked me up five minutes early in a fun shirt, jeans, lots of cologne and his hair gelled back. He looked very different and I liked that he was on time. He did not stop talking the whole way to dinner and was surprisingly very funny. I found him easy to be with and could not get over how complimentary he was the entire evening. It was extremely flattering and I felt beautiful with him. What stood out was how respectful he was. Not once did he seem interested in anyone else in that restaurant but me. His compliments seemed to be natural and sincere, but I still felt a little guarded not knowing how authentic he was. I was still healing from being married to a narcissist and it was my own shortcoming that caused my caution. I had a really great evening with Greg and accepted a third invitation for dinner that week. It was during that time that I realized that I really liked him but, more importantly, felt that I could trust him. He was genuine and kind. I felt happy when I was with Greg. I felt beautiful, I felt respected and I felt like he really cared about me. Over the next few months I grew to quickly trust him and felt a great sense of emotional safety with him. He spoke lovingly about his mother, his father who had passed, his daughter and his son. Greg had a nice circle of friends and as I started to meet them it told me a lot about his character. Not once did he say an unkind thing about his ex-wife. I loved that. He always talked about her with respect and referred to her as the mother of his two children. Any time he mentioned her in my presence to other people he said that they just grew part. He continues to support and encourage a healthy relationship between his children and their mother. This further confirmed to me that he was a man of impeccable character.

When I think about what my boys had to hear from their father I find it most upsetting and disgraceful in comparison. At some point, Peter will face retribution for what he did and how he hurt our children. Greg and I are still together and get along beautifully. Greg has been an outstanding role model to the three boys. As they hear negative things about their mother at one house, they witness a beautiful and respectful loving relationship at another. Greg has been a true blessing to our family because he is setting a wonderful example to my boys on how to treat their mother, women, and people in general. He takes the time to listen to all three of them intently and has done nothing but lift them up in every single aspect of their life. They express how good he makes them feel and often look for him before me on some occasions. I love how much they have grown fond of him and how attached they feel to him, because I do too. I have been very fortunate to meet Greg and I didn't have to chase him.

Chapter 20

Meeting Greg and having his unwavering support helped our family dynamic tremendously. Things had started to shake out just as Nityama had assured me they would. The boys were changing back to who I remembered them to be, most likely because they realize that I was not the mother they were manipulated to believe I was. Martin and Michael were noticeably more respectful but were ready to challenge me at any moment. I firmly believe that Greg's presence in our lives and in my home, along with his authentic and genuine character, helped the boys to see that their mother was in fact normal and in a very loving and respectful relationship. I'm sure the reality of seeing our authentic and healthy relationship offset their manipulated views about me and perhaps even led them to speculate who really was the unhealthy parent in their lives.

As each month passed I saw tremendous progress. Michael had started seeing an amazing therapist who happened to specialize in parental alienation. It was Greg who had found him for me; he would be the therapist who ended up freeing Michael from the invisible chains of alienation. Over the following year, he earned Michael's trust to the point where he was able to peel back the layers of his pain, and provided him with the emotional and mental tools that he needed to recover. His goal was for Michael to stand up to what was haunting him. The day he was able to stand up to the person haunting him in this case, the one responsible for most of his emotional distress and pain, his own father, would be the day Michael could heal and would be the day he became a man. When Michael met his new therapist, I knew he was going to be OK. He liked and trusted him which was imperative to him healing. He was starting to speak more confidently, he seemed happier, especially around me, he started to get clarity about himself and his situation, but most importantly of all, he recognized that he had been brainwashed. His therapist was doing a wonderful job at giving

Michael the clarity he needed to see for himself what had transpired. He was not interested in winning him back for me, far from it. His only goal was to help Michael find Michael.

One day Michael decided it was time to speak with Peter about the abuse he had encountered during the divorce and how much pain it had caused him. He shared the conversation with me afterwards. During his conversation, he told Peter that he had lied and that he had brainwashed him against his own mother and, because of that, he had lost valuable time with me that he could never get back. He told Peter how he could never forgive him for what he had done, but that he had to for the sake of his own recovery. Michael also said that while he has had to forgive him for what he did, he would never forget what Peter did to him during the worst and lowest time of his life. Peter, being the great dad that he is, asked him only one thing, "Did your therapist put you up to that?" I can only imagine how that had to have felt. Opening up after way too many years and expressing to your abuser what pain they had caused you and how it had affected you only to receive a cold, arrogant and abusive response. I would have to believe that Michael finally understood, right there and then, who his dad really is. An uncaring, selfish and self-centered narcissist. Michael has expressed to me that while he will always acknowledge Peter as his father, he has shut the door on him emotionally, and vows he will never give him the opportunity to hurt him ever again. *"Let them go back to him so they can find out who he really is..."*

My relationship with Michael has continued to be healthier and stronger by the day. He called me during his last month of high school and told me that his teacher had told the class that he wanted them to call the most influential person in their life; Michael wanted that person to be me. He told me how much he appreciated me, how much he loved me, how much I had helped him during his difficult times, how much I had supported him, how much I believed in him, and how much I had elevated him. He thanked me for assisting him with his college applications and for taking him to colleges. He thanked Greg and I for helping him get a summer internship with one of the most esteemed Internet Marketing companies in the world. He learned about Marketing a business on Google and Facebook and how to measure its success that segued into writing a book with his boss based on that internship which reached #1 on Amazon Kindle and resulted in a college scholarship. I would love for you to read his book, but in an effort to protect my children, one still being a minor, I am unable to provide you with the title, however, I may provide it in my sequel. I had in fact been the most influential person to him and not the "zero value added mother" that Peter told them I was. Michael also thanked me profusely for not giving up on him during the time that he turned away from me. That call from Michael almost made the entire nightmare worth it. Just to hear his gratitude was rewarding and priceless. He apologized to me many times for several months for all the unkind things he said to me during the alienation period and at those times asked me for my forgiveness. I told him that I had long forgiven him since he had been a victim and his words to me were not his own.

Peter did not inquire or have any interest in Michael's college process at all. Michael was a disappointment because he would not be able to attend a "good" college because of his high school attendance, medical leave and grades. Michael's basketball journey also disappointed him and, since Michael was the one destined for basketball triumphs, Peter had had nothing to brag and boast about. He didn't help Michael with his college process because he found him to be an embarrassment, and a child not worth investing in. He hadn't believed in Michael. How wrong he will turn out to be. During Michael's breakdown, his therapist at the time suggested a battery of psycho-educational testing just before he was forced back to school prematurely by Peter. Even though he was not fully recovered during that two-day testing time, and a little sick to boot, his test results came back showing Michael's IQ to be in the top 96% of his age group in the US. His academic ability was exceptional and concluded that it was his emotional state that had interfered with his high school years and his grades. Peter's prodigy was right there under his nose the whole time and yet all he had done was turn his back on him.

Greg played a huge role in repairing my relationship with Michael along with Michael's therapist. Greg is not only a successful, honest and well-respected sports agent but a skillful negotiator. Greg is, like Michael, a sensitive person by nature and was able to reach Michael because of it. He knew how to find him. His integrity, along with his ability to elevate people, made Michael feel good around him and consequently developed an unbreakable trust between them. Greg was then able to help repair the damage, not only by helping Michael to see the overall picture, but mostly by showing him the key to healthy relationships through example.

Martin's relationship with me slowly improved once he left for college. In therapy, I was advised to read a book called, "Divorce Poison"; I had to stop reading it because it scared me. It spoke about severe cases of alienation where some children actually never spoke to the alienated parent ever again, excluding them from marriages, births, grandchildren and the like. I stopped reading at that point because I vowed that that was not going to happen to me, and also because it had been too painful for me to read. I worried the most about Martin who seemed to get the major brunt of the alienation since he was the oldest. Peter had less time to drive him away from me because he was leaving for college the soonest and I believe that, because of the time constraint, he got hit the hardest. Narcissism typically, but not always starts, from trauma as a child, usually from a parent. The abuse and brainwashing that Martin received from Peter is a worrying factor to this happening in his adulthood. Martin does not appear to be a narcissist at this time, but could very easily spin off narcissistic learned behavior when feeling threatened or in a contentious situation. This could easily have been prevented through therapy, however, Martin was denied and talked out of therapy by Peter and was told that therapy causes more damage than good. He refused to go even after he turned eighteen when he was out of Peter's control of and legally could. Since he was not as fortunate as his brother to have the opportunity to unveil the abuse that was inflicted on him, I remain concerned that he will suppress this abuse and that it will surface within his own relationships later in life. Peter knew that any therapist would condemn what he was doing to them and therapy was therefore deemed a threat.

Michael's medical set-back was actually a blessing in disguise since it was the recovery process that exposed the alienation and this led to him getting the help he needed. Every child has the right to both of his parents unless one, or both of them, are a certified danger to them. A child should never have to choose between his mother or his father. He has a right to both. Martin has spent the last two summers in my home and appears to be doing very well. I still believe there is a lot of pain suppressed in his heart and soul and I will continue to urge him to release the poison via therapy but, sadly, I have to wait until he is ready. It might take relationship problems or marital problems to make him realize he needs to release his childhood wounds, and I pray that he doesn't get too hurt along the way until he does. Martin seems to struggle with trust, is wary of ulterior motives, tends to be cantankerous and is brutally opinionated. Some of his behaviors, though not bad, are indicative of low self-esteem. His choice of Chemical Engineering at college has been most impressive and has been extremely challenging. He wants to prove to himself that he can do it, but I will always wonder if he is taking on this stressful challenge to get the long-needed acceptance of his own father. Martin has taken on crew in college and has bonded well with his teammates. He is well liked and admired according to what his college friends tell me. He is a sensible and intelligent young man and has no idea how proud I am of him and how proud I am to be his mother. From the outside looking in, he looks like he's going to be just fine.

Martin took a while to warm up to Greg. I understand why. He has been hurt by the people he trusts the most and Greg needed to earn his trust. Now that the trust has been established they get along better than I could have ever imagined. They reach out to each other independently of me for sports information, game times, college games and races, which warms my heart and brings pleasure to my soul. I am so relieved to see Martin feeling free and safe around Greg and will be forever grateful to Greg, the man I love, for being the man in his life providing a safe zone, guidance, honesty, openness and trust that Martin appears to be flourishing from. Greg has brought a lot of silliness and fun into Martin's life and is adept at taking my beautiful and serious son and making him smile. This is the work and the heart of the wonderful man that I am proud to call my partner in life.

Alex seems to have come out of our family crisis unscathed. I'm not suggesting that he was not hurt by it, but he seems to have coped quite well, probably due to his age at the time. Inevitably, though he shows no remorse for it, Peter saw how much anguish he had caused Michael and the retribution that followed, and I highly doubt he will abuse Alex because of that. My fear at one point had been that once Martin and Michael left for college that Peter would start on Alex, and he still might, but I very much doubt Alex will allow it. He is a spiritually strong child and saw how much pain I suffered with losing my older boys for some time. Being a boy of great character, he would never allow that to happen to me again. Greg has been as wonderful with Alex as he has with his brothers. Alex has been fortunate to live around Greg and will leave my home one day with all the wonderful traits and respectfulness that Greg has shown him through example for the years we have been together and around him. Alex was so excited to hear that his mom had met a sports agent and is so enamored with Greg's exciting career. Alex and Greg are very close and have a lot of fun together which Greg is really good at. I do not believe I will ever have to worry about Alex.

Greg had been the best thing that ever happened to me. I believe you meet people in life at different times for different reasons. I met Greg when I had successfully put Peter behind me. It was a matter of closing one door with Peter, and another with Rob before the door opened for Greg. There is no doubt that Greg was blessed to me for all the wonderful things that followed. We have a strong, loving and respectful relationship and friendship that continues to flourish day by day. He selflessly helped me over and over again with the healing process with Martin and Michael. I will never forget how he assisted with that recovery and will always be there by his side with any and all struggles he will face. Greg starts every single day that he is not travelling by waking me with a cup of coffee. He has not missed one day in almost four years. He doesn't even drink coffee. He knows how much I love coffee in the morning and how much it means to me, especially since he wakes earlier than me. His kind morning gesture speaks volumes and goes to show that it's the small things that make such a huge difference in relationships. I have never asked Greg to do this for me. What a difference from the seventeen years that Peter refused to spend a few minutes with me over a cup of coffee in the morning only to learn of his thousands of trips to Starbucks after he left my home.

I have quickly and admirably rebounded from my seventeen-year nightmare and feel that I have healed fairly well, considering. I decided to take a healthy and forward path. I could have wallowed in self-pity, victimization, bitterness and anger, but I chose to take my life back into my own hands and wisely listened to signs moving forward that I had previously ignored. I can spot a phony with proficiency because the narcissists out there all seem to have the traits that I am sensitive to. Observing their relationships, or lack of, to their closest family members can be revealing to boot.

I have found a gentleman who I trust wholeheartedly. We talk about our days at night and what we did and what we have coming up. There is such a beautiful transparency between us that neither of us will ever have to be suspicious of the other's whereabouts – as it should be. Not once did I put my time with Greg ahead of the parenting of my boys. They always come first. Greg has never tried to compete with the time I spend with my boys; in fact, he actually likes being around them too. He joins me most of the time when we visit Martin and Michael at college and has stepped into my

225

family with ease. I have been very lucky and am truly grateful to have met Greg. My boys have benefitted tremendously in every way possible from his presence in their lives. My family thinks he's the greatest and my friends adore him. Everyone seems so happy for us.

Not only was I blessed with this amazing man, I have been blessed with all the great people in his life. He has a beautiful mother who is intelligent, perceptive, funny, sincere, loving and caring. She and I are very similar in our personalities and I speak with her all the time. Greg has two children older than mine who I get along with very well. His daughter and I talk about girl stuff, the kind of stuff that I don't encounter with my boys. I think she's a sweetheart. We talk about her boyfriend and his family and I share with her the wisdom that I have picked up along the way and caution her about what is out there. Greg's son is still finishing his education at college and has a close bond with his father. Greg's closest friends are all of good character. He chooses his people well.

Peter still refuses to acknowledge me, and refuses to acknowledge me to our three boys. I find Peter's behavior to be childish, hurtful to all and a continuation of abuse. Most children are protective of their parents, so when one is unkind to the other it continues to hurt the child. I will receive the occasional e-mail from Peter, which is always about me paying a bill. "You need to pay this..." and that is all that is written. I absolutely hate seeing his name in my Inbox since I know that I am going to get some kind of miserable reminder of a former abusive and toxic relationship.

Peter has refused to take a call from me in over four years. I am unable to call him regarding any parenting concern about our boys, and there have been many. I find his behavior to be pathetic and indicative of a very angry man. There have been a number of important things I would have liked to have discussed with him concerning our boys, but then I forget that I have no value in their lives and therefore he's not interested in what I have to say. When I attend games at school things are just as ugly. He has actually

226

walked right past me and totally ignored me on many occasions. He must consume so much energy hating me. Michael once told me that he absolutely hated basketball games because he knew that Peter and I were in the stands and it made him so uncomfortable that it affected his game. Another example of the negative affect caused by Peter's childish behavior.

For the sake of all three boys I would think he would be helping them heal by saying hello to me, even if he detested it. It would be good for *them*. His refusal to acknowledge me in any way constantly gnaws at them and if he cared one little bit for their emotional wellbeing he would change. The reason he doesn't change is because he doesn't love them or care enough about their lives as much as he hates me. Martin has shared with me that he gets into conflict with him about this very issue, yet he continues to tell him that I hurt him and he has cut me out... and that is that.

I have often told the boys that I am open to communication with him at any time. When Peter refuses to communicate with me about an issue they continue to say that "we" are immature parents for behaving the way we do. Sadly, they still encompass me into that statement because they are afraid to stand up to him and his wretched behavior. They know full well I am not playing that game.

Greg's conversations with my boys about his ex-wife allows them to see that Peter's behavior is not normal, is dysfunctional and indicative of a very angry and mean person. If Greg treated his ex-wife the way Peter treats me and if he spoke as unkindly about her as Peter has of me, I would not be with him today. Peter went on to meet a young girl who had no idea of the narcissist partner she had just met. I could not understand how she could want to be around a man who spoke so disgracefully about the mother of his three children, in front of his children, and still want to be with him. I knew her to be an intelligent young woman and was surprised that she wasn't curious as to what other people thought of my parenting. She seemed to have formed an opinion of me only from Peter and the angry boys that he had inflamed. If he could do that to me, he could easily do that to her. He had not been honest with her from the beginning and was dating other women behind her back, according to friends of mine. One of my boys told me that she would laugh about me with Peter in front of them and obviously had a very poor opinion of me.

Now the joke is on her since he acquired property just before they were married, which, of course, is known as a "non-marital asset". She also did not get to have her baby; no surprise since Peter had had a vasectomy, which she probably didn't know about. They filed for divorce less than a year into their marriage. My immediate thought when I heard was how happy I was for her. God had saved her and her unborn child--which had been a prerequisite of hers before getting married. I don't know if she will ever realize how lucky she was.

I caution any woman or man reading this book to think long and hard about your partner if he/she treats their ex, or you, with an unacceptable level of disrespect, since it is a huge red flag about *them* not the ex. A good man will treat women respectfully regardless of the situation. He might not like her any longer or like something that she did, but he will treat her with some level of respect and dignity.

When I have shared my stories with people, I know many of them must have wondered why I stayed with such a cruel man in such an unhealthy relationship for as long as I did. The primary reason is that I stayed for my children just like most people suffering in narcissistic relationships do. The majority of parents with a narcissistic spouse feel the need to stay to protect their children, just like I did. I always hoped that he would change, but the truth is they will never change. They will not change because they do not think there is anything wrong with them; they only believe that you are the problem. Once that realization settles in, you have a choice. Stay or go. We all know the miserable consequences of staying and unconsciously we know the hell that faces us by leaving: "You won't see your kids, I have more money than you and will take full custody of them, you won't get any money from *my* assets, you will have to leave the house since you want to get out, and I will make your life hell."

Many women in particular, but men too are afraid of these threats which they know their narcissist partner will follow through on. I eventually had the strength to leave my miserable marriage once the boys became older and was confident that if they all had each other they would be fine. So much for that thought. All I wanted was an opportunity to be free, to be back in control of my own life, and bask in happy and healthier years ahead of me that I felt I so desperately deserved. I had absolutely no idea of the intensity and of the unnecessary destruction that lay ahead of that decision.

I wrote this book initially for cathartic reasons and to help expel the poison from my soul. It helped me since I no longer need to hold onto the abuse now that I have released it in writing. I have talked about my marriage with so many people and am flabbergasted at how many other people like me are out there suffering silently in the same miserable and abusive relationships. I originally felt that writing my story was a recovery step and necessary for me, and perhaps one day my boys. Now I believe there is a much greater need for it for other narcissistic victims. I want you to know you don't have to live in despair and always feel that you are the blame for your partner's sickness and abusive behavior. I want to be an advocate for people feeling hopeless in their turmoil with nowhere to turn. I appreciate there are many professionals that understand the wrath of this destructive disorder, but only a survivor can really help another wanting to survive. Not only do I want to try to help people in narcissistic marriages and relationships where there are children involved, I want to strongly caution those who have not yet committed to the narcissist or yet had a child.

To the person in a relationship with a narcissist who is living miserably day after day, or who has decided to self-medicate through prescription pills, drugs and /or alcohol to cope, I urge you to seek the help of a therapist who specializes in narcissism. If you have been left with no choice but to leave your marriage or relationship, I would like to firstly commend and congratulate you on your decision. I know it was not easy for you. Please find a therapist, preferably one who specializes in alienation, and seek it secretly if you have to. Your partner is going to punish you and will start with your heartstrings, your children. Prepare yourself and your children for the upcoming punishment, but do not alienate them yourself. Remember when you alienate them from their parent you are only hurting them. You will need all the support you can get, but continue to parent them as you always have and love them the same or more. They will always remember how you behaved and that will dictate who they will choose to remain close with even if you lose them for short periods of time. Do not worry. *"Let them go back to him/her so they can find out who he/she really is..."* Remember strong for them because they need you the most.

I am not a supporter of divorce and struggled for many years to leave Peter because of it. However, there comes a time when you get tired of the fight and lack of positive change and sadly give up. Giving up on my marriage was the saddest day of my life, but was necessary for my own peace, happiness and sanity.

My happiness eventually became more important to me than my marriage. I believe that everyone in our entire world deserves to be happy. You deserve happiness too. In an effort not to repeat my mistakes, I needed to change what I was attracting. I could no longer attract a co-dependent partner. As much as I want to help the world, my job is not to change anyone - that is their job. I spent too long trying to support that damaged little boy in Peter, but the little boy didn't want to be helped. After I steered myself away from the bad boy-damaged-energy was when I finally attracted the perfect mate.

To anyone reading this book who is with a narcissist, not yet married and does not yet have children, get out as fast as possible. If you have seen more than one sign of meanness, lack of empathy for you or others, blame for things that you know you haven't done, telling you that you are imagining things that you know you saw, telling you that you are insecure for not trusting them when you know you have good reason not to trust them...please, please, please leave. If you don't, plan on having a very long and miserable amount of years together which will only end in a torn family, wounded children, and years of abuse post-divorce as punishment for leaving. I wish I had known more about narcissism when I was younger and been mature enough to heed the warnings if I had. I do not feel there is enough known about the narcissist and his/her demented and destructive personality. We do not always know what we have until it is too late, or there's a marriage or child involved. Perhaps it's time to spread the word, give the name a warning sign, push for laws on child alienation (child abuse) making it a crime like any other abuse, and maybe it's time for all of us to look at ourselves and who we are attracting to us. I know that half this lesson was for me and that I had a lot to learn about myself. No more co-dependency relationships for me.

Today I am in a very happy, healthy, respectful and loving relationship with Greg. He is not only caring and loving towards me, but to my three boys, my family and my friends. Everyone loves him--and me the most. He would never do anything intentionally to hurt anyone, especially me. I feel safe with him on every level and felt that I needed to change myself and the path I was on so that I could open the door to meeting Greg.

Not only do I feel happy and free again, I feel more feminine and beautiful now the cloud of evil has moved away. My personality has shifted to a softer stance. I had become a little tough in order to cope and since I am no longer in a war zone I no longer needed to be in fight or flight mode. I have been kinder to myself and ultimately to everyone around me. I'm sure that I was kind before but I am genuinely kinder now. I have learned to love myself completely and by doing so I will never allow anyone to impact that wall of love and self-respect.

My three amazing boys are doing well in their respective lives. I stayed true to myself, and loved my boys unconditionally throughout our horrible divorce and I truly believe that is what brought them home.

I beg anyone who, unfortunately and for whatever reason, has to get divorced from a narcissist partner to leave your children out of your divorce. They are innocent, they love you both, they are not in your fight, they will be left wounded and scarred from your selfishness, and it will affect their own relationships, marriages and challenges later in life.

Don't involve the children – please.

God Bless.

Printed in Great Britain
by Amazon

26440001R00138